DEMOCR

Democracy is today universally considered to be a good thing, yet in history has been frequently criticised. Ross Harrison argues the merits of democracy by tracing its history from the works of Plato, Aristotle, Hobbes, Locke, Rousseau, the American Federalists and Hume, Bentham, the Mills, Hegel and Marx. This historical perspective provides a repertory of specific problems where democracy converges upon the values of liberty, equality, knowledge and welfare. These same values can be used to argue the benefits and demerits of democracy. Any overall assessment must therefore take account of such complexity. **Democracy** shows us how we may navigate between these moral conflicts, by examining the paradoxes and problems that arise and arguing their resolution.

Ross Harrison provides a clear analytical justification of democracy, informed by facts and detailed knowledge of the work of major thinkers of the past. This book is ideal for both those with an interest in the arguments for democracy and readers in politics or philosophy who will find this an excellent introduction to the term.

'The author is at his best, and most original, when he picks out of the debris of history a few of the concepts of democracy such as majority rule. He is especially good on what the Founding Fathers of the US had to say. . . . This is a very good book, with a useful bibliography.'

Henry B. Mayo, Canadian Journal of Political Science

'Clear writing and a conversational tone make this book accessible to general readers. Highly recommended for public and academic libraries.'

Choice

'The reader finishes each chapter with a feeling of accomplishment.'

Philosophical Books

Ross Harrison is Reader in Philosophy and Fellow of King's College, Cambridge. He is the author of *Bentham* (1983) for Routledge's The Arguments of the Philosophers series, and *On What There Must Be* (1974).

The Problems of Philosophy

Founding editor: Ted Honderich
Editors: Tim Crane and Jonathan Wolff, University College London

This series addresses the central problems of philosophy. Each book gives a fresh account of a particular philosophical theme by offering two perspectives on the subject: the historical context and the author's own distinctive and original contribution.

The books are written to be accessible to students of philosophy and related disciplines, while taking the debate to a new level.

*Also available in paperback

Democracy

Ross Harrison

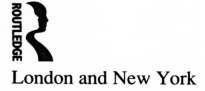

London and New York

First published 1993
by Routledge
2 Park Square, Milton Park, Abingdon, Oxon, OX14 4RN

Simultaneously published in the USA and Canada
by Routledge
270 Madison Ave, New York NY 10016

First published in paperback 1995

Reprinted in 1996

Transferred to Digital Printing 2006

© 1993 Ross Harrison

Typeset in Times by
Ponting–Green Publishing Services, Chesham, Bucks

British Library Cataloguing in Publication Data
A catalogue record for this book is available from
the British Library

Library of Congress Cataloguing in Publication Data
A catalogue record for this book is available from
the Library of Congress

ISBN 0–415–03254–7 (hbk)
ISBN 0–415–13080–8 (pbk)

Publisher's Note
The publisher has gone to great lengths to ensure
the quality of this reprint but points out that some
imperfections in the original may be apparent

Contents

Preface, Principally on History

In accordance with the general house style of the series in which this volume appears, it is divided more or less equally between the history of the problem and a contemporary attempt at solution (or resolution, or explanation). 'History' means many things to many people, so I would like to start with a word or two of explanation of what I am, or more importantly, what I am not, trying to do with it in this volume.

Proper history is an attempt to describe a period as it was, not just to raid it for present purposes. One such present purpose is an attempt to acquire validation for one side of a current dispute. Another is to acquire quaint ornaments to place on the mantelpiece and display cultural sophistication. Proper history eschews this. Unfortunately, proper history also takes time and requires considerable background knowledge. Partly because of this, proper history is not what happens here. Both the enquiry in the second half of the book and the history in the first half are problem-driven. These problems connect. So this is a raiding effort, in an improper or unhistorical mode; just as it used to be in the bad old days of the history of philosophy. It is Whig history. The justification of the so-called historical part of the book is to set up the problems; to provide a greater variety of thoughts or solutions; and to enrich the contemporary subject matter. Other than that, it is not history at all.

As described so far the problem of the relation of an active subject to its history is the same as in other parts of philosophy. However, there are special problems which arise with political philosophy. For this area has a more intimate connection with action; and the question of its history therefore brings up the question of which kinds of thought of the past should be studied; that is, how closely these thoughts should be connected with political action. For example, we might study thought as exemplified in real political action; that is, in the actual exercise of (past) politics, or (past) political systems. These set problems or give suggestions which may help with more abstract current philosophical questions about the nature or value of democracy. In this case the history used (or abused, or raided) would be normal political history. Or the subject matter could be thought rather than action. But there are many sorts of thought: the agents were also thinkers, in some cases writers. Around the agents are a host of pamphleteers, commentators, propagandists, making sense of events in a nexus of ideas; ideas which also contain implicit or explicit prescriptions about the good polity. This is political thought; and it might also be raided. Then there is political philosophy, more narrowly so called, the sort of thing written, it might be supposed, by people like Locke or Hume.

However, Locke and Hume were both engaged actively in politics; they were also both essay writers or commentators, more concerned to understand or influence their own societies than build ideal commonwealths. Locke's *Two Treatises on Government* is a work called forward by a particular, crucial, political occasion; so also were the American *Federalist* papers. In one way this just means that someone doing the intellectual history of these areas has to be more open to a full, rich, political history (and vice versa). It increases the difficulty of raiding them for philosophical purposes. But on the other hand, it means that we shouldn't approach the thought of the past with too strongly entrenched an idea of what counts as political philosophy, as opposed to essay-writing, or political commentary, or propaganda or political speeches. It means that we can raid what we want, where the criterion of what we want is that it helps us with current problems.

My rationalisation of my practice is therefore that the variety of past writing and action means that we can raid what we want, so long as it does help us with present purposes. In the historical first half of this work, I have unashamedly talked about people like Aristotle and Rousseau, Marx and Madison (and Locke and Hume), where any proper study of them would take many more pages than I have at my disposal here and more knowledge than I possess. I have raided them for present purposes: to set up some of the questions for the second part of the book. I have tried to be as accurate as I can, and not just used the names as counters to be pushed round the board in a contemporary game ('advance the Locke to Mayfair'; 'send the Marx directly to jail'). But I have used primary texts rather than secondary ones; and the essential historical background is missing not just from the pages of the book but from the mind of the author.

With this due warning about what I am trying to achieve, I hope that you enjoy it. I hope, that is, that you discover that there are still difficulties in thinking about the problems of democracy in an abstract or philosophical manner. Democracy is now thought very generally to be a good thing. It is much harder work to see why or whether this thought should be justified.

Fuller information about references and reading is given for each of the chapters in the Notes section at the end of the book.

I am grateful to Robin Osborne for saving me from even more errors about the Greeks.

Ross Harrison

CHAPTER I

Self-rule

Philosophy tends to think about things which, otherwise, would seem to be so totally obvious that they were not worth thinking about. Given the manifest and pressing problems of life, to spend time deciding whether tables and chairs really exist or whether people have feelings can seem like being trapped in the difficult and tedious business of trying to answer the questions of a small child who should have gone home long ago. Showing how the answer can withstand full intellectual scrutiny is not easy; nevertheless the answers themselves seem to be totally obvious and generally agreed. We agree that there are tables, chairs and other people. Similarly, we agree that democracy is a good thing and that the political system inside which we currently operate is a democratic system. Democracy surrounds us like tables and chairs and the air we breathe, normally totally taken for granted. Right across the world, in obviously different political systems, the form of government is taken to be democratic and democracy is unquestionably taken to be a good thing. Except then as mere speculative play, further examination of democracy and of its value might seem to be idle or naive.

The very variety of systems that call themselves democratic, however, seems to raise a philosophical problem in the way that the existence of tables and chairs does not. Furthermore, in cases like democracy, what the term actually refers to more obviously depends on what we think that thing to be than in cases of tables or stones. For, just as what people are actually doing depends in part on what they think they are doing, so, in part, which political system a group of people are actually in depends upon which system they think themselves to be in. Furthermore, what they think about it cannot just be told by examination of the word that they use; it also depends

1

upon what sort of actions they think this word legitimates or makes possible as well as the reasons why they think that the system is of value. On the recent reunification of Germany a country which many thought not to be democratic, the DDR, disappeared. Yet this country had 'democratic' in its official name. Both it and the country it joined thought themselves to be democratic; yet they were clearly quite different kinds of country. Both liberal and socialist systems use the same word, but in the different systems it legitimates or explains different types of behaviour. Hence it is not obvious that they are referring to the same thing by the same word.

The same word is used in these quite different systems and languages because, as a word, it has a long history. 'Democracy' is a Greek word meaning 'rule by the people'. It is natural, therefore, to start an examination of democracy by starting with the Greeks. This, however, is not just because the word is Greek. Many scientific terms are Greek but this does not mean that a history of these sciences should start with the Greeks. The importance of the Greeks is that, as well as the word, the Greeks invented the idea and the practice. Some of the ancient Greeks for some of the time actually lived in a political system which both they and independent commentators described as democratic. This last fact should cause more surprise and commentary than it normally does, living as we do in a world in which democracy surrounds us like air. For, after the Greeks, the practice of democracy more or less vanishes for two millennia. In the intervening period, generally speaking, societies were not democratic, did not think themselves to be democratic, and, in so far as they thought about democracy at all, thought democracy to be a thoroughly disreputable thing. So, once we introduce an historical dimension, the apparent agreement between widely spatially and culturally separated systems vanishes. It is only in the twentieth century and some few previous isolated political societies that democracy has been thought to be a good thing and people have thought, often in a completely unquestioning manner, that they lived in societies which could be called democratic.

With the introduction of an historical dimension and the disappearance of agreement, comes also the disappearance of obviousness. Democracy can no longer be assumed to be like air when it is found to be much more temporally specific or relative than air. The question inevitably arises whether democracy is after all such a good thing. This question reinforces the question of whether the apparent

2

agreement about democracy between different political systems might be more than superficial. Once we consider these two questions, we have also to consider the question of what exactly democracy is. However tedious or idle intellectually puzzling questions about tables, chairs and other minds might be, these questions about democracy have a real grip. If we try to answer them by looking at what people have formerly thought, we find that most people have not only disagreed with each other but also with what we presently think. They cannot all be right; and if we decided (democratically) by taking the majority view, we would lose the vote. So the problem of the value and meaning of democracy, once raised, cannot just be brushed aside. In the rest of this chapter, as a prolegomenon to the detailed historical and analytical treatment which follows, a first attempt will be made to sketch, in a highly outline fashion, some of the problems.

Let us start with a direct analysis of the possible meaning of the word 'democracy' itself. As mentioned, the word is originally Greek, which explains why it appears in the same form in so many different languages. The meaning of it in Greek is that the people (the *demos*) rule; it is rule by the people. Now ruling is an activity which must have an object as well as a subject. If the people rule, they must rule something. Yet the only possible object of rule is the people who form the state or political system being considered. Hence the rulers in a democracy, the people, are also the ruled, namely the people again. So the meaning of the word 'democracy' can be given most perspicuously as being that the people rule themselves. This gives three terms to look at: *the people*, *ruling* and *themselves* (that is, the people again under another description). Each term has problems in itself, and the combination of the three generates some more.

To begin with *the people* or the *demos*. This has an ambiguity, more pronounced in Greek than in English, between meaning the people as a whole (that is, everyone) and the most common basic group of the people (that is the normal person or, as we say in English, the common people). In Greek this meant that commentators and objectors to the system could move easily from a description of it as rule by the people as a whole to rule by a particular group of the people, namely the poor, low, vulgar mass of the people. Democracy could then be understood as the rule of this vulgar mass over the beautiful, rich and good. As a specific problem

3

in Greek thought, this will be discussed in the next chapter. However, it relates to a more general problem in democratic theory: the domination of the minority by the majority.

The ambiguity of 'demos' sounds a warning that a phrase like 'the people' does not necessarily and uncontentiously refer to everyone. In fact, even if 'the people' is taken to refer to everyone, there still remains a problem about which set of people is meant. For as long as there is more than one state in the world, what is meant by the people being the rulers of a state is not that all the people in the world are but, rather, the people which belong to that particular state. This means that any theory, or state, has to lay down some criterion of membership so that it can distinguish between the people who do, and the people who do not, belong to that state. Furthermore, this cannot just be the simple criterion of all the people who happen at any one time to be in the geographical area controlled by the state. All states must be able to allow for visitors, so that it can recognise its members even when they are abroad and recognise that some people in its area are not full members. This part of the general problem of what 'the people' refers to is not so easily soluble as might appear at first sight. However, in what follows it will be ignored and 'the people' taken to mean 'the people belonging to the particular state being discussed'.

Another dimension of the problem of what *the people* refers to arises once we consider what is involved in ruling. Suppose we think of ruling as being an exercise of power. For someone to exercise power is for their wishes to be effective. So someone is a ruler if it is the case that what happens happens because it is accordance with their wishes. If, then, the people rule, this means that the people's wishes are effective. However there are two ways in which we can understand the idea of someone's wishes being effective. In the first, the expression of the wish causes its fulfilment. In the second what is wanted happens, but its happening does not depend upon the expression of the wish. If the people rule in the first sense, then what happens happens as a result of their wishes being expressed. So we need a mechanism, such as voting, which links the expression of the wishes with the result. If the people rule in the second sense, what happens must still happen because it is in accord with their wishes; but the mechanism which achieves this need not depend upon their wishes being expressed; for what happens does not have to be caused by the wishes being expressed. On this second account the people rule, or have power, if they get what they want; even if the reason why they get what they want is because of the benevolent management of a third party.

In the first of these options, which is the one most familiar to us, the people rule if there is a mechanism connecting the expression of their wishes with what actually happens. The normal such mechanism is voting. Yet, if we understand the people's wishes being effective in this familiar way, we again run into problems about what is meant by 'the people'. The natural thing is to assume that 'the people' means all the people; so that the people's wishes are effective if they all participate in the mechanism; that is, if they all vote. However, two problems immediately arise. First, if people are offered any kind of free choice about voting, they will normally not all vote. Second, and independently, those that vote will normally not all vote the same way. It is only if absolutely everyone votes and if absolutely everyone agrees that there are no problems. Then, assuming that their expressed wishes determine what actually happens, the people can be said to rule because, for each of them, the wish they have is effective; hence, for all of them, their wishes are effective. Yet for everyone to vote and everyone to agree is obviously a highly abnormal case. It is also an uninteresting one. All the real questions of power and government start when people are being forced to do things which they otherwise would not wish to do. Once these questions arise, as happens if there is disagreement and the majority view is followed, then it is problematic how, even if they all vote, it can be said that the people rule. For if 'the people' means all the people, and if the wishes of a majority of the people are the ones which are effective, then it is not the case that the wishes of all the people are effective, for the wishes of the minority are not.

If, in the normal case of majority decision just described it is nevertheless said that the result is the wish of the people (as it usually is), then the reference of the term *the people* is starting to depart from being all the people. Or, if it is still held that it refers to all the people, then the meaning of *ruling* is no longer that an expressed wish is effective because it has been expressed. A quite different idea is starting to emerge whereby the wishes of the people as a whole are represented by the expressed wishes of another group, which is smaller than the people as a whole. This group is is the majority. The wishes of the majority are now taken to express the wishes of the people as a whole. Yet this seems to be obviously problematic or paradoxical. The minority explicitly disagree with the decision. It seems perverse, therefore, to say that their wishes are being represented and are effective, and yet the minority are part of the people as a whole.

The same problem comes up, if in a less severe or obviously paradoxical form, if not all the people vote. For the decision which results, even if it is effective, only represents the wishes of those who vote. The non-voters, although part of the people, do not have wishes which are connected with the result. So, again, a part of the people (the voters) represent the whole. So, again, it stretches the meaning of the term to describe the result as being a decision by the people. Of course, what happens may be exactly what the non-voters want; and, indeed, knowledge that this will happen may be exactly why they don't vote. However, if we take their getting what they want as a reason for saying that the non-voters' wishes are nevertheless effective, then we are shifting to the second way of understanding the idea of being effective, whereby a wish is effective if the wished-for result occurs independently of the wish being expressed.

On the normal way of understanding power and effective wishes, therefore, there are problems in saying that the people rule, even if there is a voting procedure and absolutely everyone is entitled to vote. For unless they actually do all vote and do all agree, then the wishes expressed by some of these votes are going to be effective in a way that other wishes (expressed or not expressed) are not; and if the result is still taken to be a decision of the people, then 'the people' is being understood in a different, or representative, sense whereby one part of the people is taken to represent the people as a whole. The decisions of this group are being taken to be the decisions of the people as a whole.

There is a way of putting this which may make it seem less paradoxical. This is to query the original assumption that 'the people' naturally refers to all of the people, as if it was just a collective noun which picked out a group of similar individuals as the expressions 'the animals' or 'the petitioners' might. Rather, it might be supposed, 'the people' should be taken as a singular term referring to a special kind of individual or entity, which was not to be identified with a collection of people. This special individual, the-people-as-a-whole (or, perhaps, the spirit of the people) makes decisions when certain actual people do certain things, such as vote in elections or whatever. Another advantage of this way of looking at it is that it alleviates the problem of reflexivity which seems to arise once we consider as well the third term, the 'themselves' in the expression 'the people rule themselves'. For we could take the people as ruler as being this super-special entity and the people as ruled as being the collection of all the individual people. Since these are not identical, there is no longer a problem in how it could be meaningful to say that one of them rules the other. Such a special entity also alleviates the problem of partiality which seems to arise when a part of the people (the majority or the voters) decide for the whole. So, if 'the people' is thought of as some kind of super-singular person, then many problems are eased.

However, this easing is only at the cost of creating a cloud of new problems. For now we have a new type of entity, whose nature, desires and conditions of identity are all deeply uncertain. There is a metaphysical problem about whether such a thing could exist at all. There are practical problems about how exactly its will should be determined (which we would have to do if the point of democracy is to put the will of this strange entity into effect). Furthermore, even if we introduce this new special kind of entity, we are still faced with problems of representation; that is, of why the desires or decisions of some actual people should be taken to be the decisions of 'the people'. For there still remains the question of which actual decisions of which actual people are going to be taken to represent or constitute the decisions of the super-entity.

Most decisions made in any country of familiar or modern size can only be taken by relatively few people, and these decisions, if they are decisions of government, will then be taken to apply to the actions of all the people in the state. Everyone, that is, will be made to obey them. If these decisions are nevertheless taken to be decisions which are made democratically, or in some sense by the people, then clearly some doctrine of representation has to be relied on whereby the decisions of a few people can be taken to represent the decisions of the whole. So, if modern states are democracies at all, then they are clearly representative democracies; and one problem to be considered is whether this expression is not a contradiction in terms, so that once representation starts, democracy ends. However, it follows from the preceding paragraphs that representation is not just a problem for large or modern democracies. There is a problem of representation however small or direct the political unit is. For as soon as people disagree, something like representation will be required.

Solutions to this problem have to explain how the decisions of one group of people (such as the majority) may be taken to be decisions made by the people as a whole. One way to attempt a solution is to weaken the connection between the actually expressed wish of someone and the idea that these wishes are (in some sense) effective in decision. One way that this could be done is by moving to the second way described above of understanding power, or of wishes being effective; whereby someone's wishes are effective if they get what they want, whether or not this is brought about by the direct expression of the wish. On this way of understanding power, there will be democracy, or rule by the people, if the rule gives the people what they want. The problem of representation will then be alleviated, because any intervening body (the majority, a particular political party or whatever) could make the actual or effective decisions, providing only that these decisions led to the people getting what they wanted. The representatives would then be those people, or that group, which had sufficient knowledge about what the people wanted.

This solution, however, has obvious problems. There is the problem of whether getting what you want in this manner is really an exemplification of power (or ruling). There is also still the problem of what happens when the people's wishes diverge. For, however benevolent the intervening body might be, if people's desires diverge, it will not be possible to satisfy them all. The benevolent body will have to choose to satisfy some rather than others. This means that the ones not satisfied do not get what they want, and hence do not rule, even in this second way of understanding power. So the same problem recurs.

On this second way of understanding power there is a natural, if somewhat drastic, solution to this problem of divergence of desire. This is to adopt an account of desire whereby everyone comes out as really having the same desires. Some theory of human nature is relied on to tell what people (*qua* people) are like; that is, what they really desire. These real desires, which are part of human nature as such, will diverge in particular cases from the expressed or felt desires. This, however, is no longer a problem; nor is the corresponding diversity of apparent desires. For these conflicts are only in, or among, the apparent desires. The real desires can be taken to be the same for everyone. Hence they do not conflict. Hence, if the intervening benevolent entity knows what these real desires are, it can arrange for these desires to be satisfied. Hence everyone will be satisfied, or get what they (really) want. Hence all the people will have power (in the second sense). Furthermore, if the benevolent entity knows better what these real desires are than individual people taken at random, then there is every reason for putting decisions of the benevolent entity into effect rather than the expressed wishes of the people. For if people do not know what they really want, then to follow their expressed wishes would not be to satisfy their real desires. Hence, the representative status of the intervening body would be fully justified and the worst method to rely on if one wants to be fully democratic (to give the people power or make their wishes effective) is elections.

Starting, therefore, from a position in which elections can seem to be the paradigmatic expression of democracy, we can reach a position in which elections are incompatible with democracy. This goes some way towards explaining the great variety of systems, noted at the beginning, all of which describe themselves as being democratic. It is also something that will emerge when we examine the history of democratic theory in the first part of this book. For this history can be seen as falling into two general traditions which differ on democracy as much as they differ on various associated notions, such as freedom. In one of these traditions, which could be called the classic liberal tradition from Hobbes and Locke to Rawls and Nozick, people are the best judges of their own wants. They are free when these wants are realised. Freedom is something which individuals can ideally have on their own, and is only limited by others and the state. The wants of different people are varied and incompatible. So the state has the role of holding the ring between these incompatible desires; its main task is, as far as possible, not to get in the way of the realisation of these pre-existing wishes. This tradition stresses voting, and elections are taken to be one way of holding the ring.

In the other tradition, by contrast, which links Rousseau (on one way of looking at him) to Hegel, Marx and the later idealists, wants are not just taken as given by expressed desires. People may be mistaken about their real interests. Freedom consists not in the arbitrary play of desire but in achieving what is really wanted. People may be helped to achieve this by others, or by the state. So the state can have a positive role in the creation of the right kind of desire, giving people what they really want rather than just what they think they want. People may (in a famous phrase of Rousseau's) be forced to be free. On this account, realisation of the people's will depends much less on elections than on having the right kind of structure to ensure that these real desires become effective.

One advantage of the theory by which a particular group could represent the people as a whole, interfering on behalf of their real interests and giving them what they really want, was that it seemed to explain why it was not trivial to talk of a group, the people, ruling themselves. In such a case there would be real ruling, since the group which represented the people would as really control the people as a whole as would a group or individual in quite other forms of rule such as oligarchy or dictatorship. On the other hand, if 'the people' is just taken to mean all the people taken collectively, then it might seem purely trivial to talk of the people ruling themselves. For if this just means that they all make themselves do what they all want, then it might seem that no making (or ruling) could enter. The people just do what they want and all talk of rule is redundant.

However, without any special ideas about real interests, sense can be made of the idea of the people ruling themselves. The analogy to start from here is an individual person and the corresponding problem, or question, is whether we can make sense of the idea of someone ruling themselves (commanding themselves, ordering themselves and so on). One answer might be to think of a person as split into several parts, such as the conscience or the emotions. Then, if one of these parts were dominant it could be said to rule ('he's ruled by his emotions'). Then there is self-rule. As ruler the person is identified with the ruling part, for example the conscience. As ruled, they are identified with the whole. This obviously is more acceptable if it is the reason or conscience which is ruling. Someone is said to be master of themselves when their reason or conscience determines what happens rather than being merely prey to passions. So we can make sense of individuals ruling themselves without resorting to special kinds of interests. Unfortunately, however, this is not a very helpful analogy of how the people as a whole could rule themselves. For it depends upon a part ruling the whole, and so reproduces all the problems when one part of the people is taken to represent the whole.

Perhaps, therefore, it is more useful to consider analogies in which a person is not split into parts. The question now becomes whether a person as a whole could ever be meaningfully be taken to be the ruler of themselves as a whole. At first sight, at least if we think of ruling on the model of issuing orders, this seems to be absurd. It seems that there could be no difference between a person ordering themselves to do something and doing it just because they want to. Yet, at second sight, it is possible to think of cases in which individual people control themselves in an analogous way to the way in which they control other people. The best dimension to work with is time, so that a person at one time controls what happens at another time. For example, knowing that I shall return this evening half-drunk and in a weak-willed state, I now, being at present fully sensible and sober, lock the drinks cupboard and hide the key. This means that when I return home in the evening, however much I want a drink, I can't have one. My self at that time is being controlled, or ruled, by myself at the earlier time; and such control or rule is just as meaningful (it impinges just as directly on my immediate desires) as if it had been exercised by someone else.

It is possible, therefore, to talk in a non-trivial way of individual persons controlling, or ruling, themselves; so the analogous extension to a group of people should also be possible. In the case just described, however, although the person was not fragmented into a controlling conscience and subordinate passions, it was still an essential part of the case that the views or understanding of the person at one time was taken to be superior to their views at another time. There was, even if implicitly, a split into a superior and an inferior self. This is not surprising if we wish to give force to the idea of self-rule, but it does mean that in looking for an analogy in the social case, we should look for one situation, or aspect, in which the society (or the people) have a superior understanding and another situation, or aspect, in which their understanding is inferior. Then, if when they are in the superior aspect, they control what happens while in the inferior one, they can genuinely, comprehensibly and justifiably be taken to be ruling themselves.

It can now be seen how it is natural to stress discussion and formal debate in democratic theory. For, just as it is natural to take thought, or perhaps conscience, as the superior aspect of man, and think that it was reasonable for a cool, thinking self to take steps to block irrational future actions, so, for a group of people, it would seem equally reasonable to think that the views that they arrived at when they were all thinking carefully about the matter should be allowed to control what happened when they were not. Hence it would be reasonable for a group of people to meet together and decide, after careful discussion, to institute rules or controls which were designed to block their activities when they were not thinking so carefully. For example, a group of people might be using a parking space in a way that was mutually disadvantageous, in that no one who really needed it could get in. They might meet together and decide (all of them, unanimously) to institute a series of fines or controls designed to prevent all but urgent parking. On leaving the meeting they would then be controlled by their decision in just the same way as if the fines had been imposed by someone else. They would have blocked, or controlled, their future action. They would have ruled themselves. Yet this would seem to be perfectly reasonable, or natural, since the decision they take together is probably better for them than what happens when they act in an uncoordinated way. They can all see that it is really in all their interests to control themselves in this way. Looked at even from each person's individual point of view, they can all think that their better, or higher, self was effective when they were engaged in joint discussion and decision, and that this better self then properly controls their less good desires in just the same way as they might lock the whisky cabinet against themselves.

It is possible, therefore, to give content to the idea of a group of people ruling themselves without relying on some notion of a part representing the whole, and even to put this in the form that the better self of each person is expressed or exposed when he or she meets in equal discussion with others. Yet, analogously with before, once we have got this far, it is quite natural to go on to a point at which this better self, or real self, only exists in the debate or discussion, and the decisions of such an assembly may rightly be taken to be decisions of the whole people, even if it is no longer the case that everyone is present or everyone agrees with each other. In other words, we naturally come back to the idea of representation, and then again reach the point that, even when discussing, the average person is not as good at assessing his real wants as some kind of expert. There is then the danger that we then move from a position in which citizens in a special reflective assembly think of themselves as superior to themselves not in assembly, to the position that they need not get into assembly at all because their better or higher selves are sufficiently well represented by someone else.

The exact turns and possibilities inside the territory which has been laid out with very broad sweeps of the brush in this chapter will be investigated in what follows, first following the fortunes of the two very broad traditions just delineated, with their very different ideas of freedom, desire and value; then by more analytic or direct attack on the problems of democracy itself. In the first part we shall explore democracy and concepts connected with it and discover problems which provide material for the second part. Before then, however, we naturally start with where democracy itself started. Before the traditions diverge, and to find where both the practice and the ideas originally come from, we have to start with the Greeks.

CHAPTER II

The Greeks

One evening the news suddenly reached Athens that Elateia, a key city giving access to the main body of the Greek peninsula, had unexpectedly been attacked and fallen to Philip of Macedon. There was sudden commotion in the streets, the Council members attempted to clear the way to the Assembly and there, next morning, the citizens of Athens met, waiting and ready before the Council appeared to give the news. As Demosthenes describes it: 'The herald then voiced the question, "who desires to speak?" No one moved. The question was repeated several times without a man standing up, although all the generals were there and all the orators.' This far from impartial reminiscence is merely a lead-in to the voice for which they have all been waiting. For 'it appeared that the occasion demanded not merely patriotic feeling and wealth, but familiarity with public affairs from the beginning and a right judgment of Philip's aims and motives'. Hence, the narrator modestly concludes, 'I was the man who showed such capacity that day. I came forward and addressed the Assembly' (*Dem* XVIII 170; 172–3). Here we have Athenian democracy in action, even if in response to the threat which eventually closed it down. The citizen body as a whole meets to decide what to do. Typically the issue is one of immediate policy, specifically foreign policy, rather than of creation of law. Although all are called on to speak (the herald standardly first asked for those over 50, then for the others), in fact some are listened to, and expected to speak, more than others. Finally, Demosthenes is not addressing these reminiscences to the Assembly itself but is instead defending his policy in a legal suit brought against him in the Courts. These are all features of the first and most famous democracy of them all, the democracy of ancient Athens. In the last chapter it was observed that democracy was not only a Greek word and Greek idea but that, for at least some of the ancient Greeks for at least some of the time, they actually lived in a form of government which both they themselves and also independent commentators described as a democracy. They had, as noted, surprisingly few imitators in the succeeding thousands of years and seem also to have had no predecessors, for democracy seems to be a form of government which they themselves invented. Since the restless fertility of Greek invention also produced political theory, it might be thought that there would be a neat match between these two exemplifications of their genius, so that the people who first practised democracy were also the first people both to explain and defend it. This, however, is not what happened. The principal commentators whose works survive were anti-democratic in inclination, and although they attempted to explain, they did not defend. This is the case both for the principal historian, Thucydides, with his brilliant analysis of the progress of the actual events, and also for the principal philosophers who considered the theory, Plato and Aristotle. Since such commentators came, almost necessarily, from the leisured, propertied (one might say, thinking) classes, and since these classes felt themselves to be threatened by democracy, this hostility is presumably not completely accidental. Nevertheless it poses a problem. For, while we can easily find powerful and important criticism of democracy in Greek thought, we have to look at the practice itself as well as the arguments reported by hostile commentators in order to extract any kind of defence, or even sympathetic explanation, of it. This is one reason for starting with the practice rather than the theory, and in this chapter two things will be attempted. First, ancient Athenian democracy will be described so that we have before us an actual working example of democracy as a basis for future discussion. Then the theory inspired by this practice will be introduced, theory which has had a deep influence on the discussion of democracy from the time of the Greeks up to the present day.

Another link between theory and practice is provided by Aristotle, the Greek genius who inevitably dominates this chapter. For not only did Aristotle write the best work of political theory; he also wrote the best extant account of Athenian political practice. In this work, the *Constitution of Athens*, Aristotle plots eleven changes of constitution leading up to his own time and showing 'ever-increasing power being assumed by the people' so that now 'they have made themselves supreme in all fields; they run everything by decrees of the Assembly and by decisions of the courts in which the people are supreme' (XLI 2). Although there is this progress toward ever-increased democracy, it is reasonable to say that some form of democracy existed for about two hundred years from its original introduction at the end of the sixth century BC until Athens itself was closed down as an independent state by external forces at the end of the fourth century. There were two brief interruptions (or reversions to oligarchy) at the end of the fifth century, mainly precipitated by reverses in the long war against Athens' great rival, Sparta; the chief theoretical interest of these is that on one of these occasions the democracy itself voted for its own abolition. In this chapter the position in Aristotle's day, that is, in the fourth century, is described; but the differences from the previous century are minor.

Athens, like other Greek towns of the same period, was a wholly independent city-state. This meant that the final unit of government, or as we now say the state, was, in modern terms, extremely small. It meant that both in the physical distances and in the number of people involved, it was possible for all to participate directly in the processes of government. This brings us to the next noticeable feature which was that, as a democracy, Athens was a direct democracy; each citizen was himself directly involved rather than being represented by others. Of course, to be in this position he had to be a citizen, or full member of the state, and this was a quite different thing from happening to live in the geographical area. As noticed in the last chapter, all states necessarily impose some criterion of membership which is distinct from just being physically present in the territory. However, in Athens this was extremely strict. To be a citizen, both of one's parents had to be citizens. If one's parents were not citizens, one could live in the territory and carry on quite a normal life, be wealthy or intellectually influential (many famous Greek thinkers who worked in Athens, such as Anaxagoras or Aristotle himself were like this), but one would not be a citizen. This group are known as the metics; they formed a fair proportion of the residents of Athens. Next (and in terms of present-day ideas, notoriously) women were excluded from full citizenship. The metics had other states of their own, to which they could at any stage return. However, the women married to the Athenian citizens would normally have no other state with which they were connected (and, indeed, as just noticed, they had to be citizens if their children,

16

male or female, were to be so). Nevertheless they were excluded from political rights. After women come the slaves. These had no political rights. Unlike the metics, they were obviously not free to go as they pleased although like them they were non-Athenian (and, indeed non-Greek; barbarian). So once these elements, together with the male children, are excluded from the population normally living in Athenian territory we find that the actual full members of the state, exercising their direct democracy, were a minority of the population. In Athens, a particularly large Greek city-state, they numbered something of the order of 35,000.

Although all were favoured compared to those who were excluded, the full citizens formed a highly heterogeneous group of people, ranging from men of property and leisure on the one side to poor peasants and artisans on the other. The former had considerable property and depended upon the labour of slaves for their leisure. The latter, however, had nothing apart from their own and their family's resources. They were sometimes illiterate and they had to work hard to stay alive. Nevertheless they were equally full citizens. Indeed, they were by far the majority, standardly known as 'the many' (*hoi polloi*). It was their entry into the processes of government, in the middle fifth century, which marked the accomplishment of complete Athenian democracy, when they gained important political rights. The first of these was that they were now fully protected by law, having equality before the law, or what the Greeks called *isonomia*. Herodotus, who lived through the time just described, describes in his *History* a debate between upholders of different forms of government which he ascribes to Persia but could clearly only sensibly be taken as applying to Athens. The spokesman for democracy says 'the rule of the many has a name that is the most beautiful of all – *isonomia*' (III 80). Similarly, Pericles, in the famous funeral speech reported by Thucydides, says that 'in law, as it touches individuals, all are equal' (II 7).

Equality before the law was clearly one kind of important form of protection and equality for citizens in a democracy, but also important for the democratic Athenian citizen was equal freedom of speech, or *isegoria*. Later in his *History* Herodotus comments on the rise of Athens that 'the Athenians grew in strength, and demonstrated what a fine thing equality is' (V 78). The word used for 'equality' here is *isegoria* which has as many connotations of freedom as of equality; in the standard nineteenth-century translation 'freedom' appears at this point. The quotation from Herodotus about the Athenians continues that before the institution of democracy 'they were like men labouring for a master: unwilling to make an effort; but when they had been liberated each man had his own incentive for working hard'. Similarly Pericles is reported as saying 'liberty marks both our public politics and the feelings which touch our daily life together' (Thuc. II 7). Moving on into the fourth century, liberty is frequently identified by commentators as the chief aim of democrats. Aristotle lists in his *Politics* the two supposed defining features of democracy as being 'the sovereignty of the majority and liberty' (1310 a 30); more baldly, in the *Rhetoric* he states that 'the end [goal] of democracy is freedom' (1366 a 4); ('liberty' and 'freedom' in all these quotations translate *eleutheria*). Plato earlier makes Socrates say: 'in a democratic country you will be told that liberty is its noblest possession', adding tartly that in a democracy 'the whole place is simply bursting with the spirit of liberty' (*Republic* VIII 562 c; d). These are remarks of hostile commentators, and all have the overtones whereby unbridled liberty becomes licence. However, the freedom implied by *isegoria* (rather than the more general concept of *eleutheria*) was much more specific. It meant the equal freedom of all citizens to make their views known in public debate, so that they could all contribute, if they wished, to the process of making decisions. What this meant was that they all had an equal right to address the Assembly of all citizens, the *ecclesia*.

The *ecclesia* met forty times a year in the fourth century, starting at sunrise and often finishing by noon. The quorum was 6,000 and (in this century but not before) citizens were paid for attending (at the rate of a modest day's wage). Voting was by show of hands so that, given the numbers involved, the estimation of results can only have been approximate. Although all citizens had the equal right of addressing the Assembly it seems clear that it was in fact dominated by particular speakers who had the leisure and inclination to devote themselves in a much more full-time way to politics. This can be seen from the story told by Demosthenes about himself with which the chapter started. In Demosthenes' story, although all are called on to speak, in fact some are listened to, and expected to speak, more than others. Similarly, going back to the so-called demagogues of the previous century, Plutarch reports the following story about the most famous of them, Cleon. Once, or so Plutarch recounts it, when he had kept the Assembly for a long time sitting on the Pnyx and waiting for him to address them, he appeared towards evening, garlanded for a dinner-party, and asked them to adjourn the session until the following day. 'Today', he exclaimed, 'I am not free to give you my time'.

The reported reaction of the Athenians was laughter and dissolution of the Assembly (*Nicias* 7). This is only a story and Plutarch is writing hundreds of years later. However it fits in with the feeling produced by Demosthenes' own contemporary account; however equal in theory the right of all citizens to address the Assembly, in fact some were much more able to get listened to than others. Politics in Athens, just as in later states, was in the hands of a group of professionals who had the time, ability, and knowledge to devote themselves to it. Analogously, the leaders who were taken to be representing the general, common, people were not themselves of them, either in terms of background nor in terms of current financial resources. The previously mentioned Cleon, who was derided in a socially snobbish fashion as an artisan, in fact possessed considerable financial resources; he did not himself tan but possessed slaves who did it for him. Pericles, with whom he was contrasted, also took a popular line in the Assembly, yet he himself was one of the landed, propertied classes. The commentators of these classes who admired him contrasted his control with those that followed. In Thucydides' view, with Pericles 'what was nominally a democracy became in fact rule by the first citizen' (II 65 9).

The Athenian assembly was therefore open on an equal basis to all of the full citizens, although to be such a citizen one had to be an especially favoured inhabitant, and even then not all citizens seem to have counted equally in the Assembly. The business for the Assembly was prepared for it by the Council (*boule*); the story with which the chapter began showed them attempting to do this in a rush when they were caught unawares. The Council was much smaller than the Assembly and also met much more frequently, both of which might be thought to have given it more power. Whether this is true or not, it was still representative of the citizen body as a whole in that its 500 members were selected by lot, fifty being taken each year from each of the ten tribes of which the citizen body was composed. Furthermore, it was only permissible to serve for two years, and it seems in fact to have been rare to serve beyond a single term, so a fairly large part of the citizen body would have served at one time or another. Selection by lot is a striking and characteristic feature of Greek democracy, identified by contemporary commentators as being particularly democratic. In democracy, Plato notes in the *Republic*, 'the officials are usually appointed by lot' (557a). By contrast, elections were thought to be aristocratic, since they involved choice of the best (*aristoi* in Greek) rather than giving every one an equal chance in the way that a lottery does. Commenting on the Spartan constitution Aristotle says that it has several oligarchic factors; 'for example', he says, 'the magistrates are all appointed by vote, and none by lot' (*Politics* 1294b); just before this he notes that 'the use of lot is regarded as democratic, and the use of the vote as oligarchical'. Nearly all the officials in Athens were selected by lot. The Assembly, for example, was presided over by a citizen chosen purely arbitrarily for that day. Only a few, although admittedly the most important of positions such as that of the generals (*strategoi*), were filled by election.

Aristotle devotes a lot of space in his description of the Athenian constitution to description of the Council. However, it does not seem to have been as important as its small size might lead one to expect. The turnover in its membership, together with the arbitrariness of their selection, seems to have meant that it was not in much of a position to exercise independent political force. In any case the provision that people could not serve more than two years, no doubt designed to prevent domination by a few individuals, meant that the domination which did take place took place elsewhere. In Athens, people like Pericles, Cleon or Demosthenes were clearly important, yet they were not members of the Council. The ultimate power either lay with the Assembly or with the courts.

These courts are the remaining instrument of government to be described. If, from a political point of view, the Council was perhaps less important than one might have expected, the courts were more so. Aristotle's description of the domination of the courts by the people has already been quoted, and in the *Constitution of Athens* he says that 'when the people have the right to vote in the courts they control the constitution' (IX 1). The members of these courts were selected by lot from the citizen body as a whole, in a way which again gave equal representation to the ten tribes. Jurors had to be over 30 years of age and were selected from among those who turned up. They were paid. The juries selected were large by modern standards, always over 200, normally 500 (as in the case of the trial of Socrates) and sometimes over a thousand. The voting was not by show of hands but was done with tokens which were counted exactly. From a political point of view, the important thing is that they not only looked at straightforward judicial cases but also acted in effect as a review body for proceedings in the Assembly. In modern terms they were more like a supreme court, with the power of striking down legislation. They could set aside decrees of the Assembly and, indeed, in the fourth century, the Assembly only had the power to pass decrees rather than laws. Laws (that is, general regulations not specific to a particular person or occasion) could only be passed by a special committee set up by the courts themselves, the *nomothetai*. So in effect, this meant that the Assembly was more like a supreme executive body, making immediate decisions, particularly with respect to foreign policy, and doing so inside the context of established law, which was upheld by the courts and which could be appealed to if someone felt that any measure or politician had gone too far. This means that much of the proceedings of the courts was what we should now regard as political; and most of the preserved political speeches made by fourth-century orators such as Aeschines or Demosthenes were in fact made to courts, not the Assembly. The speech of Demosthenes quoted at the start is an example. Demosthenes was defending his conduct in a prosecution brought by Aeschines, and Aeschines had started his own prosecution speech in this case by stressing how democracy is subservient to law: 'In tyranny and oligarchy', he says, 'government depends on the whims of those in power, but democratic government depends upon established law' (III).

Aeschines here stresses the subservience of democracy to law because it was part of the criticism of opponents that in democracy all established laws were overturned and everything happened because of the whims of the mass of the citizens gathered together in the Assembly. So, for example, Aristotle can talk of 'those forms of democracy where the will of the people is superior to the law' (*Politics* 1310a). He is particularly thinking of times at which demagogues like Cleon took over; for, as he says earlier, 'it is popular leaders who, by referring all issues to the decision of the people, are responsible for substituting the sovereignty of decrees for that of the laws' (1292a). However here the control of the courts by the people, also stressed by Aristotle, becomes important. For even if the people meeting in Assembly were thought to make bad decisions, the courts allowed the people themselves to control this form of decision-making. If they were rash when in one guise, under another guise they could control themselves. So, in considering the workings of Athenian democracy, it is important to consider the workings of all three central bodies, the Assembly, the Council and the courts. To restate how these worked: in the government of Athens all full members had the right to attend and address the Assembly; the Assembly voted on the central, important decisions although business was introduced to it by the Council; most officials operating the system were chosen by lot, including the jurors in the large courts; and these courts had considerable powers of judicial review.

These are the facts about what happened. In assessing the value of democracy as a whole, and of this example in particular, it would also be useful to know how successful it was. Yet it is difficult to know how to measure this. One measure of the success of societies, as of other entities, is by how well they survive. Athenian democracy in the fourth century was remarkably stable and, if it had not been closed down by external forces, it is possible to suppose (although this is disputed) that it could have survived indefinitely. In that sense, as a form of government it was possible or operable; that is, it did not immediately and inevitably decay into another form. Arguing a priori, Plato thought that democracy was unstable, whereas Aristotle thought that it was more stable than oligarchy. In fact, while democracy was (or at least could be) stable, quite different sorts of societies were even more stable in the ancient world. Oligarchies such as Corinth and, particularly, Sparta survived for centuries.

Another, and related, way of measuring value might be taken to be the success of a society in competition with other societies, either in economic competition or in war. While Athens seems to have been fairly successful in the former, it was notably unsuccessful in the latter against its great rival Sparta. It is exactly this which Thucydides took to be the central point of his criticism of democracy; the disasters of the Sicilian expedition were attributed by him to a decision procedure in which a group of citizens in Assembly could vote for an expedition with no knowledge of what it really involved. On the other hand (quite apart from the fact that the Sicilian expedition seems to have been in fact as well prepared as it could have been by any form of government), war is not obviously a good measure of the worth of societies. Quite repulsive societies (measured on other grounds) seem sometimes to do well in war and vice versa. Furthermore, when societies, democratic or otherwise, fight wars they often change their form of government in order to do so; whether this shows the weakness of a democracy, in that, for the sake of efficiency, it has to turn itself into a temporary dictatorship or oligarchy, or whether it shows the strength of democracy that it is democratically able to change its form like this, is unclear.

Lacking a clear empirical measure of success, therefore, we have to turn to theory, ancient and modern, in order to assess the value of Athenian democracy. The first question here is whether it can really be called a democracy at all. For, as noticed, only a minority of the population who lived in the territory of Athens actually had the right of participating in government. Some of those excluded, such as minors and metics, are categories which nearly every state will have to exclude in some way (even if the lines are drawn in different places). However, this still leaves slaves and women as excluded groups. An answer from the theoretical point of view to the objection that no state excluding such categories could count as a democracy might be to take the Athenian state not as a direct example of a democracy but, rather, as a model which displayed certain democratic features, even if not itself one. That is, if such groups as slaves and women are ignored, then it could be thought that we have a working model of what one kind of democracy is like. However, if Athens, omitting slaves and women, is to be used as a model of what a real democracy (including slaves and women) might be like, then it is important to know how accidental is the omission of the omitted groups. For, to take the extreme case, if it were absolutely essential to the working of a government that certain groups were excluded, then this government could not be taken as a model of what would happen if these groups were included. As Aristotle puts it, commenting on the free-floating political inventions of Plato, 'we may admit that it is right to make assumptions freely; but it cannot be right to make any assumption which is plainly impossible' (*Politics* 1265a).

In the description above it was seen that attendance at all the central bodies of the state was paid (Council and courts in the fifth century and after, the Assembly in the fourth). It seems to be pretty generally agreed both by contemporary and more recent commentators that this payment was essential for the working of the democracy in that it enabled the poorer people (that is, the great mass of the population) to attend and work in these bodies (although Aristotle does distinguish between different kinds of democracy and thinks that some kinds, preferred by him, work without pay). So the next thing to examine is the preconditions of this payment; that is, where the money actually came from. In the fifth century, Athens headed a league of states united as a defence measure against the Persians. It was effectively an empire and Athens taxed her client states as the cost of providing protection. This was the source of the money used on the famous buildings of fifth-century Athens, and it has been argued that the money used to finance the democratic machinery had the same (essential) source, so that democracy at Athens was only possible at the cost of colonial exploitation elsewhere. However, the figures behind this argument do not really add up, for the expensive period from a democratic point of view was the fourth century when the Assembly was also paid and it was in just this century that Athens lost her empire and its tribute money. Furthermore, the cost of the democratic machinery was at no time in any way comparable with the cost of military operations. So it does not seem that a necessary condition for the operation of Athenian democracy was the exploitation of those outside.

There remains the more important question of the exploitation of those within. The argument here would be that the operation of Athenian democracy required leisure in its members so that they had time to participate in the Assembly, Council and courts. This leisure, it might be argued, was only available to the Athenian citizens because they possessed slaves who did the essential work and so gave their masters the time needed to engage in politics. Hence Athens could not be used as a model of a democracy. Aristotle says that 'it is generally agreed that leisure, or in other words freedom from the necessity of labour, should be present in any well-ordered state' (*Politics* 1269a), and he then goes on to discuss the conditions necessary for its achievement, such as the possession of serfs or slaves. However, since Aristotle thought that leisure was part of the good life and that a really ideal state was one in which all of its citizens were participating in the good life, it followed that no democracy could satisfy his absolute ideal since, at least in the way in which he thought of it 'a state with an ideal constitution . . . cannot have its citizens living the life of mechanics or shopkeepers, which is ignoble and inimical to goodness' (1328b). If we descend to a less exalted plane, and ask whether it was or could be possible for people without slaves to have enough leisure to operate the machinery of a democracy, then the actual practice of Athens shows that it could. For, as was seen above, the great mass of people had no slaves, and yet they engaged in politics. Aristotle himself talks elsewhere of the latest form of democracy as one in which 'the facilities of leisure are provided even for the poor by the system of state-payment' (*Politics* 1293a). Of course the great working mass were not full-time politicians, but, once public pay is introduced, there seems to be nothing in principle which would prevent some of them from being so. Even though lack of slaves might prevent people being the best possible people, it does not prevent the operation of a working democracy.

The very idea that Athens at this period was not a democracy would have seemed highly paradoxical to contemporary commentators. They thought that it was an obvious, or indeed extreme, example. Aristotle says that the 'present form' of the Athenian constitution was 'extreme democracy' (*Politics* 1274a). For them, if Athens was not a democracy, it was difficult to see what could be. However, even if we disagree with them about this, it seems that there is nothing in principle which prevents us from taking it as a full working model of democracy. So, either way, it works as a good example for considering the value of democracy. For it is with the question of its value that the real problems start. Neither Plato nor Aristotle were in doubt that what surrounded them in Athens was a democracy. However, they did not doubt either that what surrounded them was not an exemplification of the good, at least in its highest form.

The question of whether a particular form of constitution is of value, just like the question of whether any other particular thing is of value, is a question in applied ethics, and the ethical theory of both Plato and Aristotle is complex and sophisticated. Nevertheless, their central criticisms of democracy can be put simply in a way which presupposes little specific ethical theory. Indeed, it is best to put the criticisms like this, since it is good simple ideas which are the most devastating. Mere subtlety may always be eluded as smelling of sophistry and, since detail gets lost in transmission, it is also the simple root ideas which have been remembered and have been influential. At the centre of both Plato's and Aristotle's thought are extremely powerful criticisms which apply to both the theory and practice of democracy as they have occurred in the last two thousand years. All that is required for presentation of these ideas is, for Plato, a simple and widely-held view about the status of value judgments and, for Aristotle, some simple, and also widely held, views about the nature of justice. They also share with Greek thought in general an assumption about the relation between moral and political theory.

To start with the latter. The Greeks made the assumption that the measure of value (of the good) is from a human perspective. What is good is good for people. So the value of a particular kind of state, just like the value of any other particular kind of thing, is assessed by its value for the people who inhabit it. A good state is one which will allow its citizens to flourish or be happy. As Aristotle puts it in the *Politics*, 'the end and purpose of a *polis* is the good life, and the institutions of social life are means to that end' (1280b); or, just before, 'what constitutes a *polis* is an association of households and clans in a good life, for the sake of attaining a perfect and self-sufficing existence'. This may make it sound as if in Greek thought, as happens in much later political thought, we start with an idea of the nature of man, already fully formed and pre-existing, and then ask which societies would be good for such a man (or, in certain versions, which societies he would choose to enter). However, such use of the idea of pre-social individuals, with its related fantasies of the use of a state of nature and of original contracts, is not prominent or central in Greek thought. This is because although the value of states is assessed by their value to individuals, individuals are standardly assumed only to possess their highest value when they are members of states. To take Aristotle again: he is quite clear that the end, or goal, of man is to live in society; that is, living in a state is the natural condition of a properly developed individual just as being an oak tree is the natural state of a properly developed acorn ('Man is by nature an animal intended to live in a *polis*' is a better translation of the famous remark habitually translated as 'man is a political animal' (*Politics* 1253a)). So, although the good of the state is measured by its good for individuals, this does not mean that we can take already formed, pre-social individuals and see how good a state or particular types of state might be for them. Instead, we have to compare actual and possible states and see which one gives the greatest possibility of fulfilment or good to its citizens.

If, then, as Aristotle puts it, 'the end of the state is not mere life; it is, rather, a good quality of life' (1280a), it has to be seen which kinds of state promote this quality, and it is here we run into the objections of both Plato and Aristotle. The central idea involved in Plato's criticism is that there is a truth about matters of value, so that whether or not something is good does not just depend upon whether or not somebody thinks that it is. If people disagree about matters of value, then it is possible that some of them are right and some of them are wrong; it is not that every opinion is as good as every other. Or, to put this another way, it is possible to have knowledge about the good, so that those who know are better placed than those who do not know. Now, if the central aim of democracy, as of any valuable political system, is to promote the good life for man, then it is important that it does, or brings about, those things which are in fact good for man. That is, if someone's views are followed with respect to what ought to be done, those views should be followed which lead to the right things being done. Presumably, if some people have knowledge about the good and others do not, then the views of those with knowledge should be followed. Yet, in a democracy, it is not the views of those with knowledge which are put into effect but, rather, the views of the people as a whole (or, more realistically, since the people as a whole are unlikely to be in unanimous agreement, the views of the majority of the people). If the views of the people (or the majority) coincides with the views of the people who know, this would seem to be entirely accidental. So the problem for democracy is how it can be other than pure accident or pure luck that it manages to promote the assumed end of all states, the good for man. To meet the challenge, it seems that it would have to be shown that the majority naturally or normally are those who possess knowledge.

This is the root of Plato's challenge. As far as the empirical facts were concerned, he tended to assume that the majority did not have such knowledge. Just as Thucydides saw the contemporary democracy making what he felt to be wrong decisions, Plato talks scathingly in passing in the *Republic* of the populace crowding into the Assembly and 'clamouring its approval or disapproval, both alike excessive' (492b). He gives the same impression that the members of their own class, the so-called beautiful and best, knew better about things than the people at large. However such purely empirical assumptions are an optional extra to the central thrust of Plato's criticism. Nor, though he was anti-democratic, and in favour of rule by a few, did this mean that Plato was in favour of a hereditary aristocracy or of rule by a few rich people. For the central point of the whole account is knowledge, and the few that should rule are those with knowledge. This is why the *Republic*, ostensibly a work of political theory, devotes so much space to pure philosophy and to topics such as education. The important thing is to show that there could be knowledge of the good, and the long education which would be needed to acquire it. Based on this is the idea that the perfect state will only arise if, in the famous phrase, 'either philosophers become kings or those who are now called kings and rulers come to be sufficiently inspired with a genuine desire for wisdom' (437d). For Plato, the masses could never become such rulers, for 'the multitude can never be philosophical' (494a).

The *Republic* contains an extensive sketch of an ideal state run by such carefully educated philosophers, the guardians. However, again the details are additional to the basic criticism, which arises quite naturally from the fact that democracy is a decision procedure. Plato displays how strange such a decision procedure would look in apparently analogous cases, such as the navigation of a ship. If we supposed that there was no knowledge about navigation, then perhaps everyone could argue with everyone; however, since there is knowledge, 'it is not in the natural course of things for the pilot to beg the crew to take his orders' (489b). Similarly, since the philosophers have knowledge, 'it would be absurd not to choose the philosophers whose knowledge is perhaps their greatest point of superiority', in deciding which views to follow in questions of state (484d).

It was noted earlier how Plato commentated unfavourably on the freedom that was rife in democracies, and in the *Republic* there are splendid descriptions of a state in which everyone was free to do what they wanted. What is brought out in these graphic descriptions is the consequence, as Plato sees it, of allowing equality between those that are unequal. Even the animals, he thinks, are too full of themselves in democracies; and the pupils no longer listen to their teachers. Modelling the state on an individual, he tries to show up the absurdity of treating every person's opinions equally by considering how absurd it would be if someone were to hold that every one of his own desires and beliefs were to be treated equally, that is considered to be equally good and given equal rights. Plato has other things in mind, such as the danger of the decay of democracy into either anarchy or tyranny, but the central idea is the same. In democracy, all opinions are held to be of equal value; hence the majority view is followed. But, if there is knowledge, all opinions are not of equal value; hence adopting the views of the majority is not the right way to make decisions.

Answering the objection that his description of the guardians would seem to leave them leading such a deprived life that they could not possibly be happy, Plato has Socrates remark that 'our aim in founding the commonwealth was not to make one class specially happy but to secure the greatest possible happiness for the community as a whole' (420c). In Plato's ideal state, the people who know would work not for their own but for the general interest, hence promoting both fairness (or justice) and harmony in the state. The need for fairness or justice is a presupposition also made by Aristotle, and is the central assumption on which he builds. He assumes that a political system is not aimed at the good if its decisions are made in the interest of one particular part of the state rather than the state as a whole. He then shows that this is what in fact happens in democracy. So the core of Aristotle's criticism is that democracy is the rule by a particular group of people in its own interests. This particular group is the majority. In a democracy their views prevail. So, if they act in their own interest, a democracy serves the interest of the majority and not the people as a whole.

At first sight this might look to be a merely formal objection. Obviously if there is disagreement some view has to be chosen, and the best way of treating everyone's views equally, as democracy requires, is to adopt the views of the majority. However, this is not Aristotle's point. It is not just that the views of the majority are followed, but that this majority is in fact composed of a particular class of people identifiable in other ways. In other words, independently of whether or not they formed the majority, the group which happens to form the majority could be identified. Hence decisions made by the majority are decisions made by, and in the interest of, this separately identifiable group. Hence rule by it will be rule by this separately identifiable group rather than rule by the people as a whole. The group in question is the great mass of the poor people. So democracy is identified as rule by the poor in their own interests. This thought was already present before Aristotle; Plato had said in the *Republic* that, in civil conflict, 'when the poor win, the result is democracy' (557a), and before that the writer now referred to as the Old Oligarch, or Pseudo Xenophon, said 'when the poor, the ordinary people and the lower classes flourish and increase in numbers, then the power of the democracy will be increased' and explained, at least from the point of view of these people, that it was not desirable for the 'ablest' or 'respectable' to rule instead, for they would then draw up laws in their own interest and 'as a result of this excellent system the common people would very soon lose all their political rights' (*The Constitution of the Athenians* 4; 9). However, Aristotle gives the general idea its most developed form.

Aristotle's *Politics* is a deep and dense work covering an enormous variety of questions about political theory and practice. One remark from it about restricting philosophy to the possible has already been quoted; however as well as the possible, Aristotle was also very interested in the actual, and the *Politics* not only considers ideal states, or the 'absolute best', but also 'what is the best in relation to actual conditions' (1288b). Aristotle even considers such things as climate, water supply and ideal geographical situation (a single strong acropolis for monarchies, a plain for democracies and many separate strong points for aristocracies). Five different kinds of democracies are distinguished and a variety of mixed constitutions. Faced with all this detail the present account inevitably restricts itself to a few short and central points.

The overall structure of Aristotle's treatment depends upon his classification of states. He makes two kinds of distinction and then combines them to give him the matrix of his classification. He distinguishes states according to how many people form the sovereign (or rulers) and according to whether they are aimed at their proper object or not. Rule can be by one, few or many; the state may be aimed at its proper end of justice or not. So this gives him three 'right' kinds of state, called by him, according to how many rule, kingship, aristocracy and 'polity' (*politeia*), and, corresponding to them, three 'wrong' kinds of states, or 'perversions', tyranny, oligarchy and democracy. Democracy is hence a perversion of proper government; directed, as Aristotle puts it, 'to the interest of the poorer classes' (1279b). However this classification reveals that there is something very like democracy, something indeed which other people might call democracy, which is not perverse in this way. This is the so-called 'polity' (otherwise variously translated as 'constitutional government' or 'constitution') which is also, like democracy, rule by 'the masses', only now governing 'with a view to the common interest' (1279a). The fact that Aristotle's classification allows this perfectly proper form of government by the masses shows how his objection to rule by the many does not depend upon some factor necessarily connected with such rule but, rather, with an extra and merely contingently connected fact. This is the fact that the masses will tend to pursue their own rather than the general interest; and so it is here that Aristotle's general sociological analysis becomes important. An account has to be, and is, added of classes, class interest and money. This is what he undertakes immediately after the general classification, and it is in terms of this that it emerges that 'the real ground of the difference between oligarchy and democracy is poverty and riches' (1279b).

There are, therefore, two quite separate factors operating in Aristotle's analysis and criticism, each plausible but each also contestable and in need of defence. The first is an account of the ends of the state, whereby a general criterion of value is proposed which can be used to distinguish between good states and bad. The second is an account of what happens in actual states, whereby it is held that specific groups or classes can be distinguished on economic grounds and that each of these groups tends to operate in its own class interest. Not much more can be said about the latter, proto-Marxist point, which must in any case depend in the end upon the observation of actual societies. Those whose political theory lives by the facts may also die by the facts. However, on the former, general evaluative point, more can be said and more is said by Aristotle himself. For it can naturally be asked why we should operate with a criterion of value which concerns more than self-interest. The answer, to take Aristotle's own term, is because we have an idea of what is just (*dikaion*). However, this is only the start of an answer, because there can be different ideas of justice. Justice, after all, is connected with equality and it has already been seen that equality is one of the prime virtues presupposed and promoted by democracy. Yet Aristotle is aware of this objection, and it is the way in which he holds to and manages such objections which displays the continuing relevance and sophistication of his analyses. Commenting on the conflict between oligarchy and democracy (the few and the many), he holds that each side has its own idea of justice. The democrats think of justice in terms of equality but the proper idea of justice is giving things equally to those who are equal, not giving things equally to those who are unequal. People are not, in this way, equal; so it is wrong to respect them equally.

This reply could be taken as a way of making the Platonic objection, and both as such and as an analysis of the crucial central idea of equality it will be looked at in the second, analytic, part of this book. However, the idea of justice also has its independent force in Aristotle's account, as when he takes it that it is unjust for any group, even the majority, to rule in its own interests. For Aristotle, 'the good in the sphere of politics is justice; and justice consists in what tends to promote the common interest' (1282b). He tests whether this is what happens in democracy by asking what we would think 'if the poor, on the ground of their being a majority, proceeded to divide among themselves the possessions of the wealthy', asking 'will this not be unjust?' (1281a). He then imagines two replies, such as might be given in an argument on this topic. The first is that of a democrat who is taken as saying that it is not unjust because it 'has been justly decreed so by the sovereign'. This is not in fact fully relevant to the question as asked, although Aristotle does not bring this out immediately, since the question concerns the abstract, or moral, justice of an action, not its legitimacy according to a fixed law. Instead he moves directly to the other side, which replies with the rhetorical question, 'but if this is not the extreme of injustice, what is?' As a rhetorical question, this will not convince anyone who does not already hold the view; yet it is clearly the side which Aristotle thinks should be convincing, as emerges when he adds some argument. This is that justice, as a good, cannot have bad consequences. Yet 'whenever a majority of any sort, irrespective of wealth or poverty, divides among its members the possessions of a minority, that majority is obviously ruining the state'. Hence, such a law 'cannot possibly be just'. Yet there are at least two problematic features in this argument. First, it is a pure assumption that all good things will converge or coincide, so that something good cannot have bad consequences; indeed it is more normal to think that justice is precisely one of those virtues that may very well not have good consequences (but that, to cite another ancient tag, one should do justice even if the heavens fall). Second, it is not clear that the consequences of the expropriation of the property of the rich is as ruinous to the state as Aristotle assumes.

The example of expropriation is, however, one to which Aristotle keeps returning. 'It is clear', he holds, 'that all these acts of oppression are mean and unjust' (1281a), and yet he constantly holds that such acts of oppression are exactly what are liable to happen in democracies, particularly those of the worst sort. As he sums it up, towards the end of the *Politics*, 'if . . . justice is made to consist in the will of a majority of persons, that majority will be sure to act unjustly, as we have already noted, and to confiscate the property of a rich minority' (1318a). Hence follows the idea that the rule of a majority can be exactly like the rule of a self-interested tyranny. Earlier Xenophon (the real one this time) had reported a supposed conversation in which Alcibiades had argued that 'whatever the assembled majority, through using its power over the owners of property, enacts without persuasion is not law but force' (*Mem* I ii 45). Aristotle's own eventual reply to the claim that what was enacted by the majority, because it was enacted by the sovereign, must be just, is that if this made something just, then 'the tyrant's acts too must necessarily be just; for he too uses coercion by virtue of superior power in just the same way as the people coerce the wealthy' (1281a).

The problem which Aristotle leaves to subsequent theorists or defenders of democracy is, therefore, how democracy can be other than dictatorship by the majority; or sectional rule by a group of the people in its own interests. His criterion of a proper form of government, that it should be such 'that there is no single section in all the state which would favour a change to a different constitution' (1294b), is likely to be generally acceptable; as is the factual presupposition on which it rests, that states are composed of different groups or classes of people with different interests. So the problem is how democracy can be a just or fair government of a mixed society, given that by the nature of the case government in a democracy can only be by normal individuals (and not any super-trained guardians wound up from birth to aim at goodness) and that in such a mixed society there are inevitably conflicts of interests and opinions, so there is no way of trying to rule by unanimous decision. The problem posed for democracy as a means of deciding such disputes is that it seems to put the wrong people in charge because they lack both sufficient knowledge and also, since they will aim at their own rather than the general interest, sufficient goodness. This problem, or these problems, will have to be resolved in the second part of the book.

CHAPTER III

The Negative Liberal Tradition: Hobbes and Locke

People choose between possibilities; possibilities are constituted by knowledge; and knowledge is based on what has happened before. The theory and the practice of the Greeks have provided models which have been copied, abused, and adapted from the time of the Greeks to the present day. They have been possibilities moulding what followed, even though what followed has rarely been democracy. In the period between the classical Athens and the relatively recent past it is the theory rather than the practice of democracy, and indeed of government more generally, which is important for our purposes. The theory we are particularly interested in is theory which frames and explains our present understanding of democracy, and so, luckily for us, not all important political theory needs to be considered. This chapter in fact jumps over two thousand years from the last. On the other hand, not all theory important for the present understanding and assessment of democracy is itself democratic theory or specifically about democracy. The thinkers centrally considered in this chapter are important for us because of their influence on the actual nature of our present democracy and because of the possibilities they offer us for understanding it. Yet they did not think of themselves as democrats.

When considering self-rule in the first chapter it was noted that we would examine two rival traditions of thought. Both traditions agree in giving a value to liberty, and so in considering how society might allow or promote this aspect of human value. However, since they disagree in their understanding of what liberty amounts to, they disagree about the nature of such promotion, and so about the nature of a government which would promote it. We would expect liberty to go with democracy. If people are liberated from the rule of others, then, it seems, there is nobody left to rule them but themselves. And we saw in the last chapter how democratic Athens arose from such a liberation; and how the accounts of it stressed liberty.

We also saw how these accounts stressed equality. If democracy is rule of people as a whole, then it inevitably gives equal significance, at least in one respect, to all the citizens of a country. It is true of them all (that is, it is equally true of them) that they are part of the sovereign power. More specifically, for classical Athens it was seen that the particular equalities which citizens possessed were equality before the law, equal right to address the Assembly and equal chance of being a member of the Council or of holding political office. Described as rights, the first two of these were freedoms allowed to the citizens; that is, there was no legal or constitutional impediment to their being judged according to the laws, or their addressing the Assembly. So the equal spread of power characteristic of a democracy goes with the equal spread of certain rights or privileges. Everyone is equally granted certain freedoms of operation. To understand these liberties is to acquire insight into the democracy they represent. The freedoms which democracy enables or prevents give a measure of its legitimate basis and of its appropriate limits. The two traditions to be described, differing as they do over liberty, hence also differ over these.

This later thought was influenced by its own contexts and hence differed importantly from the thought of the Greeks. Just as the Greeks were influenced by, and partially commenting on, the situation in their own day, so subsequent political theory has not been thought up in a vacuum, but has been a response to particular and local conditions. These conditions however were viewed in terms of the existing possibilities of thought at that time, so that the context of the thought has been not only immediately political but also historical. If we jump over two thousand years from the Greeks, the thought which we arrive at was influenced not just by the ideas of classical Athens, but also by later Greek and Roman thought and its transmission through the thinkers of the medieval church. It is, however, the classical context that is most influential in a classically educated civilisation, which is what Europe was until the present century. Knowledge of this classical world is one thing which unites such diverse thinkers as Hume and Marx, both of whom wrote about the ancient world as well as the modern. Rousseau may have been the son of a watchmaker, but he was brought up with Plutarch.

Machiavelli's chief work was a series of discourses on Livy. Hobbes translated Thucydides and frequently referred to Aristotle. It was in this way that ancient thought provided a continuous model.

It might seem that these later thinkers would be able to make little use of classical thought. On grounds of size alone, the form of state discussed in Athenian thought was quite irrelevant to later thought and practice. The modern world exists in enormous nation-states with little resemblance to the small, face-to-face, world of classical Athens as described in the last chapter. However, even in the modern world some of the influential later thinkers grew up in, and had acquaintance with, small city-states not completely dissimilar to the ancient variety. Machiavelli did so, and also Rousseau. Even when they did not, as is the case with the two people principally studied in this chapter, Hobbes and Locke, what happened in these much-studied and hence familiar ancient states formed an argumentative resource, or model, on which these classically educated thinkers could draw when faced with the problems of their own society. In *De Cive*, for example, Hobbes takes as his object of study what he calls 'the city'. He draws the possible kinds of government, democracy, aristocracy, monarchy, directly from Aristotle. His model of demo-cracy is a state in which all have equal access to address a single assembly; that is, it is exactly like the classical Athenian model discussed in the last chapter.

Hobbes and Locke both faced problems in their particular society which they needed arguments, that is, a normative political theory, to resolve. Hobbes saw a country torn apart by civil war, brother destroying brother; Locke the apparently unbridled power of a king which seemed to require resistance by his subjects. These are converse problems: on the one hand the problem of what would legitimate the removal of such civil strife; on the other the problem of what could legitimate rebellion against a properly crowned hereditary monarch. Yet the arguments they deployed to meet these real and pressing problems have a certain similarity as well as important differences.

One similarity between the approach of Hobbes and Locke which makes them both strikingly different from the thought of the Greeks discussed in the last chapter, and which is noticed as such by Hobbes himself right at the start of his *De Cive*, is that they approach political theory from the standpoint of the value for individuals of states or other political structures. Of course, value for Plato and

Aristotle was also value for individuals; and it was the freedom or equality of individuals which the ancient democratic commentators took to be of value. However, as was seen, Plato and Aristotle thought that human beings attained their full perfection, or highest value, in a community. For them little could be understood about the final or complete good for man unless he was thought of as a member of a political community. However Hobbes (and, following him, Locke and later thinkers) thought that a perfectly good sense could be given to the highest good for man even if he was regarded as an individual independently of all political society. Human worth or value could be looked at in itself, and it then became a quite separate question of which forms of state or political organisation would promote this separately understood value. This helps to locate the importance of liberty in their thought because since man has value when he is independent of (that is free of) a government, the problem becomes how much of this freedom he is able to preserve on entry to political society. Freedom is thought of as freedom from interference, either by government or by other individuals.

The independent worth of human beings also explains the use of the myth, or story, of the state of nature in these thinkers. Since civil society (or organised government) is supposed to be a human artifact, it is contrasted for analytical purposes with a supposed natural state in which there is no such artifact. As both Hobbes and Locke stress, they are not very interested in the historical facts about whether there ever was at any period such a pre-political state. Yet description of such a state is prominent in both of their thought, serving as a model which enables them to identify and analyse those features only present in political society. Since the values of human beings are the values they can be supposed to possess in the natural state, it can then be asked whether entry into the artificial, political society might promote those values. One way of testing this out, and hence testing whether a given political society is of value, is to ask whether people placed in the natural state would agree to enter that political society. If they would, this tends to show that it improves on, or at least preserves, the values which man would have in the natural state; if not, not. The contract models the supposed mutually beneficial advantages of a transition from natural to political society; and so the question of whether or on what terms the transition would be beneficial can be decided by deciding whether or on what terms such a contract would be made. Societies which would be contracted into are societies that are good for man; hence the goodness of a particular form of society for man can be determined by seeing whether it would be contracted into.

Hobbes wrote two books about government, his *De Cive*, which appeared in 1642, and the more famous expansion and rewriting of it and other material, the *Leviathan*, which appeared in 1651. In both he talks of a law of nature, but this does not really have the moral tone of most invocations of natural law, either before or after him. Hobbes thinks of the individual good for man in much more self-interested terms, and the law of nature refers much more to how human individuals actually do behave than to how they ought to behave. As Hobbes puts it, 'of the voluntary acts of every man, the object is some *good to himselfe*' (*Lev* xiv 93). These goods, or needs, start with life and the protection of the body against attack. These are the basic values for individuals, and so the first values which an individual would be seeking to protect or promote if he chose to enter civil society. It is protection, his first need, which makes him obey the state; as Hobbes puts it, 'the end of Obedience is Protection' (*Lev* xxi 153). The famous phrase in the *Leviathan* about the condition of man, that it is 'solitary, poore, nasty, brutish and short' (xiii 89) describes the supposed state of man in natural, or pre-political, society. This is the state which Hobbes thinks of as the state of war in which there is complete liberty and anyone is free to devour anyone else. It is to avoid such an unpleasant state, therefore, that man enters society. Or (to put this another way) the benefits of society can be measured by seeing how much a man's life is superior to being nasty, brutish and short.

Political society for Hobbes is an artificial construct in the sense that it has been created by man as a replacement for, or improvement on, natural society. It can arise (for him) in basically one of two ways. Either a group of independent (and in that sense equal) people can meet together and agree with each other to have such a political society or else someone (or some group with superior power) can conquer the others and subject them to political authority. The former Hobbes calls a state formed by institution; the latter a state formed by acquisition. Perhaps surprisingly, the final result in each is very similar in terms of the power and entitlement of the sovereign and the obligations on both sovereign and subject. This is because Hobbes thinks of them both as arising from some kind of agreement. Even if a state is formed by acquisition, Hobbes still thinks that this represents the agreement of the conquered people to obey their conquerors. It is precisely this which distinguishes such subject people, or servants, for him from the condition of slavery. A slave is fettered, has to be forced to work by purely physical means, has made no agreements and so is fully entitled to kill his masters if he gets a chance. By contrast a servant is unfettered and has agreed to obey; the fact that the agreement might have been achieved by the use of force does not invalidate it in Hobbes' eyes and indeed is explicitly held to be irrelevant. In both kinds of states, therefore, agreement is involved. So although Hobbes realises very well that most states arise through conquest he can still look at the construction of a state through agreement between equals in order to expose the logical structure of obligations inherent in all states.

Whatever is thought of Hobbes' particular solutions, the general structure of argument which he here adopts has had a perennial appeal. The central idea is that the value of a social institution can be determined or calculated by reference to how well it supports the pre-existing values or desires of individuals. It is assumed that pre-eminent among these is security, or bare survival. Yet there is a problem about how individual, self-interested, people can ensure such security. The problem can be expressed in terms of modern games theory. Each individual is taken to be a purely self-interested atom only concerned to protect himself; he enters political society only for the good which he individually gets out of it. There is an incentive for him to do so in that no one person has strength to secure himself individually. Even the strongest go to sleep; as Hobbes puts it, 'as to the strength of body, the weakest has strength enough to kill the strongest' (*Lev* xiii 87). Hence it seems that everyone should in his own interest agree with others so that they all mutually ensure each others' protection. Yet it is just with such an agreement that from this self-interested or games-playing point of view that the troubles start. For although a particular individual would be better off in a system with agreement about security than no system at all, he would be even better off if everyone else guaranteed his security and he could do what he liked. Put in terms of promises, or contracts, he will be best off if others keep their promises to him but he does not necessarily keep his to them; so that they protect him if he is asleep and he does not need to protect them if they are asleep. However, everyone is in the same position, and so there will be a temptation for everyone to break their promises. Therefore the individual self-interested action of each person is likely to end up with everyone back in the original state of nature position in which life is nasty, brutish and short.

The problem here is called in modern terms the prisoner's dilemma: if everyone keeps faith everyone will be better off, yet when each individual calculates his own advantage, he cannot trust everyone to keep faith, so he acts in his own immediate interest, and this has the result that everyone is in the end worse off. Hobbes, even if not in these terms, is aware of the problem since he provides an answer to it. There is no suggestion in either *De Cive* or *Leviathan* that mere agreement is all that is required to take people out of the state of nature and into an instituted society created for their mutual benefit. For, as Hobbes puts it, 'the bonds of words are too weak to bridle men's ambition, avarice, anger, and other Passions, without the feare of some coërcive Power' (*Lev* xiv 96). Keeping one's agreements is indeed the right thing to do but he holds that it cannot be expected that this will happen in the state of nature. So this is why we need something which frightens people into keeping their agreements. As Hobbes puts it, 'the Passion to be reckoned upon, is Fear' (*Lev* xiv 99). In Hobbes' terms we need the power of the sword. 'Covenants, without the Sword, are but Words', he says (*Lev* xvii 117). The sword, or fear frightening people into obedience, is provided by the state. Hence people in agreeing to have a state agree to have a power sufficient to frighten them into obedience. There is no question of them being left to rely on their and each other's words; instead they all agree to have a power which allows them no choice. Hence the great power of the Leviathan, the state, is constructed and this power is absolute, bound by no external conventions or laws. The individuals have no rights against it, and it has full power of interpretation and control of thought, not permitting the private judgment of individuals to stand over against it. There is no way now in which the prisoner's dilemma can arise in which each person being tempted into his own particular good provides less good for everyone including themselves. His own interest, his own fear, frightens him out of a such a short-sighted course. The power each individual has agreed to create for his own protection binds and terrifies him as much as it does anyone else.

These considerations are about government or political authority as such, so it might well be asked what significance they have for the study of democracy. The first significance is that they provide a clear statement of an important and generally understood measure of value to individuals which can then be used to assess the worth of various systems. Self-interest (or the life, welfare or happiness of the agent) is a recognised or self-understandable motivation for action. Later on it becomes stipulative of what is considered to be rational behaviour, or at least of what is more narrowly called economic rationality. So the problem it sets for the assessment of democracy is to show that participation in democracy is actually in the interests of the participants in this way; in later formulations this becomes the question of whether it is rational (in this economic sense) for someone to be a democrat. In terms of the original contract, this can be put as the question of why it should be rational for anyone to contract into a democratic society.

This is a general problem bequeathed by Hobbes' evaluative starting point, but he also bequeaths a particular answer which is both clarificatory of and also opposed to democracy. The clarificatory point is that since the reason why anyone would find it rational to engage in society is protection and because such protection would be unavailable without unquestioned authority (the power of the sword), democracies just like other systems have to have a single, coercive authority. So although the method in which decisions are arrived at may be different from monarchies, both the method itself and decisions arrived at by the method must be as beyond the control of individual choice, as separated from individual judgment about whether or not to obey, as the products of the most coercive dictatorship. Otherwise any point of having a state at all would disappear. As Hobbes puts it, 'it is requisite that, in those necessary matters which concern peace and self-defence, there be but one will of all men' (*De Cive* v). He goes on to say that it could be subject to a council, as in a democracy, but subject it must be. So Hobbes, if he is right, severely limits the understanding of what is possible in a democracy, and hence what the attractions for its citizens might be. However, as well as such clarifications, Hobbes is himself explicitly opposed to democracy. When he specifically discusses it he thinks that decision-making is both more certain and also more likely to be addressed to the good of the people as a whole if a single person such as a king is in charge rather than competing democratic factions or people who make speeches to the assembly for effect; here he is effectively following the sceptical Greek commentators such as Thucydides.

41

The other importance of Hobbes' thought for the discussion of democracy is the use of the idea of a contract. This, as seen, is a less moralised device in Hobbes than in either earlier or later thinkers. However, once the idea of obligation based upon contract or agreement is established, the question arises of what sort of agreement or contract is present specifically in democracy. Immediately after the remark just quoted about submission to one will Hobbes says that such submission is made by a group of people when 'each one of them obligeth himself by contract to every one of the rest, not to resist the will of that one man or council, to which he hath submitted himself'. The one man is monarchy, but the council is the democratic case, so Hobbes sees democracies being instituted by a universal agreement between all men that they will be bound by the council. Since few, if any, states are founded by such explicit agreement or institution, the question is what importance if any such an idea of contract can have for other democracies. It was seen above that he also assumed that contract worked in the case of conquest; however, what is a more powerful idea for subsequent analysis is the idea that the contracting does not have to be a once-and-for-all gesture at the institution of a state but, rather, is something which can be presumed from subsequent actions. For as well as explicit contracts, Hobbes says that there are tacit contracts. He says of a citizen that 'if he voluntarily entered into the Congregation of them that were assembled, he sufficiently declared thereby his will (and therefore tacitely covenanted) to stand to what the major part should ordayne' (*Lev* xviii 123). In other words, the mere entry into the assembly is taken as a sign that someone is willing to be bound by the results of the deliberations of that assembly, and that he is properly subjected to these results even if he does not like them. This is a very powerful result because one chief problem for democracy is how the kind of anarchy Hobbes portrays is to be prevented. If this involves some way of making dissenting citizens bound by a single community will, it would be very convenient if such binding could be seen to arise from some earlier agreement on the individual's part. But explicit agreements are normally lacking; so it would be even more convenient if some other action could be taken as expressing tacit agreement. Hobbes takes here entry into the assembly as such an action; a later attempt might take the participation in a democratic procedure such as voting. So Hobbes' idea has potentially powerful consequences. If on the one hand Hobbes is right about the authority which any state needs, but on the other hand no such agreement, explicit or tacit, can properly be found, then it seems that there cannot be any effective democracies.

As the last remark shows, Hobbes assumes that the will of the majorities in assemblies ought to prevail. The question therefore arises as to why the majority should be supposed to have such rights over the minority. This can be taken in Hobbes, as the remark also shows, as arising from the agreement of those persons who happen to form the minority. However, if that is the only source, anyone in the original position of agreement could have agreed on any decision procedure which ought to be followed by the assembly: two-thirds majority, universal agreement, drawing lots for a spokesman and so on. Yet Hobbes talks as if there were something peculiarly natural or distinctive about following the majority will. The question arises for him even if his preferred government is monarchy rather than democracy; that is, government by one man rather than by assembly. For when the state is originally set up, at that time at least it is (as he recognises) a sort of democracy. All the people assemble together and decide what to have, even if they decide to have monarchy. So in this original assembly there has to be some decision procedure, and Hobbes assumes that it is by majority vote. He starts the chapter in *Leviathan* on the rights of sovereigns created by institution by saying that a commonwealth is instituted when all agree that whatsoever man or assembly the majority will select shall be the sovereign (xviii). Here the source is still the agreement of all, but it is also assumed that this is what all will agree about. Such agreement of all to have majority decision is also mentioned in the earlier *De Cive* (vi. 2), and there Hobbes says that 'we understand that to be the will of the council, which is the will of the major part of those men of whom the council consists' (v. 7). Although Hobbes' invocation of an original universal agreement can provide an answer about the source of the authority of the majority, other thinkers seem to think that they can assume it without any such prop; and in any case agreement may prove to be an unreliable support particularly if it is taken to be tacit rather than explicit. So this relatively unquestioning assumption of the rightness of the majority representing the view of the whole council or assembly is another problem bequeathed for subsequent concern.

Locke, who disagrees in many things with Hobbes, follows him in the assumption that it is reasonably straightforward to suppose that the wishes of a group can be identified with the wishes of the majority of members of that group. Yet the other differences are such to make this a considerably less comfortable supposition for him than it is for Hobbes. The chief of these differences is that Locke's state of nature is moralised again, so that description of what people are like in a natural, or pre-political, state becomes a description of what they are like bound by a natural, moral law. Hence the question of their entry into a political state, by agreement or otherwise, becomes now not just the question of why it might be of advantage to them, but also the question of whether it is morally permitted, obligatory or advisable in terms of this pre-existing and over-arching moral framework.

Locke's chief political work is the *Second Treatise of Government*, which he entitled *An Essay concerning the True Original, Extent, and End of Civil Government*. It appeared anonymously in 1690, just after the so-called bloodless revolution in which James II had been replaced by William III (although it was probably written earlier with another proposed revolution in mind). Its first main chapter is devoted to the state of nature and Locke is immediately concerned to assert that the 'state of nature has a law of nature to govern it which obliges every one' (ii §7). This law prevents assaults on others' lives and lesser possessions, and Locke thinks that, as well as the law of nature, there is also a right to punish in the state of nature by which this law can be enforced. Indeed he thinks that it is precisely this right to punish which individuals transfer to government when they enter civil society. So for Locke the most important things which individuals have on the basis of this pre-political law of nature are rights. Like property, these can be looked at as moral assets of their owners; particular advantages an individual possesses which are protected (morally) against the depredations of others. Such are life, liberty and possessions, all of which Locke called 'property' ('his property, that is, his life, liberty, and estate' (vii §87)). Hobbes talked of rights or freedoms in the state of nature, but all he meant by this was that, in the state of nature, everyone was free to do what they wanted; having a right meant that someone might do something if they could and would. It was a type of moral permission. In Locke, by contrast, having a right means that others are morally prevented from interfering with the right; rather than permitting the right-holder, the right lays obligations on others. The difference can clearly be seen in the case of property itself, understood in its normal or narrower sense. In Hobbes, no one has any moral entitlement to private possessions in a pre-political state. In Locke, by contrast, there is an entire chapter of the *Second Treatise* explicitly designed to show how entitlement to private property could have arisen in a state of nature.

So in Locke man has property and other private rights before entering into a political community. If, therefore, he agrees by contract to do so, he already has much more than in a Hobbesian state of nature (which Locke calls a state of war). Since he has much more to preserve on entry to the political state, this constrains more sharply the kind of society which he might agree to enter and the terms on which the entry might be made. Of course, for the advantages of state protection, people might be represented as (explicitly or tacitly) giving up all these more substantial rights just as Hobbes took them to give up his lesser ones. However, even on the assumption that it is possible to do so, to will such rights away might seem to be a bad bargain. To suppose that someone would hand themselves over to a Hobbesian absolute sovereign who could not be checked in any way would seem, in Locke's words, 'to think that Men are so foolish that they take care to avoid what Mischiefs may be done them by *Pole-Cats*, or *Foxes*, but are content, nay think it Safety, to be devoured by *Lions*' (vii §93). Uncertain as the depredations of polecats might be in the state of nature, depredations would become more certain in a political state run by a lion.

Whether someone having such rights should choose to leave the state of nature is a matter of calculation; and Locke himself writes at times as if people so calculating would not relinquish their rights on these conditions. However the more important and interesting point is whether it is possible for people to relinquish the rights at all even if they wished to. There are two views about this in general rights theory, which will be picked up in the second half of this book, in Chapter 8. Locke himself supposes that there are certain rights which people could not relinquish on entering the political state, even if they wished to. He does not think that it is possible, for example, for anyone to sell themselves into slavery nor, therefore, to bind themselves by contract to a certain kind of absolute ruler. As he puts it, 'a Man, not having the Power of his own Life, *cannot*, by Compact, or his own Consent, *enslave himself* to any one, nor put himself under the Absolute, Arbitrary Power of another, to take away his Life, when he pleases' (iv §23). Locke hence becomes a leading representative of the tradition in which it is assumed that, to quote the American Declaration of Independence, all men are 'endowed by their Creator with certain inalienable rights'. Being inalienable, these rights are such that even if someone would, he could not give them away.

When Locke is understood in this manner, he becomes sharply distinct from Hobbes, and Hobbes' problem comes into sharp focus. For Locke, government is a matter of trust. Individual citizens have relinquished the exercise of certain rights to the government, explicitly or tacitly, on the understanding that the government will exercise them in certain ways. They still hold the rights and can resume individual exercise of them if they judge that the government has broken this trust. So all the things which Hobbes thought had to be swept away if a state was to be possible at all, such as a fundamental law outside the power of the sovereign or the ability of individuals to exercise private judgment about this fundamental law are maintained in Locke. Hence, as Locke wanted and Hobbes did not, we can have justification of resistance and rebellion, when an individual (or at least the people as a whole) judges that a state has broken its trust. This, however, still leaves Hobbes' problems. A state that is so subject to the views of individuals is always liable to dissolve into anarchy. Anyone may think that the state is a good thing as long as it agrees with them; but then remove consent or support when it disagrees. Locke, it is true, does talk of individuals in political society relinquishing their private rights of judgment; however, once the threatening force of the Hobbesian sovereign is removed, the instability of the prisoner's dilemma returns.

The most interesting as well as the most historically important case of an individual's rights is property itself. For if people are thought to agree to enter political society preserving their inalienable rights, and if these rights include property, then every individual is entitled to a continuous say about everything which happens to his property. This means that no government or state can take control over parts of its citizens' property without consulting them, indeed without getting their explicit agreement. Otherwise it would be illegitimate theft; the violation of that individual's property rights. As Locke says about men in society, 'no Body hath a right to take their substance, or any part of it from them, without their own consent; without this, they have no *Property* at all' (xi §138). Since any realistic government will need resources to do whatever it wishes to do, and since it will normally have to have recourse to its citizens for such resources, this means that most states will naturally have to consult with or obtain the agreement of its citizens. Yet such extensive consultation is effectively to behave as a democracy. So even if Locke himself did not write in a particularly democratic manner, the logic of his position, leading to the slogan that there should be no taxation without representation, ends up with a democratic conclusion whereby only a government which can consult with, and gain the agreement of all its citizens, is legitimate.

Even though this is democratic, it does not yet help much to justify actual democratic practice in that it has not yet been able to justify majority decision. As long as everyone universally agrees that their property should be used to such-and-such ends, this is fine; but, as this stands, no action is possible with less than universal agreement. Here we have a particular example of how, once such inalienable rights are granted, we have the tendency of any state to descend into anarchy or impotence. For there will be no effective government unless the state can act with less than universal agreement; this, after all, is just why Hobbes thought that the Leviathan had to be beyond all subsequent control by its citizens. Locke accepts this. Indeed he says that, if the consent of every individual were required before an act became the act of the whole body, then 'such a Constitution as this would make the mighty *Leviathan* of a shorter duration, than the feeblest creatures' (viii §98). Hence he argues that there has to be majority rule and that therefore (just as in Hobbes) people must be taken to have agreed on majority rule when contracting into society. As Locke puts it,

> when any number of Men have, by the consent of every individual, made a *Community*, they have thereby made that *Community* one Body, with a Power to Act as one Body, which is only by the will and determination of the *majority*.
>
> (viii §96)

This is just as in Hobbes, when all agree that they all will follow the majority. The question, however, is whether Locke, as opposed to Hobbes, is entitled to do this. If people have rights which they cannot give up, so that they have to be consulted about the disposal of their property, then it is not clear how they can give their rights up to the majority. On the other hand, if they are allowed to hand over such rights, then it would seem that all rights of resistance would have been given away and we would be back with the Hobbesian state in which, because of our fear of polecats, we deliver ourselves over to a lion.

In spite of these problems, the kind of view represented by Locke is of central importance in understanding and criticising democratic theory. The most important element in this view is the understanding of human rights as a kind of moral possession which someone has independently of society and which they continue to have while in any legitimate society. This constrains the understanding of democracy in two contrasting ways. On the one hand, it places a limit on the exercise of democratic government, just as it does on any other legitimate government. There are certain things which the government is not permitted to do to individuals, however democratic it might be, since these things would be against their rights. It has just been seen that if this is taken seriously it creates a problem inside Locke's own thought, since it would seem to give a minority the power of blocking anything the majority wanted. However, even as a problem, it is something bequeathed to subsequent democratic thought; it is, in other words, a problem which has to be solved.

The other way in which this kind of use of rights has a continuing significance works in favour of democracy rather than in limitation of it. This is that if everyone has and maintains such natural rights, then the views of everyone have to be respected in society. As seen, their property cannot be removed from them by a government without their consent. Yet this equal right of all to have a say, and to participate in the decision-making of a state, is exactly what typifies democracy. So this idea of equal moral rights can be used as a foundation for democracy, giving it moral legitimacy. Taxation in a democracy respects the independent and equal moral standing of individuals; taxation in an absolute government does not. As such, the idea of human rights, which are equally possessed by all, has had a powerful and continuing effect in the criticism and reform of government. It stands behind the two great revolutions of some hundred years after Locke, the American and French revolutions, which will be examined later, in Chapter V. In both cases, specific lists or claims of human, natural, rights were produced as the legitimating document which justified the revolution; and in the American case this got built into the written constitution which still mediates the operation of this democracy. Many sources can be found for these thoughts, and it is an over-simplification to make

Locke, who was in any case drawing on his own contemporary thought, especially significant. But what is clearly important is the central idea of the equal moral value of human beings as the possessors of rights. This legitimates pressure for change of particular societies, ultimately for rebellion or revolution. It also determines that the hoped-for succeeding, and better, society pays more attention to the separate individual worth of human beings. This it can only do by moving in a more democratic direction, so that equal respect is granted by equal consultation.

So after the use of the rights of man by Locke and others we get Thomas Paine's *Rights of Man* of 1791, and after Paine's rights of man we get Mary Wollstonecraft's *A Vindication of the Rights of Woman* of 1792. The invocation of rights unleashes an equalising force with which the new states had to struggle to keep up; however radical the new states might be in certain directions, slaves and women were not granted equality even though both human beings and so, presumably, also possessors of natural, human rights. The argument, the rhetoric, behind the foundational use of rights produces continuing problems and continuing pressure for change which leads up to the present day. However, this change has continuously been in a democratic direction, if democracy is understood as giving an equal role, or an equal say in government, to all the people in the area of a particular state. It was seen in the last chapter that, for the class of citizens, the advent of Athenian democracy was described as the advance in equality of these citizens so that they possessed certain political rights equally; or, putting it another way, certain of their freedoms were equally protected. The idea of a state of nature, which can be used to contrast with and provide legitimation of the political state, incorporates in itself an idea of equality. Thus Hobbes says that 'all men equally, are by Nature Free' (*Lev* xxi 150) and criticises Aristotle for holding that men are naturally unequal (xv); Locke says that men are 'by Nature, all free, equal and independent' (viii §95). The state of nature was obviously, as they understood the notion, a state of liberty in which equal people were free to act without government interference. So the central question for them is how these liberties and equalities might be preserved on entry into a state. In Hobbes, where natural man has less, and natural conditions are more savage, man gladly loses the liberty and equality in order to preserve the basic benefit of life or security. However, in Locke, where man has a greater natural moral endowment and the natural pre-political state is correspondingly represented as considerably less ferocious, man seeks to preserve this original liberty and equality on entry into political society. He has, and wishes to maintain, natural rights. It would seem that the only kind of state that could possibly fully do this, is a complete democratic state in which the equal respect which such rights imply is granted equally to all the citizens of that state.

CHAPTER IV

Rousseau

Rousseau stands in a middle position between ancient and modern thought about democracy. On the one hand we have the person brought up on Plutarch's lives, who was proud to be the citizen of a small city-state, and who looked back to classical thought for concepts and categories. On the other, we have someone whose influence was felt by Kant, by the thinkers of the French Revolution, and so by the modern world. As preserver of the ancient, we have the emphasis on the civic virtue of living the life of a small *polis* as a full member, regularly attending the assembly of all citizens, and, in general, having an existence which was shot through with communal, or political, activity. It is in this nostalgic spirit, whereby man is not so much defined as abjured to be a political animal, that we can find Rousseau talking about the 'assembly' (*assemblé*): 'The people in assembly, I shall be told, is a mere chimera. It is so today, but two thousand years ago it was not so. Has man's nature changed?' (*Social Contract* III xii). Whether or not man's nature has changed, his circumstances clearly have. Rousseau had, indeed, one point of contact with the ancient world which was missing for most of his own contemporaries, and even more for our contemporaries. He came from a small city-state, the city of Geneva. However, the France in which he spent much more time and which was influenced by him, was a large nation-state. Such states dominate the modern world. If Rousseau's thought is to have relevance, therefore, it has to be applicable to such states.

This is not to say that Rousseau's thought has been rendered irrelevant by the change of scale between modern states and Rousseau's Geneva; or even to say that he was insensitive to the problems of scale. In fact, benefiting from Montesquieu's thought,

Rousseau was particularly sensitive to the different needs of different types of peoples and governments, climate, temperament and, particularly, size. Democracy is held to be suitable only for states which are small. (The precise interpretation of what Rousseau means by 'democracy' in such a context will be considered later.) So the point is not that Rousseau ignores scale. Instead the point is that it is better to start with, and concentrate on, those aspects of Rousseau's thought which, while they may share connections with the ancient world, also do so with the modern. Luckily his fundamental principles, at least nominally, can be held to be such. For the central ends which Rousseau thinks that it is the business of government to promote are liberty and equality. This resonant pair are, of course, prominent in ancient thought, as was seen in Chapter II. They also echoed through the last chapter. However, they were also inscribed on the French revolutionary banners shortly after Rousseau wrote; and they are central and foundational in our contemporary thought about politics.

Focusing particularly on this pair of ends, or ideals, this chapter will concentrate on his most famous work, the *Social Contract*. Rousseau wrote other important works, but the *Social Contract* is both the central document in Rousseau's posthumous image and also a convenient and sufficient text with which to set central problems and ideas about democracy. In it we find that Rousseau prominently and precisely identifies the two ideals mentioned. He writes 'if we ask in what precisely consists the greatest good of all, which should be the end of every system of legislation, we shall find it reduce itself into two main objects, liberty and equality' (II xi).

Of this pair, liberty is especially important for Rousseau. The *Social Contract* opens with the ringing declaration that 'man is born free; and everywhere he is in chains' (I i). The task of the work is to show how, by contrast, man can preserve, or indeed even increase, the liberty with which he is born, by living in a properly organised political society. The social contract for Rousseau hence plays a similar role to the social contract for Hobbes in that it models how it might be rational for someone to exchange a non-political for a political state in order to gain some sort of protection. Yet for Rousseau protection alone is not enough. Liberty must also be preserved. So a Hobbesian solution, whereby someone hands himself over to the dreadful dictator or Leviathan, exchanging liberty for (relative) security, is no good. As Rousseau himself puts it, the solution must be one in which 'each, while uniting himself with all, may still obey himself alone, and remain as free as before' (I vi).

That someone's liberty should be preserved by entering political association might seem to demand a rather special sense of 'liberty', for nothing would seem to be more paradigmatic of what we understand by this term than the supposed state of nature in which no one is under any kind of government control or interference. Yet it was noted in Chapter I that there are two different traditions of understanding about freedom; so it is natural to see Rousseau as propounding a different idea, or concept, of freedom than Locke or Hobbes. Whereas freedom for them was 'negative' in that it'essentially consisted in being left alone, freedom for Rousseau is 'positive' in that someone is only held to be free if he is capable of doing certain things. Notoriously Rousseau declares that 'whoever refuses to obey the general will shall be compelled to do so by the whole body. This means nothing less than that he will be forced to be free' (I vii). A freedom into which one can be forced and which arises from compulsion by the whole body is obviously different from the freedom which consists in being left alone. Indeed, it would be natural to go further and say that it is not just a different idea of liberty but that it is not liberty at all. So the first problem in understanding Rousseau is that of understanding his apparently special idea of liberty.

Some help can be got in this by considering Rousseau's remark that 'the mere impulse of appetite is slavery' (I viii). From this it follows that, for Rousseau, it not good enough merely to get what you want in order to be free, you must also want the right things. For Rousseau, freedom consists in the exercise of one's will in the right way, in prescribing laws to oneself. So merely giving way to appetites, such as it is supposed happens in the pre-political state of nature, is not enough to guarantee freedom. It follows that for Rousseau people are free only in states. The problem is no longer how they can preserve their natural liberty, but rather how they are to acquire liberty. This they do by entering into states; for 'the strength of the state can alone secure the liberty of its members' (II xii).

There are two, not necessarily incompatible, ways in which states might provide such security and hence liberty. One arises if liberty is thought of as getting the right things rather than being mere exercise of choice, for these things may only be available in states. Liberty, that is, can be thought of as a sort of power; a human good. Initially it is natural to think that this power is exemplified most centrally when people choose what they are to get. So the paradigm of freedom looks like a state of nature in which people's choices are not constrained by governments or other political entities. However, on closer examination, it is plausible to assume that in such a situation people do not get what they want, or what they really want. They do not therefore really have power over their circumstances. So the political control which states provide increases their liberty rather than reducing it, because it now enables them to get certain things they want (possessions, security, freedom from attack) which were unavailable in the natural condition.

The second way in which liberty can be increased is less obvious and more contentious. This is that someone's power is increased if they also want the right things. If liberty is getting what you really want, then it can be increased both by changes in what you are able to get and by changes in what you are able to want. It may be that people have to be in states or societies if they are going to be able to discover what it is that they really want. So it is only in states that they discover what is really good for them. So being in states increases rather than diminishes their power or liberty. This obviously is the point at which the idea of being forced to be free starts to resurface, in that, in states, people may be forced into such an increase of power. Explained like this, it may still seem paradoxical to talk of people being forced to be free, yet it no longer seems to be wilfully self-contradictory. Yet such an explanation is one way of understanding Rousseau's solution to his original problem.

After setting his original problem about how each 'while uniting himself with all' may 'remain as free as before', Rousseau gives his first statement of the solution. This is that 'each of us puts his person and all his power in common under the supreme direction of the general will [*volonté générale*]' (I vi). The key term here is obviously the 'general will', and both the adequacy of Rousseau's solution to his own problem and also the adequacy of his account of freedom will depend upon the understanding of this elusive concept. It might be thought that the general will was just something produced by a combination of particular wills, so that when individuals combine in society, their individual wills are accumulated to produce a general will. However, as Rousseau understands the term, the general will (*volonté générale*) must be distinguished from the will of all *(volonté de tous)*. As he remarks in Chapter 3 of Book II, 'there is often a great deal of difference between the will of all and the general will'. He then goes on immediately to distinguish them saying that the latter (the general will), 'considers only the common interest, while the former takes private interest into account, and is no more than a sum of particular wills'. Rousseau follows this with a rather obscure mathematical illusion, which can be variously interpreted, about arriving at the general will by cancelling out the pluses and minuses of the particular wills. However, without trying to sort out exactly what he had in mind by this, the general shape of the distinction is clear. The general will aims at the general, or common, interest; particular wills aim at particular interests; the former is not merely the sum of the latter. The question whether we can make sense of Rousseau's general will therefore boils down to the question of whether we can make sense of the idea of a common interest for a group of people joined into a political association.

'It is solely on the basis of this common interest that every society should be governed', claims Rousseau (II i), and for him it seemed obvious that if there was society at all, then there must be a common interest; for 'were there no point of agreement', 'no society could exist'. Yet, if the general interest is only what is literally common to members of a society, then it may not offer much of a target at which the general will may aim. People coming out of the Hobbesian state of nature through fear may have a common interest in having the Leviathan who will so terrorise them that they stop killing each other. Yet they may have nothing else in common; the incompatible desires which would lead them to want to kill each other still exist. Perhaps this merely illustrates Rousseau's point. The more the society is really a society, the more there will be on which the general will can work; by contrast, the more it is an accidental collection of individuals, the less use there can be for the idea of a common interest. Thus, if society is just like a group of people collected in the lifeboat or on a desert island after the ship has gone down, then they have a clear common interest in survival, but they may have nothing else in common at all. Then the development of Rousseau's idea would be to delimit the kinds of conditions which would improve the existence of a common interest and make society more really a society. If these conditions were satisfied, then we could make more sense of the people as a whole exercising their general will; that is, to put it into a democratic context, of the people as a whole uniting to become the ruler so that we have a society in which the people rule.

Taking the general will as aiming at what is literally common in people's interests is part of an answer to the question of what the common interest might be. When Rousseau talks of the artificial moral person composing the state, it would then be thought of as constructed of the intersection of people's prior individual desires. However, another answer is also available, which gives more status to the artificial moral person than the pale intersection of independent desires. This answer depends upon introducing the other end of good government mentioned at the outset, equality. Another way in which the common interest can be understood, in addition to being the literal commonness of interests, is as being the interest that could be willed in common by the various members of a society. That is, if everyone were taken indifferently (or equally) and it was asked what they could all equally will as being something willed for all, then we might find out a common interest as well as the separate individual interests, and something furthermore which was not just a sum of these separate interests. Handling Rousseau in this way may be something of a constructive reinterpretation. However, it is not a forced one, given the number of times that Rousseau closely identifies the general will with equality. He says, for example, that 'the particular will tends, by its very nature, to partiality, while the general will tends to equality' (II i), or that 'the general will, to be really such, must be general in its object as well as its essence; that it must both come from all and apply to all' (II iv). As he sums it up,

> From whatever side we approach our principle, we reach the same conclusion, that the social compact sets up among the citizens an equality of such a kind, that they all bind themselves to observe the same conditions and should therefore all enjoy the same rights. Thus, from the very nature of the compact, every act of sovereignty, i.e. every authentic act of the general will, binds or favours all the citizens equally.
>
> (II iv)

From this can be derived both a general and a more specific lesson or suggestion. The general lesson is that what characterises the general will, or what characterises the appropriate way in which people should gather together to make political decisions, is that they adopt a special way of thinking. In this they do not see

themselves as bargaining in terms of their own separate and particular interests. Instead, they have to think together about a
common interest; the general will comes from merging their individual wills into one that is general, and this is not done by adding
them together or even by finding the common ground between their
separate particular wills. Instead, they all should think from the
standpoint of the people thought of as a collective entity. Of course
it helps if there is considerable common ground between their
particular wills, but, thinking like this, they may well reach conclusions, or will results, which are more than such common ground.
This could be what Rousseau has in mind when he says that 'as long
as several men in assembly regard themselves as a single body, they
have only a single will which is concerned with their common
preservation and general well-being' (IV i). Partly this is common
ground, in that they are all concerned with common preservation and
general well-being. However, they are also thinking in a special way
in that they are regarding themselves as a single body. They are not
just bargaining with their independent wills but regarding themselves as part of a single, moral entity with its own separate will.

As well as this general lesson, that people have to think in a
special way in the state, there is also a particular lesson about the
form that this special thinking should take. This is that everyone who
is thinking in this special sort of 'general will' way, will take himself
to be willing those things which he can prescribe equally. The idea is
that instead of just prescribing the things that fulfil what happens to
be his own particular interests, he thinks what could be prescribed by
an independent, or impartial, spectator who considers the interests of
all equally. Obviously, such an idea has a Kantian flavour in which
man as a practically rational being is supposed to will those things
which can become universal laws, but Kant was a great admirer of
Rousseau, and this seems a reasonable interpretation of Rousseau's
own thought. Certainly it gives another way of interpreting the
general will. We only need the addition, in Kantian style, that this
will comes from the rational self, to think that it has a superior
authority or worth than motivation based on mere desire. And we
only have to think that this higher self is the real self to think that
what it wills is what that self really wants. Then we get the case that
what fulfils this rational universal law is what the real, that is the
rational, self really wants. So we arrive at the conclusion that what
fulfils this law is what someone, indeed anyone, wants and which

thus makes him (really) free. Of course, any particular person may not think that he wants this, but then he will have to be forced to be free.

It might be thought that what has been said about Rousseau so far has very little to do with democracy. However if we understand democracy to be the form of government in which people rule themselves instead of being ruled by a small group (oligarchy) or a single person (monarchy), then any study of the general will is bound to be very important. For if we can understand the general will, then we can understand how the people as a whole can have a voice. The expressions of this voice, that is the commands or wishes emanating from this voice, can then be said to be the commands or wishes of the people. The people, that is, would rule, which is democracy. On the other hand, as was seen in the first chapter, the idea of the people ruling themselves, just like the idea of anyone ruling themselves, might seem to be a misleading form of expression, as meaning no more than that people do what they want. Yet if they just do what they want, there would seem to be no ruling at all going on; at least in the sense of people being forced to do what they otherwise would not want to do. However, in Rousseau, the general will, which expresses the view of the people as a whole, may bear so strongly on the will of a particular individual that he can be forced to be free if he disagrees. This removes the problem. For if someone can be forced to be free, then he is really being ruled; even if he is in some sense ruled by himself. So, in Rousseau we get a solution to the problem posed in the first chapter of how people could sensibly be said to rule themselves. For him the people can both be thought of as a proper ruler, forcing recalcitrant individuals into line, and also as being themselves so forced.

So far, so good. However it is a solution which comes with costs. One, as has been obvious throughout, is the coherence of the idea of freedom which is involved. Another is that when Rousseau himself talks about democracy, he seems to think that it is a form of government which would only be suitable for super-human beings. 'Were there a people of gods, their government would be democratic', he writes, 'so perfect a government is not for man' (III iv). Let us take these in turn. The paradox, or danger, in the idea of being forced to be free turns on how well people understand what they really want. It is only if people do not understand what they really want, or what is really in their interest, that they can be forced into getting this, and so (if freedom consists in getting what you want) be forced into being free. So people, thought of as part of the general will, might know better what they (individually) want than they would if thought of merely as separate wills. Therefore, as · a collective entity, they might force themselves, as individuals. Yet this could only be justified if the people as a whole, that is, the people meeting in assembly and thinking of themselves collectively in a special way, have a correct view of what is in their real interests. However, although Rousseau does think that the people as a whole are more likely than not to be right, he does not think that they are infallible. It is true that when he asks himself the direct question 'whether the general will is fallible', his answer is that the 'general will is always right'. However, he then immediately adds that 'it does not follow that the deliberations of the people are always equally correct' (II iii).

The general will is right; but people may not discover the general will. As Rousseau puts it in the next paragraph, 'our will is always for our own good, but we do not always see what it is'. So he clearly allows the possibility of mistake, and this is at the social as well as the individual level, since he talks here about 'the people' being 'often deceived'. Therefore, as he puts it later, 'the general will is always in the right, but the judgment which guides it is not always enlightened' (II vi). So he preserves the general will itself from error by the merely formal device of defining or understanding it as being whatever acts in the general interest. However, the more important question is whether this general will can be known or discovered by actual people, for example by the people meeting in assembly. Here this series of remarks shows that it is certainly possible that it cannot be so known or discovered; indeed that this might even be the normal condition. So the problem remains of the relation of democracy and knowledge; the problem of why what the people decide should be put into effect, if the people are not gods and may well have the wrong answer.

Rousseau can get round part of this problem by holding, as he does, that the people are more likely than not to be right. However I think that his final search for a solution tempts him into a *deus ex machina* to resolve it. This is the splendid figure of the legislator who appeals by a kind of charismatic authority and, without using reason, gets the people to adopt the right answer. Godlike, he sees the right answer; and, godlike, he gets others to see that it is. He therefore speeds along the plot to its happy ending in which the people are allowed to decide without the unfortunate problem of their coming up with the wrong answer. This is all very well; but it is exactly the sort of cheat, or short cut, which has led to criticism of the implicit totalitarianism in Rousseau. Just like any other dictator, or would-be dictator, he acts in the name of the people; however, it is only in the name of the people rather than by consultation with the people, since it is only the dictator who knows what the people really want or what is good for them. Here we do reach the problematic or sinister implications of forcing people to be free. A divine dictator or legislator acting in the people's interests looks to be no more genuinely democratic than any other agent who is meant to have a hot-line to the truth acting in the people's interests. Rousseau reveals how natural it is to fall into such an idea while still thinking that the right thing is that the people's will prevail. The people are supposed not to know their will or interests. It is natural, but it is also sinister. Rousseau reveals that the key problem is not so much our understanding of freedom but rather our assumptions about people's knowledge of their own interests. We saw in Chapter II that knowledge was important in the Platonic argument against democracy. The people's knowledge will also feature centrally in the next three chapters.

Such are the general problems of what we would call democratic theory, in the way that this is treated by Rousseau. However when Rousseau talks about what he himself calls 'democracy' in the *Social Contract* he usually has something more limited in mind. It is in this context, as noted at the beginning of this chapter, that he remarks that democracy is only suitable for very small states 'where the people can readily be got together and where each citizen can with ease know all the rest'. In addition, rough equality of wealth, virtue and absence of luxury, are all required. Yet even all this, it seems, would still not be enough, since 'it is against the natural order for the many to govern and the few to be governed' (III iv). So the thing would seem to be impossible. Indeed Rousseau himself says that, taking the term in a strict sense, there has never been a real democracy. However, in understanding Rousseau here, it is important to distinguish between government as a law-making body and government as the executive agent of decided laws. When Rousseau is talking about forms of 'government' (*gouvernement*) in Book III of the *Social Contract* he is concerned with the executive functions of government. As maker of law the people may still be sovereign. It is just that the people as a whole are the wrong body for putting these laws into effect. So, again, as was seen for the Greeks, even if there are no problems about how to choose representatives for the assembly, there is still the problem of how to choose executive officials. For Greek democratic theory, such selection was by lot. It remains to be seen what alternatives are on offer; or what they have to offer. In any case, it is clear that even the general decision-making process can only be done in small, face-to-face societies, where everyone knows everyone. With the large nation-state, it would seem that the question, or problem, of representation has also to come in with the original decisions. The laws, it seems, have to be made, as well as be executed, by representatives. It is to these problems of larger states and of representation that we now turn.

CHAPTER V

Revolutions, Liberty and Law

The last two chapters have been concerned with proposals made at times when there were no significant democratic governments. We now come to a period when we get a reappearance of actual and important regimes which have some claim to be called democratic. This is the period of the American and French revolutions; revolutions in government which replaced kings with something much more like rule by the people. It is a period in which thinkers no longer have to rely on ancient exemplars. It is a period in which important thinkers about democracy may not be engaged in merely theoretical enquiry. Indeed, the theorists who form the central concern of this chapter were practising politicians. They could think abstractly and they could refer to authorities. But they also had to mould, oppose or advance real political happenings or possibilities. This was action; and their writing was part of the action. Writing about democracy was itself an engagement in it.

The central concern of this chapter is more with America than France, and more with the creation and ratification of the American Constitution than the declaration of independence from Britain. The War of Independence had left America with thirteen separate states loosely connected in a confederation. The Constitution was drafted in 1787, as it says in the first line, 'in Order to form a more perfect Union'. Its ratification was then debated both in the press and in specially elected ratification conventions convened in each state. A great volume of speeches and pamphlets was produced, both for and against ratification. The most significant of these are the eighty-five short essays, known as *The Federalist Papers*, which were written in an attempt to persuade the New York convention to support ratification. They were nearly all written by Alexander Hamilton and

James Madison, two men who had been at the convention which drafted the constitution. So the *Federalist* forms an early defence and explanation of the constitution by two people who knew it from the inside. Hamilton, a New Yorker, set the project up; and then brought in Madison, a Virginian who also had to argue for the constitution in his own state's ratifying convention. It is Madison, who has a claim to be considered the father of the constitution, who will form the central focus of this chapter.

In the year of the American Declaration of Independence, 1776, the English thinker Bentham started his first important book with the thought that 'the age we live in is a busy age; in which knowledge is rapidly advancing towards perfection' (*A Fragment on Government*). The modern world, with its newly successful science, was now out-doing the ancient world. The founding fathers knew and used their classical authors. But in the play, or competition, between the ancients and the moderns, they were on the side of the moderns. Not just in science, but in matters of history and government, thinkers could feel that there were new truths, unknown to the ancient world, and that the ideal to be aimed at was not restoration or renaissance, but new development. Even the idea of revolution itself changed in this sense, from meaning a return to a previous state to the production of a new and uncharted world. As Hamilton said, in *Federalist* 9, 'the science of politics, however, like most other sciences, has received great improvement. The efficacy of various principles is now well understood, which were either not known at all, or were imperfectly known to the ancients' (119).

In previous chapters we have seen the lure of the ancient world in the thought of Hobbes and Rousseau. We have also investigated the prime example of a practising democracy, classical Athens. Yet, in the modern world, with new knowledge and developments in economy and society, the question was whether this form of government was any longer practical. This theme was later most fully developed by Benjamin Constant, writing as a man who had lived through the French revolution and its aftermath. In a famous lecture of 1819, 'The liberty of the ancients compared with that of the moderns', Constant contrasted two kinds of liberty, the liberty of the ancient world, which consisted in participation in government, and the liberty of the modern world, which consisted in being secured by government in one's own separate and private enjoyments. In these terms it can be seen that Rousseau, as discussed in the last chapter, was holding to the liberty of the ancients. Constant thought that this was a mistake, a mistake also made by the French revolutionaries. They were trying to restore a kind of liberty which was no longer appropriate to the modern commercial world. Society had moved beyond a point in which it was possible to recreate Sparta, Athens or early Rome.

As well as changes in the economy, there were changes in the sizes of states. Defending the French revolution, Thomas Paine, in Part II of the *Rights of Man*, writes 'what Athens was in miniature, America will be in magnitude. The one was the wonder of the ancient world; the other is becoming the admiration and model of the present' (202). Again we have an ancient and a modern example. But, again, we have not just comparison but also contrast. This time it is representation which makes the difference. As Paine put it, 'by ingrafting representation upon democracy, we arrive at a system of government capable of embracing and confederating all the various interests and every extent of territory and population' (202). Here are two crucial, interconnected, differences. We have the difference between direct and representative democracy; and we have the difference between a small and a large state.

The ancient city republics had been just that, cities. They had been small. It was natural to suppose that their republican form had been connected with their size. As Montesquieu put it (in 1748),

> By its nature a republic has but a small area, otherwise it cannot easily continue to exist. In a large republic, there are large fortunes, and, therefore, but little moderation in the minds of men. Its resources are too considerable to be entrusted to a citizen; interests become increasingly individual.
>
> *(Spirit of the Laws* 8.16)

Rousseau connected this explicitly with representation. He said that 'the moment a people allows itself to be represented, it is no longer free: it no longer exists', and immediately went on to say, 'All things considered, I do not see that it is possible henceforth for the Sovereign to preserve among us the exercise of its rights, unless the city is very small' (*Social Contract* III 15).

This idea was absolutely standard. For better or worse, like them or loathe them, democracies had to be small. To take an example almost at random, Algernon Sidney was considered in the eighteenth century to be a republican martyr (he had been executed in 1683 for suggesting that people might be permitted in certain circumstances to depose their kings). The manuscripts on the basis of which he was tried were subsequently published as the *Discourses Concerning Government*. And any well-thinking modern-minded republican, for example an American rebelling against George III, could read there that 'as for democracy, he may say what pleases him of it; and I believe that it can suit only with the convenience of a small town, accompanied by such circumstance as are seldom found' (426). If the rebellious American, or the American constructing a constitution, was trying to construct something which looked to be democratic and was yet in a state the size of a continent, this would seem to be an impossibility.

People arguing against ratification of the American constitution could and did use this as an argument. A good example of such an Anti-Federalist (as they were called) is George Mason, of Virginia. Like Madison and Hamilton, he was a delegate to the constitutional convention which drew up the document. However, although he attended the debates to the end, he was one of the very few who refused to sign it. Arguing against ratification (and against Madison) in the Virginia convention, he said, on 4 June 1788,

> It is ascertained by history, that there never was a Government, over a very extensive country, without destroying the liberties of the people: History also, supported by the opinions of the best writers, shew us, that monarchy may suit a large territory, and despotic Governments ever so extensive a country; but that popular governments can only exist in small territories.
>
> (VIII 937)

We have met one of these best writers, Montesquieu. Montesquieu and the English jurist Blackstone were cited far more than anyone else in the ratification debates and papers in Pennsylvania. He is called the 'oracle' in the *Federalist*. And we have seen what he said about large states.

If the essential nature of democracy is that all the citizens are able to assemble together in public discussion, then it indeed has to be small. We may have New England town meetings, but there is no hope for this in something the size of France or England. But nor, as the Federalists pointed out, was there then hope for this in something the size of Virginia or Pennsylvania. When we get on to something the size of a continent, to the United States, we need a new device.

This was representation. The substitution of representative for direct democracy allows democracy in a large, modern, state. This is the great invention of the moderns. This was the device which James Mill was later to call 'the grand discovery of modern times'. It is one of the new principles listed by Hamilton in *Federalist* 9. For Madison, his *Federalist* partner, we shall see that representation was not just a grudging second best but something positively to be preferred.

So if there are two sorts of liberty, there are two sorts of democracy to match. The ancients found their liberty in direct democracy, and the liberty of the moderns is served by representative democracy. This is very neat; but it is too simple. It cannot just be representation, the grand modern discovery, which makes all the difference. For, in the year after the ratification of the American constitution came the revolution in France. This produced another modern example to be learned from. It produced a series of regimes which were republican, or democratic. Furthermore, the type of democracy was representative. However, as a series of examples, it seemed to many commentators more like an awful warning than a positive exemplar. Just as for the hostile commentators in ancient Greece, it seemed that an attempt to put democracy into effect had merely exposed its flaws; and the modern device of representation had not saved it. The king had indeed been removed; but rule by the people had seemed to lead eventually merely to rule by Napoleon. And before Napoleon there had been the little matter of the terror, which made people think that the French had not got their form of government absolutely right. The people did not seem to possess liberty, however republican their government, when they were under terror. Unlike the American, the French constitutions did not seem to be a success.

Success or failure has to be measured by goals. One goal is survival. Here the United States was obviously successful, whereas the governments bounded by the French revolutionary constitutions failed. Another goal, or measure, is prosperity. Here again America has seemed to score well, and economic performance has clearly been a strong motor towards a desire for democracy (or what is thought of under that name) in our own time. But, at the time here being considered, a supreme value is liberty. The measure of success in a government is whether it preserves or whether it endangers liberty. So, in assessing kinds of government, or kinds of democracy, we return to liberty. We return to Constant. Writing after the restoration of the monarchy in France, Constant connected Rousseau with his criticism of the French revolutionaries. A love of liberty, of the wrong sort, had in practice led to despotism. Of Rousseau he remarked that 'this sublime genius, animated by the purest love of liberty, has nevertheless furnished deadly pretexts for more than one kind of tyranny' (318). At the beginning of the experiment, long before the terror, Burke diagnosed the new regime as being a democracy. He then cited Aristotle as holding that 'a democracy has many striking points of resemblance with a tyranny' (121). Liberty may have been written on their banners; but the central failure of the French was a failure to secure liberty.

If liberty is better protected in America, the question is whether this is because they had a better kind of democracy; or even whether they had a democracy at all. Another objection Burke had was to the man who thinks that he can 'consider his country as nothing but *carte blanche*, upon which he may scribble whatever he pleases' (153). One possible reason for the relative success of the Americans was that they adopted and developed indigenous material rather than trying to build a perfect new world, fully-fledged, from first principles. They pushed into service an eclectic mix of what they could find. They adopted and adapted English common law. Blackstone, as well as Montesquieu, was an oracle. Prominent in the descriptions of the British constitution by both Blackstone and Montesquieu, was the idea of checks and balances. The British constitution was supposed to be a balanced constitution and it was thought that this went closely with liberty. However, the British constitution was not a democratic constitution.

The first influential exposition of the British balanced constitution was in fact a king, Charles I. Admittedly, he was a king under pressure. In 1642, at a late stage of his conflict with parliament, he proposed that

> There being three kinds of government among men (absolute monarchy, aristocracy, and democracy), and all these having their particular conveniences and inconveniences, the experience and wisdom of your ancestors has so moulded this out of a mixture of these as to give to this kingdom (as far as human prudence can provide) the conveniences of all three, without the inconveniences of any one, as long as the balance hangs even between the three states.

Radical for its day with respect to Britain, and not what Charles himself either wanted or believed, the idea that the best constitution was a mixed constitution was standard enough in the ancient world. Polybius commented of Lycurgus that he

> did not make his constitution simple and uniform, but united in it all the good and distinctive features of the best governments . . . [so] that the force of each being neutralised by that of the others, neither of them should prevail and outbalance another, but that the constitution should remain for long in a state of equilibrium like a well-trimmed boat.
>
> (*Histories* VI 10 6–7)

In the modern world the stability of the Venetian Republic was thought to derive from its mixture of the three elements.

Even if Charles I (or his draftsmen, Colepepper and Falkland) was before his time with respect to the British constitution, his view was standard by the time the Americans declared their independence. The special excellence of the British constitution was supposed to lie in its mixture of the three forms of government, with the king giving monarchy, the house of lords aristocracy and the commons democracy. Each of these elements was supposed to check the others, and action and liberty to result from all three. Or as Blackstone put it,

> like three distinct powers in mechanics, they jointly impel the machine of government in a direction different from which either, acting by itself, would have done; but at the same time a direction partaking of each, and formed out of all; a direction which constitutes the true line of liberty and the happiness of the community.
>
> (*Commentaries* I 155)

'And here indeed', he said, 'consists the true excellence of the English government, that all its parts form a mutual check upon each other.' After Montesquieu, he recognised that the king was the executive; and hence we reach the result that 'it is highly necessary for preserving the balance of the constitution, that the executive power should be a branch, though not the whole, of the legislative' (154). It is this sort of language which Pitt the Elder could use, in arguing to the House of Commons on 20 February 1784 that it had no power to block the king's appointment of ministers,

if the constitutional independence of the crown is thus reduced
to the very verge of annihilation, where is the boasted equipoise
of the constitution? Where is that balance among the three
branches of the legislature which our ancestors have measured
out to each with so much precision?

So this is the language of the period for an American concerned
with liberty and wishing to use the materials to hand. Such a person,
taking liberty as a goal, might dismiss his king; or, more accurately,
revolt from the control of a distant king in parliament. The problem
was what he should do next; particularly if he had learned that
checks and balances were the guarantees of liberty. It was not clear
that he should be democratic. The British constitution was not a
democratic constitution. Indeed, that was precisely why it was
balanced; and therefore why it preserved liberty. So one way of
presenting the problem was whether this balance, and the resulting
liberty, could be preserved in a more democratic form. Or, to put it
another way, if king and aristocracy are removed, the problem
becomes what could be put back in their place.

For the Federalists, this problem was solved by the new American
constitution. In this chapter so far, it has been assumed that this was
a democratic solution. Yet this, and the promiscuous movement
above between the terms 'democratic' and 'republican' might reasonably be held to be a mistake. With no king we have a republic. It does
not follow that we have a democracy. Furthermore, Madison, in the
most famous *Federalist* paper of them all, the tenth, took particular
care to distinguish these two terms. For him 'democracy' means
direct democracy; or as he puts it, 'a pure democracy, by which I
mean a society of a small number of citizens, who assemble and
administer the government in person' (126). This is not what he
wants. What he wants he calls a 'republic'; or, to quote again from
the same paper, 'a republic, by which I mean a government in which
a scheme of representation takes place, opens a different prospect
and promises the cure for which we are seeking' (126).

So, it might be thought, the Federalists solved the problem by
refusing to be democratic. Although, as will emerge, there may be
some ground for this conclusion, it would be a mistake to rest it
merely on their use of language. In understanding what they say,
and thinking about it, we are inevitably influenced by our own use
of these words. And, in our own use, a representative government,

such as that of the United States, is a democratic government; indeed for some the paradigm of what it is to be 'democratic'. So, as we use the language, it is not necessary to follow Madison. What he is talking about is what we would call democracy even if he said that he was not.

The problem remains; the problem of whether the rich language of checks and balances can be adapted to a kingless condition. This language is not only rich but also confused; indeed there are several languages. There is the language of checks and balances; the language of separation of powers; and the language of the mixed constitution. There is a distinction between different orders of society (or estates), king, lords, and commons; and hence the idea of their mixture. There is the distinction between different functions or powers of government, legislature, executive, judiciary; and hence the idea of their separation. This is the way Montesquieu analyses the British constitution. And, over all, there is the idea of checks and balances. As Montesquieu put it, 'to prevent the abuse of power, things must be so ordered that power checks power' (*Spirit* 11.4). From these ideas the American founders in general, and the writers of *The Federalist Papers* in particular, had to make their new construction. From the idea of using power to counter power we get Madison saying that 'ambition must be made to counteract ambition' (*Federalist* 51; 319). But we have still to see in what way their constitution was mixed, balanced or separated.

The balanced constitution protected liberty because it was an example of what Montesquieu called moderate government. Since power checked power, there was no absolute power threatening liberty. But constructing such a constitution was difficult. As he says,

> To construct a moderate government requires that powers be combined, regulated, moderated, and set in motion. Ballast must be placed in one power to make it capable of resisting another. This can be done only by a masterpiece of legislation which rarely occurs by chance, and which prudence is seldom given the opportunity to attain.
>
> (*Spirit* 5.14)

In an essay first published six years before Montesquieu, David Hume similarly remarked that 'to balance a large state or society, whether monarchical or republican, on general laws, is a work of so great difficulty, that no human genius, however comprehensive, is able, by the mere dint of reason and reflection, to effect it' (*Essays* 124). Yet this is what the Federalists were doing. They were constructing a constitution, a written constitution, a balanced constitution, a constitution preserving liberty. Hamilton, indeed, quoted from this passage of Hume in the very last paragraph of the *Federalist* (85; 486).

This reference by Hamilton to Hume is not accidental. Both Hamilton and Madison were influenced by his essays. But Hume was not a republican, or what we would call a democrat, any more than Montesquieu. Both Montesquieu and Hume presented the idea that a moderate monarchy might preserve more real liberty than a republic. For Hume the index was the security, under law, of individuals and their properties. In other words, in Constant's later language, the liberty of the moderns. Hume was on the side of the moderns. In his essay called the 'Populousness of ancient nations', he drew up a balance sheet comparing the ancient with the modern world. The ancients had only 'feeble and languishing' commerce and manufactures. And, as regards liberty, he notes, 'these people were extremely fond of liberty; but seem not to have understood it very well' (408). So, as he puts it elsewhere,

> to one who considers coolly on the subject it will appear, that human nature, in general, really enjoys more liberty at present, in the most arbitrary government of EUROPE, than it ever did during the most flourishing part of ancient times.
>
> (383)

In spite of the ancient people's greater interest in civil liberty, Hume noted the connection between this and slavery, commenting that 'domestic slavery (is) more cruel and oppressive than any civil subjection whatsoever' (383).

In his pamphlet in favour of independence, *Common Sense*, Paine said that 'for as in absolute governments the King is law, so in free governments the law *ought* to be King' (98). Freedom was the rule of law. The contrast was between the predictable course of law, which secured property and expectations, and the unpredictable course of will, such as of an absolute monarch. Arbitrariness was the thing above all to be avoided. In his essay called 'The rise of arts and sciences' Hume thought that one question was whether 'a monarch could possess so much wisdom as to become a legislator, and govern his people by law, not by the arbitrary will of their fellow subjects'

(*Essays* 117). He decided that, in a primitive condition, this would only come with republics;

> Here then are the advantages of free states. Though a republic should be barbarous, it necessarily, by an infallible operation, gives rise to LAW, even before mankind have made any considerable advance in the other sciences. From law arises security: From security curiosity; And from curiosity knowledge.
>
> (118)

Notice the same key contrast here, law against arbitrary will. But, in course of time, thinks Hume, a monarchy may become moderated, so that it rules through law. Then, as he puts it

> a species of government arises, to which, in high political rant, we may give the name of *Tyranny*, but which, by a just and prudent administration, may afford tolerable security to the people, and may answer most of the ends of political society.
>
> (125)

So, as he says in another essay, 'It may now be affirmed of civilized monarchies, what was formerly said in praise of republics alone, *that they are a government of laws, not of men*' (94).

Montesquieu was also in favour of a moderate monarchy. Taking the British constitution as a model of liberty, the key, he felt, was the separation of powers. He says that

> when both the legislative and executive powers are united in the same person or body of magistrates, there is no liberty. For then it may be feared that the same monarch or senate has made tyrannical laws in order to execute them in a tyrannical way. Again, there is no liberty, if the power to judge is not separated from the legislative and executive powers. Were the judicial power joined to the legislative, the life and liberty of the citizens would be subject to arbitrary power.
>
> (11.6)

Notice here the same contrasts. This is why Montesquieu drew the conclusion that there might be less liberty in a republic where there was no such separation. As he says, 'in the Italian republics, where all three powers are combined, there is less liberty than in our monarchies' (11.6).

So when we come to the Federalists, one key to the solution would seem to be to have a republic and then make sure that the powers were separated. This should provide checks and balances, controlling power and preserving liberty. And the American Constitution, to some extent, separates powers with independent congress (the legislative chamber), president (the executive branch) and judiciary. Madison quotes the bit of Montesquieu just given after commenting himself that

> no political truth is certainly of greater intrinsic value, or is stamped with the authority of more enlightened patrons of liberty than that on which this objection is founded. The accumulation of all powers, legislative, executive, and judiciary, in the same hands, whether of one, a few, or many, and whether hereditary, self-appointed, or elective, may justly be pronounced the very definition of tyranny.
>
> *(Federalist* 47; 303)

Notice he takes it itself as tyranny. This might just be Hume's 'high political rant'. For Montesquieu didn't remark that it was in itself (that is, necessarily) tyranny but that 'apprehensions may arise lest *the same* monarch or senate should *enact* tyrannical laws to *execute* them in a tyrannical manner' (to give it in the translation quoted by Madison).

So the difficult construction of the balanced constitution seems to consist in placing these powers in different hands. Certainly the strong independent executive and judiciary distinguished the American constitution from the succeeding French ones (at least until the one Constant himself framed, Napoleon's last constitution). The French revolutionaries ran all power together into the assembly, and, from this perspective, checks can seem to be nothing other than checks on the power of the people; that is, on democracy. Looking back, Constant pronounced that 'it is in fact the degree of force, not its holders, which must be denounced'. This was because, if 'the sovereignty of the people is unlimited', then 'entrust it to one man, to several, to all, you will still find that it is equally an evil' (176). The Americans had separations and checks; but the question is whether, by introducing checks, they were not only limiting power but also democracy. The Americans had moderation and the rule of law; but the question is whether this was at the cost of the rule by the people.

A good way to focus this question is to compare the American constitution with the preceding situation in the loosely confederated American states. A written constitution was not the innovation. When they were discussing it, the Americans were used to written constitutions. The colonies had been governed according to written instruments. Standardly, these consisted of a bicameral legislature, elected on an extensive franchise and a governor appointed by the crown, with executive powers. Here we see a version of the same mixed constitution as Britain. The struggles between governors and legislatures matched the incipient struggle between the Americans and the British. So when the Americans declared their independence and the colonies became separate states, it was natural to rewrite these constitutions, greatly restricting the powers of the governors. The judiciary was also now taken over by the legislatures. The result was legislative autonomy, or despotism, with popularly elected legislatures controlling all branches of government.

The states varied. Pennsylvania was the most radical, with a unicameral legislature, rotation of offices, frequent elections on a wide suffrage, and an almost total absence of executive power. This was representative rather than direct democracy; but it still gave an example of democracy, with the people in control acting through a single body, which contemporaries could study. Some states had a stronger executive. John Adams designed a constitution for Massachusetts in 1780, which still applies, in which there was a separate executive and a separate judiciary. Here the lesson of separated powers applied. Massachusetts was larger than a city state, but, in Puritan New England there was still the hope that the people might be animated and combined by the kind of virtue which was traditionally supposed necessary for republics and which Montesquieu thought could only be maintained in a small state. One of the popular Massachusetts leaders, Samuel Adams, wanted to make of Massachusetts a 'Christian Sparta'.

Support for these states, their principles of virtue, their control by the people, their bills of rights; all these were part of what motivated people resisting ratification of the new constitution, the Anti-Federalists. On the other side the Federalists not only wanted a stronger union, but were also worried about some of what had happened in these little democracies. With many or most of their people burdened by debt, they tended to issue paper money, or pardon rebel debtors, or make laws soft on debt. For those on the side of established property, it seemed that these majoritarian decisions, without check or control, produced injustice. So Madison could state near the start of *Federalist* 10 that

> complaints are everywhere heard from our most considerate and virtuous citizens, equally the friends of public and private faith and of public and personal liberty, that our governments are too unstable, that the public good is disregarded in the conflicts of rival parties, and that measures are too often decided, not according to the rules of justice and the rights of the minor party, but by the superior force of an interested and overbearing majority.
>
> (123)

This concern can be seen in Madison's writings before the constitutional convention and his speeches during it. As the convention approached he noted down the vices of the present system and wrote outlines of his presiding ideas to Jefferson and Washington. These ideas turned up again in the *Federalist*. At first what he wanted was a stronger executive which had a right of veto on any acts of the states; as he put it to Washington (16 April 1787), 'a negative *in all cases whatsoever* on the legislative acts of the states, as heretofore exercised by the Kingly prerogative' (*Papers* IX 383). 'The great desideratum which has not yet been found for Republican Governments', he wrote in the same letter, 'seems to be some disinterested & dispassionate umpire in disputes between different passions & interests in the State. The Majority, who alone have the right of decision, have frequently an interest real or supposed in abusing it' (IX 384). Earlier he had written to Jefferson (19 March 1787) that the federal veto was needed, among other reasons, to restrain the States 'from oppressing the minority within themselves by paper money and other unrighteous measures which favor the interest of the majority' (IX 318).

Here we can see how his first idea was to use the Union like a sort of king, forcing justice in the separate states. However this idea of a federal veto on state legislation did not carry the convention or pass into the constitution. Instead as Madison himself realised, and defended in the *Federalist*, the new federal government had to act directly on the individual people of the United States. It was not to be a treaty organisation formed by separate states; it was to be a national government. Yet, in such a government, it would seem that there could

75

still be 'unrighteous measures which favor the interest of the majority'. And, even if the federal government had had a veto, this would
have been no use in controlling itself. Another solution was needed.

In his list of the 'Vices of political system of the U States' which
Madison prepared for himself before the convention, number eleven
was the 'injustice of the laws of the states'. He felt that injustice
brought 'into question the fundamental principle of republican
Government, that the majority who rule in such Governments, are
the safest Guardians both of public Good and of private rights' (IX
354). For, as he wrote, whenever 'an apparent interest or common
passion unites a majority what is to restrain them from unjust
violations of the rights and interests of the minority, or of individuals?' (355). The answer was not public opinion, for that was on
the side of the majority. Rather, the answer was 'an enlargement of
the sphere' (356); that is, increasing the size of government.

So, to take a question which Madison put to the constitutional
convention on 26 June 1787, 'how is the danger in all cases of
interested coalitions to oppress the minority to be guarded against?'
(X 77). Or, more precisely, as he had just asked, 'how is this danger
to be guarded against on republican principles?' For what was
wanted, as Madison triumphantly ended *Federalist* 10, was 'a
republican remedy for the diseases most incident to republican
government' (128). The problem, as he put it there, was factions,
groups of people which would work against people's rights. Faction
was irremovable; as he put it, 'the latent causes of faction are thus
sown in the nature of man; and we see them everywhere brought into
different degrees of activity, according to the different circumstances of civil society' (124). So what was wanted was a way not of
eliminating it, but eliminating its public or political effects. If the
faction was a minority, this was simple. In a majoritarian democracy, the majority would vote it down. But the chief problem was
what to do if the faction was a majority. This was the thing which did
not seem to have a republican, or democratic, solution. For the
majority called the shots; and it did not seem that there was anything
which could properly control its power.

Madison's distinctive contribution to this problem in *Federalist* 10
consisted in expanding his ideas about 'extending the sphere' which
had already appeared in his notes, and which he had already put to the
constitutional convention. Instead of being inimical to democracy (or
republics) large states were in fact essential if they were to work

properly. We have seen that to suggest this meant working hard against the trend. But, nevertheless, someone had been there before. In his essay called the 'Idea of a perfect commonwealth', Hume wrote 'though it is more difficult to form a republican government in an extensive country than in a city; there is more facility, when once it is formed, of preserving it steady and uniform, without tumult and faction' (527). Madison took this up. In his notes on the vices of the current system, his letters to Jefferson, particularly of 24 October 1787 and in *Federalist* 10, which appeared first on 22 November 1787, he laid out what happened when the sphere was extended. For, on the face of it, if the danger was that the majority would oppress the minority, nothing would change if the state was larger. There would still be, in a large state, a majority and a minority, and there would still be the chance for the former to oppress the latter. However, when it is larger 'a common interest or passion is less apt to be felt and the requisite combinations less easy to be formed' (*Papers* IX 357); or, as he put it to Jefferson, 'no common interest or passion will be likely to unite a majority of the whole number in an unjust pursuit' (X 214). Or, as in the public *Federalist* form, 'extend the sphere and you take in a greater variety of parties and interests; you make it less probable that a majority of the whole will have a common motive to invade the rights of other citizens' (X127).

It is quite clear what Madison wants here. What is less certain is what the conditions are for him to be correct. The presupposition has to be that partialities are merely local. Now a particular person's views might be partial because of ignorance, or because they were warped by interest. If the problem is ignorance, then extending the sphere should help. Other things being equal, as long as any one person is more likely than not to be correct, the more people there are, the better the judgment is likely to be. If special knowledge is needed, widening the sphere is more likely to unearth it. But this presupposes that everyone has the same interest; that is, to find out the truth. Then, as Madison wrote to Jefferson, if people all had 'precisely the same interests', then 'the interest of the majority would be that of the minority also; the decisions would only turn on mere opinion concerning the good of the whole, of which the major voice would be the safest criterion' (X 212). However, if there is a difference in interests, then conflict may persist, however wide the sphere. In both small and large states, a self-interested majority may fail to do justice to a minority.

Madison returned to these problems and the size of a state as a solution in *Federalist* 51. 'It is of great importance in a republic', he says,

> not only to guard the society against the oppression of its rulers, but to guard one part of the society against the injustice of the other part. Different interests necessarily exist in different classes of citizens. If the majority be united by a common interest, the rights of the minority will be insecure.
>
> (321)

The same problem again. And, again, we get the same solution. 'In the extended republic of the United States', he claims, 'a coalition of the majority of the whole society could seldom take place on any other principles than those of justice and the general good' (322). But this time we have an illuminating comparison which helps him to establish his case. This is the comparison with religious sects. Madison had in fact been the chief agent behind the passing of the Virginia statute for religious freedom of 1786, a pioneering work giving everyone equal right to practise their religion. Now in *Federalist* 51 he says that

> in a free government the security for civil rights must be the same as that for religious rights. It consists in the one case in the multiplicity of interests, and in the other in the multiplicity of sects. The degree of security in both cases will depend on the number of interests and sects; and this may be presumed to depend on the extent of country and number of people comprehended under the same government.
>
> (321)

Relying on this comparison, it is important to see that Madison did not want any one faction to take control. We noted above that he sees that factions are ineliminable, just as differing religious views are; indeed, 'a zeal for religion' is noted as one cause of faction in *Federalist* 10. Yet the answer to this is not to allow one faction to have public control, or even to try and achieve some brokerage between factions so that the state, or public action, forms a resultant of the different private interests. Rather, the answer is to let the factions cancel out, so that rights which are of common interest survive. The more factions there are, the more this is likely. Hence the importance of a large territory, to enlarge their number. If there were only two factions, just like if there were only two sects, then the bigger would be a serious threat to the smaller. But if there are very many, then the great majority of them have a common interest in no single faction becoming dominant. In the religious case, that is, even if they all (or nearly all) want their own religion to be the state-enforced one, in the circumstances they were all better off with no state-enforced religion. For this at least allows them all the unimpeded practice of their religion.

The analogy with religion can therefore be reconstructed so that civil rights form the common frame inside which each person can forward their own particular interests. But, in thinking about the numbers of special interests, it shows how Madison's idea can break down, even in a large state. For, however large it is, there may still be only two overall prevailing interests, such as the debtors and the creditors; or the people with money and the people without; or capital and labour. Then we would return to the old worries about democracy, dating back to Aristotle, that the impoverished many would appropriate the property of the wealthy few. If property is thought to be a civil right (rather than just the interest of a particular group), this will lead to the majority doing injustice. However wide the sphere, the poor may pass laws against the rich. And this, in Madison's terms, would mean the majority had become a faction.

Indeed it is precisely 'the various and unequal distribution of property' which Madison, in the tenth *Federalist*, says has been 'the most common and durable source of factions'. 'Those who hold and those who are without property', he adds, 'have ever formed distinct interests in society' (124). With this in mind, consider another of his addresses to the constitutional convention, this time on 7 August 1787. He said:

> in future times a great majority of the people will not only be without landed, but any other sort of, property. These will either combine under the influence of their common situation: in which case, the rights of property & the public liberty, will not be secure in their hands: or, which is more probable, they will become the tools of opulence and ambition, in which case there will be equal danger on another side.
>
> (X 139)

So much for trusting the people; there would still seem to be a need for republican remedies for republican diseases.

This is the place where we would expect the doctrine of the separation of powers to do its work, and, indeed, the fifty-first *Federalist* comes at the end of a sequence of papers by Madison discussing the separation of powers. It is not only the last of the sequence, but is clearly the paper which is meant to give the solution, starting as it does with the words 'to what expedient, then, shall we finally resort, for maintaining in practise the necessary partition of power . . . ?' (318). Madison mentions some administrative details adopted by the constitution and designed to keep the powers separate. But 'the great security' is giving each the motive to resist; and it is here the phrase that 'ambition must be made to counteract ambition' occurs. So far, so good. We have separated powers. We have checks and balances. We also have a structure which works because it is in the interest of each man to do his duty (or, as Madison puts it here, 'the interest of the man must be connected with the constitutional rights of the place' (319)). Structures connecting duties with interests will be discussed more fully in the next chapter. What we would now expect is that Madison would show how the separated powers, that is the legislative body or congress on the one hand and the executive body or president on the other, both had the interest and power to check the other. But this is not what happens.

Instead Madison says that 'it is not possible to give to each department an equal power of self-defense. In republican government, the legislative authority necessarily predominates' (320). There were hints of this conclusion in the earlier papers, when he was mainly concerned to show that the American system, in which there was some mixing of power, did not offend seriously against Montesquieu's principles; for example, he remarks in *Federalist* 48 that 'the legislative department is everywhere extending the sphere of its activity and drawing all power into its impetuous vortex' (309). So it is not the balance between legislature and executive that will finally to do the work, because this balance is not ultimately sustainable. 'The tendency of republican government', as he puts it in *Federalist* 49, 'is to an aggrandizement of the legislative at the expense of the other departments' (314). So the cure is different. In *Federalist* 51 he gives it. Immediately after the remarks quoted at the start of this paragraph he says that 'the remedy for this inconveniency is to divide the legislature into several branches' (320). It is not the balance between executive and legislature which finally does the work; it is an internal check or balance inside the legislature itself.

If the legislature is to be checked, therefore, it has to be checked by internal checks rather than external ones. But this was just what happened in the British mixed constitution, discussed above. There the king, lords and commons were all part of the legislature. Each exercised a veto on legislation. As well as the checks involved in the extensive sphere, Madison uses the checks involved in a bicameral legislature. We do not now have three elements, each with a veto. But we still have two, each able to check or block the other in an internally divided legislature. The two houses were to have different methods of election. The lower house was directly elected; but, in the original constitution, the upper house was elected by the state legislatures.

Here we get scope for another factor to work to cure democratic problems, namely representation. Indeed, it will be remembered that it was precisely representation which made the difference between what Madison called a republic, which he was supporting, and a democracy, which he wasn't. Representation purifies. Again, it forms part of an argument for extending the sphere. In a larger state it is possible to find better representatives, both absolutely (because there are more people from whom to choose) and also proportionately (because, with limitations on the feasible size of the legislature, each representative represents more people). Here is Hume again, amplifying his view about large republics:

> In a large government, which is modelled with masterly skill, there is compass and room enough to refine the democracy, from the lower people, who may be admitted into the first elections or first concoction of the commonwealth, to the higher magistrates, who direct all the movements.
>
> (*Essays* 528)

The idea here is one of refining. The 'lower' people are to get in, but only in a way which allows their coarseness to be refined. The same chemical metaphor was used by the Federalists, now talking of 'filtrations'. In another speech Madison gave to the constitutional convention, he noted that 'he was an advocate for the policy of refining the popular appointments by successive filtrations, but thought that it might be pushed too far' (31 May 1787, X 19).

This is typical moderate Madison. At the time he is arguing

against people who did not want the lower, or popular, representative house elected directly by the people. He did not want refinement pushed too far. On the other hand, he was in favour of refinement. In *Federalist* 10 he pointed out that representation meant that 'it may well happen that the public voice, pronounced by the representatives of the people, will be more consonant to the public good than if pronounced by the people themselves, convened for the purpose' (126). Madison's collaborators on the *Federalist*, Hamilton and Jay, were even more convinced about this. Hamilton conducts a piece of sociology in *Federalist* 35 to show that, for example, mechanics are liable to be represented by merchants; and Jay was confident in *Federalist* 3 that 'when once an efficient national government is established, the best men in the country will not only consent to serve, but also will generally be appointed to manage it' (95). In all cases a wider choice is thought to produce better results, and the assumption is that the representatives will be of a better quality than the people represented.

So first it was supposed that people would elect people better than themselves to their own state legislatures. Then these elected representatives would choose people of particular eminence or virtue to represent their states in the national congress. For it was thought they would want their states to show well in such a gathering. People of impartial, universal vision would be required, who could talk the language of, and appeal to, similar members from far distant states. Anyone pushing merely sectional state interest (or, at least, anyone who looked as if that was all that they were doing) would not be convincing. So, even if there were factions at the bottom, it was supposed that at the top there would be a place for disinterested virtue (or those who, at least, could talk its language). The president, also, was to be filtered through an electoral college. All these selections did, ultimately, start with the people. And Madison, at least, did not want anything else. 'The ultimate authority', he said, 'wherever the derivative may be found, resides in the people alone' (46; 297). Yet this ultimate authority was to be filtered to extract its virtue.

The two houses, each ultimately coming from the people, but by very different routes, were to be as different as possible from each other. These differences made them better checks for each other. Each, of course, had the constitutional power to block the other. But, more importantly, each also had the esteem. The lower house could draw its authority directly from the people. The upper house could draw its authority from the refined process of selection, which meant that it was especially selected for its wisdom and its ability to take a wider view. Each could have pride, or ambition. Hence ambition could be made to counteract ambition. The Federalists did not like mere paper checks, which they called 'parchment barriers'. Checks had to be made to work, and they would only do so if harnessed to the prevailing psychological and sociological realities. In this also they were pupils of Hume and Montesquieu; attention had to be paid to the spirit of the laws, the context which made them work.

Madison discusses the senate in detail in the following papers of the *Federalist*. Given what has just been noted we can understand why he says of a 'well constructed senate' that 'such an institution may be sometimes necessary as a defense to the people against their own temporary errors and delusions' (63; 370–1). In 57 he says that

> the aim of every political constitution is, or ought to be, first to obtain for rulers men who possess most wisdom to discern, and most virtue to pursue, the common good of society; and in the next place, to take the most effectual precautions for keeping them virtuous whilst they continue to hold their public trust.
>
> (343)

Then, in 62 he observes that 'a senate, as a second branch of the legislative assembly distinct from and dividing power with a first, must be in all cases a salutary check on the government' (366).

The sections of the *Federalist Papers* on the senate fell to Madison; but the papers about the executive and the judiciary fell to Hamilton. Even more than Madison, Hamilton thought that there were 'occasions . . . in which the interests of the people are at variance with their inclinations' (71; 410); in other words, people had to be protected from themselves. So 'energy in the executive is a leading character in the definition of good government. It is essential . . . to the security of liberty against the enterprises and assaults of ambition, of faction, and of anarchy' (70; 402). This is more orthodox separation of powers. But of greater interest is the judiciary, which has not yet been discussed. If tyranny was the government of men rather than laws, then a judicature which depended upon the legislature was a short route to tyranny. The constitution set up a federal supreme court and carefully separated the tenure and pay of the judiciary from legislative control. The supreme court justices were to be appointed by the president 'by and with the Advice and Consent of the Senate'. All this is described and defended by Hamilton.

However, in the context of the present problem of democratic defences against a mistaken majority, the most important thing which Hamilton says is with respect to the supreme court's power to review and reject acts of congress. This power of judicial review is not in the written constitution which Hamilton was defending. Nor was the enumeration of specific rights which has formed the basis of much subsequent activity by the supreme court. Amendments adding a bill of rights were adopted in 1791. The power of judicial review dates from Chief Justice Marshall's assertion of it in the 1803 case of Marbury v. Madison. However Hamilton, in the seventy-eigthth *Federalist*, writing before these events, offers a persuasive and percipient defence. 'No legislative act, therefore', he says,

> contrary to the constitution can be valid. To deny this would be to affirm that the deputy is greater than his principal; that the servant is above his master; that the representatives of the people are superior to the people themselves.
>
> (438)

Hence the supreme court could refuse to apply a legislative act contrary to the constitution. Here was another answer to the problem of defending justice against a mistaken majority.

But, surely, the objection naturally runs, if the legislature (both branches) has passed something, then that is something which the people want. If the judges then strike it down, this may happen to produce justice, but it is something which can have no democratic sanction. But this is precisely where Hamilton's argument is ingenious. As he puts it a little later,

> nor does this conclusion by any means suppose a superiority of the judicial to the legislative power. It only supposes that the power of the people is superior to both, and that where the will of the legislature, declared in its statutes, stands in opposition to that of the people, declared in the Constitution, the judges ought to be governed by the latter rather than the former.
>
> (439)

In other words, both legislature and constitution depend upon the people. So the latter may legitimately be used to control the former.

It is in this context that we see the importance of the way in which the Constitution was ratified. The convention which drew up the Constitution was clear that it had to be ratified by especially convened conventions elected for that purpose by the people. In other words, it was not a treaty between the existing States, but was to take its authority directly from the people. As Madison put it, 'the express authority of the people alone could give due validity to the Constitution' (43; 285). Or, as Hamilton said about ratification, 'the fabric of American empire ought to rest on the solid basis of THE CONSENT OF THE PEOPLE' (22; 184). Just like congress, the constitution flowed from the people. So both the supreme court and congress had a democratic mandate. If one checked the other, this was democracy checking itself. If this was what Madison called a remedy for a republican disease, then it was in that sense a republican remedy.

This chapter started with a contrast between the writing of the modern and the writing of the ancient world. The Federalists, like Hume, were taken to be on the side of the moderns. But in two connected respects the thought of the Federalists is less modern than it at first appears. The first of these is the presupposition that there are individuals who are motivated by virtue and able to take an impartial viewpoint. Care is needed in their selection; hence the interest in filtration. It is not to be presupposed that any representative (or any member drawn from a group or region to be represented) will act for the public good. But there are supposed to be some members with higher minds or nobler virtues. If there is sufficient spirit of virtue in a republic (in America this was supposed to have been demonstrated by the people's commitment in the War of Independence) and there is an appropriate representative system, then these nobler individuals can be selected. The Federalists play this theme at times, and it is one which still partakes of the ancient classical world.

The second related supposition is that factionalism, and party interest, is a defect, which is to be suppressed. It cannot be eliminated, but its public effects have, if possible, to be removed. It is not supposed that all we have in a state is a set of private individuals, all with their own private selfish concerns, all jockeying for advantage. The state is not regarded merely as a broker among these interests. Rather than having to work with or through factions, the state is still regarded as something which tends the public common interest.

Both of these connected assumptions about public virtue and private interest may strike us as more like the Greeks – or Rousseau – than the assumptions of the modern world. In the modern world, leaders in a democracy are not supposed to be any different, or any less self-interested, than anyone else. Democracy is an arena of party conflict; of clashing separate interests. Indeed we often suppose that democracy is constituted by party, or factional, conflict; the conflict between the representatives of parties at elections is for many the essence of democracy. Both individuals and leaders are supposed to have private, or partial, interests; and a properly constructed democracy works with this, rather than trying to eliminate it.

These features appear in the Federalists; but are not fully followed through. *Federalist* 10 recognises the inevitability of factions and parties. Hastily read, therefore, it can look like an anticipation of modern pluralism. But the problem it solves is the problem of removing the effects of faction, not of gaining its benefits. Similarly, the tendency of power to corrupt and leaders to betray their trust is explicitly recognised. Indeed, central to this chapter has been a demonstration of how the Federalists' thought makes use of the politics of suspicion, in which the chief object is the protection of liberty against the power of officials. Nevertheless, it is still supposed that old-fashioned virtue is available, and can be used to make the system run at the top.

Montesquieu held that democracies required virtue in the citizens, which is why he thought that they could only happen in small societies where social pressures could keep people virtuous. For the republic to work, it was supposed that it needed people concerned with the communal interest rather than with their own. This is the world of Constant's ancient liberty, public rather than private. Madison was prepared for the people to be private, but his senators were still taken to have and display public virtue. Virtue, public concern, altruism, now move up to the level of the governors. Madison, like Washington, came from the land-owning class. Perhaps this class was small enough for its members to force each other to be virtuous. But the theory of the system in this, its original formulation, depended upon people at large being represented by their betters.

It will be remembered that elections were considered by the Greeks to be an aristocratic, rather than democratic, element. Elections involve the conscious choosing of the best rather than the random, and genuinely democratic, procedure of casting lots. Here we have a political system which is precisely and self-consciously distinguished from ancient democratic systems because of its use of representation and voting (and its consequential applicability in large states). So it could be said, in ancient terms, that it grafted an aristocratic element onto the democratic one; which, of course, goes with mixing or balancing the constitution to curb the excesses of democracy; which goes with a noble-minded Senate to curb the excesses of the directly elected House of Representatives. Even one pass of representation may not get people good enough; successive passes through the filtration process are needed in order to guarantee the emergence of the natural aristocracy.

This reliance on virtue, at least at the level of the governors, places Madison with the ancients. The republic is still meant to run on virtue. Public spirit, such as was pre-eminently displayed by Washington, who impoverished himself in the public service, is required. So the question which naturally arises is whether this ancient requirement for virtue could be discarded. The question is whether it is possible to construct a constitutional machine which runs itself and in which the people rule themselves, and yet which needs no addition of a tincture of virtue. The idea would be to construct a machine in which everyone, rulers and ruled alike, is thoroughly modern. Both officials and people are to be taken to be merely self-interested. In terms of liberty, modern liberty in Constant's sense prevails throughout. People are assumed to be acting not for the good of the republic, but for their own; the wants they act upon are the wants that they think they have; they do not have to be forced to be free; but it is not supposed that they are moralised either. The question is whether modern, private, self-interested, economic man is able to run a republic. This is, or would be, the next step. Its possibility will be one subject of the next chapter.

The present chapter has centred on the defence of the American Constitution. This Constitution is important for us in that it still frames a leading democratic state; and hence is influential in one understanding of the idea of democracy. The chapter has traced its dependence on some previous ideas. This has produced another problem for democracy in that these ideas did not originate in democratic societies; nor were taken to apply to them. The mixed constitution was resurrected by an embattled Stuart king, Charles I, as a means of keeping himself in power. In both its ancient and its modern forms, its whole point was to dilute democratic elements with aristocratic and monarchical elements in order to make up for its deficiencies. As it evolved into the balanced constitution it was, again, used in defence of limited monarchies. The ideas on which the Federalists drew were ideas designed to counter and limit the excesses of democracy.

The problem that is carried forward, therefore, is that if these ideas are nevertheless pressed into democratic service as they were by the Federalists, in what sense do they really support democracy? Balance limits power. So do rights. They may work against absolute monarchy, preserving liberty. But they also work against democratic assemblies, for the same end. Similarly, rights form a limitation on all governments, including democratic ones. Madison's invocation of a bicameral legislature may, in spite of what he said, be an invocation of non-democratic elements in order to look after, and curb, the democratic ones.

CHAPTER VI

Bentham and the Mills

Jeremy Bentham (1748–1832) is commonly correctly taken as a leading example of a utilitarian thinker. He was also a democrat, arguing in favour of representative democracy. Hence he can be used to help plot the history of the utilitarian contribution to thought in this area; and to help assess the relations between utilitarianism and democracy.

Bentham worked strenuously throughout his long life, and he can be given either an eighteenth-century or a nineteenth-century image. He can be thought of as an eighteenth-century *philosophe*, who was, after all, over 40 by the time of the French Revolution. Or he can be thought of as a nineteenth-century philosophical radical, who died in the year of the great English Parliamentary Reform bill; a bill he and his disciples actively promoted. As an eighteenth-century *philosophe*, self-conscious disciple of Voltaire, Helvetius and Beccaria, he was proffering advice to an imaginary legislator, setting out a perfect system of law. If actual legislators were in question, then they were the contemporary monarchs. These were absolute rulers, even if it was hoped that they were enlightened or benevolent. It was not a natural start for a democrat.

Bentham himself was always of a practical bent, not wanting just to weave fantastical schemes but to get actual proposals into effect. His great propensity for detail gives some of his proposals a mad or impractical aura. He could not design a poorhouse without designing the inmate's hats; similarly he could not design an electoral system without planning the size of the ballot boxes. Yet these were serious proposals, which, early and late, he was trying to get put into operation. So in the 1780s he was in Russia, writing papers on civil law in French, hoping to be able to persuade the Empress Catherine to adopt a civil law code. In the new century, still offering to codify law for the world, he was still trying to hawk codes to the current Tsar, now Alexander I. However he was also in close correspondence with the new emergent regimes in Greece, Portugal and South America, as well as offering codes to James Madison, now President of the United States. And the codes on offer had expanded; as well as the old ones, there was now also a constitutional code.

A perfect system of law needs a measure of perfection, to set the goal; the criterion of goodness which Bentham adopted was utility. 'Utility' can be a mere blank or place-holder in the system, meaning different things to different people. However, it is not a total blank; it can be given some restrictions. For Bentham, as with both his mentors and his disciples, the criterion of goodness is independent of any theological underpinning. It is a secular measure of goodness for an increasingly secular world; one in which, if God is not dead, His guidance is at best uncertain. 'Utility' is what is useful to human beings. Nor does this mean 'useful' in a narrow sense, whereby things of utility might be contrasted with things of pleasure. 'Utility' is whatever people find good, that is what they would seek if given the chance. Bentham himself preferred the term 'happiness'. But this is equally a place-holder, which in practice also comes to mean whatever it is that people seek if given the chance. In what follows, we can take the terms 'utility' and 'happiness' as convertible. Bentham himself says that 'by utility is meant that property in any object whereby it tends to produce benefit, advantage, pleasure, good, or happiness (all this in the present case comes to the same thing)' (*Introduction to the Principles of Morals and Legislation*, iii).

If happiness is the end, then the next question is whose happiness. The answer to this is everyone's. Happiness should be taken as a total quantity, irrespective of whose happiness it is, and then it should be maximised. The greatest happiness, sometimes unnecessarily called the greatest happiness of the greatest number, is the goal. Bentham stated on the first page of his first main work, the *Fragment on Government*, the 'fundamental axiom, *it is the greatest happiness of the greatest number that is the measure of right and wrong*'. This axiom remained the unaltered bedrock of Bentham's thought throughout his life. For example, in the prefatory principles he drafted for the master work of his last years, the *Constitutional Code*, he wrote:

1. Position–Axiom. The right and proper end of all government in every political community is the greatest happiness of all the individuals of which it is composed.

Say in other words, the greatest happiness of the greatest number.

(*First Principles* 232)

As an axiom, it needs no defence; but it nevertheless follows fairly directly from the idea that happiness is the only good. For if there is nothing good but happiness, it follows that more happiness is better than less happiness; hence the best thing is to have as much as possible. Also, if there is nothing else of value but happiness then there is no other method of evaluation which would distinguish one person from another, such as birth, status, political position, race or class. Hence the happiness of any one person is equal in importance to the happiness of any other. Hence the best thing is the greatest happiness, regardless of who has it. As Bentham says, in his *Plan for Parliamentary Reform*, 'The happiness or unhappiness of any one member of the community – high or low, rich or poor – what greater or less part is it of the universal happiness and unhappiness, than that of any other?' (459). So, turning again to the *First Principles* , it follows that:

In the eyes of every impartial arbiter, writing in the character of legislator, and having exactly the same regard for the happiness of every member of the community in question as for that of every other, the greatest happiness of the greatest number of the members of that same community cannot but be recognized in the character of the right and proper, and sole right and proper, end of government.

(235)

We now have the criterion of correctness. The right solution to all problems of government is the one in which most happiness is produced. This applies to particular problems, like questions of what the details of the law should be or the appropriate level of punishment for an offence. It applies to administrative problems, such as how offices or prisons should be arranged or about what sort of records should be kept. About all this Bentham wrote copiously. But it also applies to the most general or political questions, such as the form of the constitution. That form of government is best which best promotes the greatest happiness.

91

This gives an end for the legislator, but a successful legislator also has to have knowledge of the materials with which he is working. He has to know about the means by which he can reach his end. This means that he has to have knowledge of his raw materials, human beings, so that he can give them the appropriate laws and institutions; so that he knows what to provide them with in order to promote the greatest happiness of the greatest number. He has to work out the right kind of structures, constitutional and otherwise, in which to place this strange creature so that the greatest happiness emerges. The assumption made here by Bentham is that man is a creature who pursues his own interests. 'Interest' is another weasel word which means many different things; it can indeed be trivialised to mean whatever it is that people pursue. But even understood like this it does not trivialise the general problem to which the legislator has to find a solution. For what he has to do is take a group of self-interested people, each pursuing their own independent happiness, and put them in some sort of structure in which the result will be the general happiness.

So the solution to the problem of good government is to produce a structure in which the way an individual person acts, seeking nothing but his own happiness, happens to coincide with what he ought to do. His interest, that is, has to be made to correspond with his duty. Bentham called this the 'duty and interest junction principle'. Such is the utilitarian theory of punishment. All punishment, as Bentham says, is in itself an evil. It is giving people pain. It can only be justified, therefore, if the evil of the (actual or threatened) pain is more than balanced by provision of happiness. But happiness can be provided by the threat of punishment; it is provided if the threat deters people from doing things which would harm the general happiness. So now we know when and how much to punish; namely, when the pain of the punishment is exceeded by the happiness gained from such deterrence. The legislator, building a perfect system of penal law, produces a system in which it is in people's interest to do their duty. The self-interested prospective criminal, wholly interested in his own gain, is nevertheless led to those things he ought to do, such as not killing and stealing, because the threatened punishments make this also in his interest.

This theory of punishment, and the idea behind the duty and interest junction principle, were available for Bentham off the eighteenth-century shelf. For example, Helvetius in *De l'Esprit*, a book which influenced Bentham greatly, says:

The legislator forms at his pleasure, heroes, great geniuses, and virtuous men . . . reward, punishment . . . are . . . divinities, with which he can always promote the public welfare, and create illustrious men of all kinds.

The whole study of the moralists consists in determining the use that ought to be made of rewards and punishments, and the assistance that may be drawn from them in order to connect the personal with the general interest. This union is the master-piece which moralists ought to propose to themselves. If citizens could not procure their own private happiness without promoting that of the public, there would be then none vicious but fools.

(1759 translation, London; 111)

Or, as Beccaria puts it: 'the legislator . . . is a wise architect, who erects his edifice on the foundation of self-love, and contrives, that the interest of the public shall be the interest of each individual' (*On Crimes and Punishments*, 1767 translation; 176). However, nobody before Bentham tried to put the general idea into effect thoroughly and in detail.

Bentham was not content to rest with reward and punishment. His legislator would not only be a metaphorical but also a literal architect, building poorhouses and prisons. The central idea, 'a simple idea in architecture', was to build them in circles, so that the guard sitting in the centre of the spider's web could see all the prisoners, the so-called panopticon. The principle of tying duty to interest also applied to the financial management; that is to the institutional structure in which the guards worked. The self-interested guards had also to be made to do their duty; that is to guard the prisoners at as little cost to the public as possible. One device which was important for Bentham here was publicity. The panopticons were to be open to continuous public inspection.

The panopticon may seem like a mad or visionary scheme, but in fact it very nearly got built. Bentham himself wished to be the first contract manager. He got the state to buy the land for it and thought several times in the course of nearly twenty years' struggle that he had got agreement to build the prison itself. In the end he never got a prison. But what he did get was a distrust of government. Both theoretically and practically he realised that he had to enlarge the net of his work. It was no good him appealing to the enlightened law-giver with schemes for perfect law or perfect institutions. The enlightened legislator was an eighteenth-century fiction. Actual legislators, actual tsars or kings, were also self-interested people. They also had to be protected against. They also had to be placed in a structure in which following their interests led to them also doing their duty. It was not just the guards in the panopticon who had to be guarded against; it was also all holders of authority.

And so we get to Bentham's interest in constitutional law, and his interest in democracy. In the 1820s his main work was drafting a constitutional code; before then he had written more polemical material about the reform of parliament. Again, he was stimulated by the thought that what he was writing might be put into practical effect. He thought that the constitutional code might be used by Portugal, Greece or one of the new South American countries. Agitation for parliamentary reform was mounting in England and he produced proposals. In fact, much of Bentham's work on parliamentary reform had been done considerably earlier. At the start of French Revolution he had drawn up proposals on voting and on parliamentary organisation both for Necker and for the new revolutionaries. (Bentham was an honorary citizen of the French republic; and the work which made his name, the *Traités de législation civile et pénale,* was published in Paris in 1802 edited by his disciple Dumont.) In 1809, when Bentham returned to and greatly amplified this material, he met James Mill, who worked for a while as his secretary. They thought together about democracy. Bentham wrote a thousand pages of manuscript. Later on, at about the same time as Bentham eventually published his *Plan for Parliamentary Reform* (1817) and his *Radical Reform Bill* (1819), James Mill wrote *An Essay on Government* (1820).

It is convenient to take the views of the two men together, even though they are not wholly coincident. James Mill's *An Essay on Government* is a short, clear work. It was regarded by contemporary utilitarians as a model of political thought, and was used as a text book by the younger politically minded utilitarians. As such, it was famously and influentially attacked by Macaulay. On the other hand, Bentham's late style is of legendary difficulty; and even worse is the handwriting in which much of this thought remained. Even when Bentham did come out into the public arena, writing pamphlets promoting reform, he was much more long-winded than Mill. Bentham's thought is more subtle than Mill's; but it is also less accessible. James Mill gets on with the job; Bentham gives the sense that there is more of a job to do.

The materials James Mill (1773–1836) brought to his solution to the problem of government are the materials we have seen in Bentham. The problem is the problem of framing a constitution in which people, following their own interests, will in fact produce the good society, that is the greatest happiness. Mill declares, with typical bluntness, that it is a 'law of nature' that 'a man, if able, will take from others any thing they have and he desires' (*Essay* 12; 61). This is also to apply to people in political power, who are, after all, people, bound by the same laws of nature. This means that

> Whenever the powers of Government are placed in any hands other than those of the community, whether those of one man, of a few, or of several, those principles of human nature which imply that Government is at all necessary, imply that those persons will make use of them to defeat the very end for which Government exists.
>
> (13; 61)

The end for which government exists is the security of one man against the depredations of another; yet if the result is depredation by the government, he is not better off. Mill therefore thought that monarchy or aristocracy, government by the one or few, led to terror:

> We have seen that the very principle of human nature on which the necessity of government is founded, the propensity of one man to possess himself of the objects of desire at the cost of another, leads on, by an infallible sequence, where power over a community is concerned, and nothing checks, not only to that degree of plunder which leaves the members ... the bare means of subsistence, but to that degree of cruelty which is necessary to keep in existence the most intense terror.
>
> (23; 67)

For Mill, 'terror is the grand instrument' (22; 66). Yet, even though Mill claimed that 'the chain of inference, in this case, is close and strong, to a most unusual degree', it looks as if something may have gone wrong with the deduction. For the world in which Mill lived was one composed of monarchies and aristocracies. Yet it did not seem that there was terror everywhere, and not everyone was living at mere subsistence level. Macaulay found it easy to make fun of this passage. However, in the subordinate clauses, the passage also includes the answer. There have to be checks. What the passage says is what will inevitably happen if there are no checks on government power. Hence, as Mill puts it later, 'upon the right constitution of checks, all goodness of Government depends' (33–4; 73). 'All the difficult questions of Government', says Mill, 'relate to the means of restraining those, in whose hands are lodged the powers necessary for the protection of all, from making a bad use of it' (6; 58). The central question, again, is who will guard the guards. Bentham did not write so bluntly; but he has the same view of the problem, and the same solution. In article 13 of Chapter 2 of the *Constitutional Code* he writes (in his more cumbrous manner):

> to render the conduct of *rulers* conducive to the maximisation of happiness, it is not less necessary to employ, in their case, the instrument of *coercion* than in the case of *rulees* . . . rulers are by the unalterable constitution of human nature, disposed to maximise the application of the matter of good to *themselves,* of the matter of evil to *rulees'*.
>
> (20)

Here we see the utilitarian tradition coinciding with the old Whig tradition described in the last chapter of the suspicion of power, in which the chief aim of a constitution is taken to be the preservation of liberty by the provision of checks or controls on the governors. We saw how this led to an interest in balancing power and in mixed constitutions. Both James Mill and Bentham poured scorn on balanced or mixed constitutions, but they were also as trenchant about the corruptions of power as any Whig. As Bentham puts it in the *Code,* 'The greater a man's power, the stronger his propensity in all possible ways to abuse it. Of this fact, all history is one continued proof' (122). In the old Whig rhetoric the abuse of power in the political sphere is corruption, the substitution of private interest for the general interest. For Bentham corruption is as universal as gravity. As he puts it, 'on this part of the *moral* world, is the *attraction of corruption* not less universal than the *attraction of gravity* in the physical world' (*Code* 78).

So, as Mill says, Lenin-style, 'what then is to be done?' (*Essay* 33; 72). How, working with corrupt human nature, do we achieve the greatest happiness of the greatest number? The answer is to place power at a point in which there can be no such corruption, that is where the power-holder, aiming at its own interest, also aims at the universal interest. This point is the people as a whole. So, following Bentham's 'Rule I' in the *Code,* namely 'the sovereign power give to those, whose interest it is that happiness be maximised' (21), we reach the conclusion that 'the sovereignty is in *the people*' (25). We reach, that is, the conclusion that 'the Constitutive authority is in the whole body of Electors belonging to this state: that is to say, in the whole body of the inhabitants, who . . . are resident on the territory of the state, deduction made of certain classes' . Or as James Mill puts it, thinking of the choice of representatives,

> the benefits of the Representative system are lost, in all cases in which the interests of the choosing body are not the same with those of the community. It is very evident, that if the community itself were the choosing body, the interest of the community and that of the choosing body would be the same.
>
> *(Essay* 45; 78–9)

We here get a quite explicit argument for democracy, described as such. Thus Bentham says in the *Plan for Parliamentary Reform,* which recommends that 'power' be 'put into the hands of those of whose obedience all power is composed' (437), that 'two words, viz. *democratical ascendency,* will, in principle, suffice for the expression of' the 'remedy' (446). It is an argument for representative, rather than direct, democracy. Both are quite explicit about this. Both cite the difficulty of getting a large people together in one place, the fact people have to make their living and are short of time. But it goes further than this, particularly in Bentham. There is a division of skill. In manuscripts written at the time of the French Revolution Bentham commented that 'were every man his own legislator laws would be as badly made as clothes would be, if every man were his own taylor'; and continued

> it is not every man that can make a shoe; but when a shoe is made every man may tell whether it fits him without difficulty. Every man cannot be a shoemaker but any man may choose his own shoemaker.
>
> (University College Bentham MSS, box 127, sheet 2)

The central principle enunciated here persists into the later work, and Bentham spent a lot of time organising systems so that the representatives (whom he called deputies) and the officials would be of high quality. 'Aptitude maximised, expense minimised' is the catchword summarising hundreds of sheets of material; and the idea, more specifically, was to guard against either moral or intellectual inferiority.

This was partly to be achieved by annual elections. Both Mill and Bentham have this. The threat of dismissal was to provide accountability. However, Bentham, unlike Mill, also added a code of penal sanctions and devoted considerable work to public opinion. For him the mass of the people, the 'supreme constitutive', as well as choosing its representatives annually, also sat in continuous judgment on them, as a kind of jury. He thought of it therefore as a kind of (fictitious) tribunal, the Public Opinion Tribunal, so that 'the Public Opinion Tribunal is to the Supreme Constitutive what the judiciary is to the Supreme Legislative' (35). 'Public opinion', he says in the *Code*, 'may be considered as a system of law, emanating from the body of the people. . . . To the pernicious exercise of the power of government it is the only check; to the beneficial, an indispensable supplement' (36). Or, 'in every situation, *moral* aptitude will depend upon the influence exercised by the Public Opinion Tribunal, as will the efficiency of that influence upon the degree of liberty possessed by the press' (86–7).

Mill does not show the same interest in public opinion and the press, and it means that Bentham was not open to one of Macaulay's objections to Mill. For the reason why Macaulay thought that kings did not terrorise their people in the way that Mill said must inevitably happen was because kings are susceptible to public opinion. They wished to guard their reputation. Bentham also allows this, holding that public opinion is the only check that there is in non-democratic regimes. 'By the healing hand of Public Opinion', he says in the *Code*, 'the rigour of the despotism may be softened' (54).

Bentham was also prepared to recognise, again unlike Mill, that there would still be a governing class in a democracy. This would, in fact, meet another of Macaulay's criticisms. As Bentham puts it:

> One point however there is – on which a representative democracy and an aristocracy-ridden monarchy do (it must be confessed) agree: under both forms of government, the possession of power is secured to one class, to the perpetual exclusion of another class. In the *character* of the *power-holding* class in the two cases, lies the sole difference.
>
> (*Code* 433)

The difference in character was that, with all Bentham's controls and protections, the governing class would be more 'apt'. So Bentham was prepared to work out much further than Mill exactly what would happen in a representative democracy, and he saw that there would still be problems to be guarded against, problems of protecting people from the governors. Severe limits were placed on those eligible for office. All prospective deputies had to have instruction in good government, and all prospective officials were not only to pass an examination but also had to bid for their offices, in a sort of Dutch auction, so that the people who would work for least got appointed. It was very important that power was split between the people elected and the officials; that is, we have the 'lodging of the supreme operative power in more hands than one' (*First Principles* 238). An elective dictatorship would not serve. Unlike Mill, for Bentham every official from the prime minister downward could be removed at any time by the direct request of a quarter of the people. He even had proposals for a militia in which the privates could vote out their officers.

So Bentham is both more democratic and more realistic than Mill. He is more democratic in allowing more direct control by the people, and by allowing more people to have that control. But he is also more realistic in realising that democracies will also be subject to the 'iron law of oligarchy', to the fact that (in Benthamite terms) government is always of the many by the few. Bentham, however, did not regard this as an unfortunate fact attending all governments. It was for him a positive feature tending to good government. It was only in this way that the governors could be of sufficient quality and have sufficient expertise. Representative democracy was for Bentham the solution to the old Platonic problem of expertise in government. The solution, however, works differently from the way that representation was described in the last chapter. We do not now need special moral expertise, or public virtue. It is Plato's problem, but it is not Plato's solution. We do not need a governing class born to the job, or guardians trained from birth. It might be thought that Bentham's purposes would in fact be better served by having Platonic guardians, specially schooled from an early age with belief in the greatest happiness principle. However, this would be a mistake. For Bentham, once it is realised that all men can be corrupted, no such guardians would be safe. The only safety is to give 'power into the hands of those of whose obedience all power is composed' (*Plan* 437). Power is to be given to the people. They will naturally tend to promote the greatest happiness of the greatest number; or at least the majority, the greatest number, naturally will. So that is where the 'sovereignty' or the 'Constitutive authority' is placed. We have a democracy. On the other hand we need expertise. Just as in Plato, governing is a skill. Not every one can make clothes. Not every one can be his own tailor. Not every one can govern. So we have representatives, with time and expertise, to do the work. So our democracy is a representative one, not just because of problems of size, but in order to maximise the good. We have both good government and also control of the governors.

We have seen how Bentham and Mill continued with Whig-like suspicions of power. Yet their solutions were different from the Whigs, and they came under attack from the more intellectual Whigs: Mill from Macaulay, Bentham from Mackintosh. Indeed, Macaulay was worried that the cause of reform would be contaminated by association with these ideas, holding it back. One difference from the Whigs has already been noted: their rejection of the idea of a mixed or balanced constitution. Another was about the nature of representation. The classic Whig view was that there should be representation of interests. Hence, as the interests changed in society (for example, with the rise of a new commercial class), so also should representation change. But what the utilitarians proposed was representation of people. Everyone, as an individual, had a right to be represented. For that they had to have the vote themselves (and there had also to be people between whom to choose when voting; Bentham is quite clear on this). Someone could not be represented by another, merely on the basis that they shared an interest; such as, for example, being a member of the woollen trade, or living off the land.

This is their view. But Mill, in the later stretches of the *Essay on Government*, rather spoils their case. For after the general argument for universal suffrage, he then starts deleting people whose interests are 'indisputably included in those of other individuals' (45). In this way he can eliminate, he thinks, women and children; and by children he means everyone under 40. For 'the interest of almost all' women 'is involved either in that of their fathers or in that of their husbands'. Macaulay, in his *Edinburgh Review* reply to Mill, also finds this simple to refute, wondering whether, for example, the 'interest of a Chinese [is] the same with that of the women whom he harness to his plough' (117). And this is an area in which Bentham, and also Mill's son, J. S. Mill, firmly disagreed with him. From the time when Bentham drafted his principles of voting for the new French revolutionaries, he could see that there was no good reason to exclude women from the suffrage; their supposed physical weakness, for example, gave more reasons why they should have their interests protected by the power of the vote rather than fewer. 'As to intellectual aptitude', he wrote in *First Principles* , 'no reason has ever been assigned why, in respect of that branch of appropriate aptitude, this half of the species ought to be deemed inferior to the other' (97).

As regards minors, Bentham recognises that there has to be some cut-off point, which he thinks should be settled partly conventionally, according to the condition of a particular society. But he is quite sure that 40 is absurdly high, noting in his private notes on Mill that when Mill was writing the *Essay* he had before his eyes a boy of 18 of high aptitude; namely John Stuart Mill. Bentham did impose one qualification, which will be noted shortly, that of literacy. However, it is reasonable to say that he really was proposing what he called 'virtual universality of suffrage'; he was not excluding great masses of people from the vote in the small print of his proposals, as did both the Mills, although for different reasons.

The question now is whether this bold proposal really follows from the principle of utility, and in what way it can be criticised. The central point of Macaulay's criticism, which was to have an important influence on J. S. Mill, was as regards method. He thought that Mill was trying to set out a wholly a priori theory of human nature, which did not correspond with the facts and which led to mistaken conclusions, such as the one already noted about the standard of living in monarchies. For Macaulay, the science of politics, like other sciences, should be placed on good inductive or observational grounds and Mill was just living in the Middle Ages. However, part of the question here is not how best to conduct the science of politics, describing what happens, but how best to conduct political theory, which is in part an evaluative enterprise. Yet even if we allow the evaluative force of the supreme principle of utility, Macaulay still has a point. For we have seen that this principle cannot be applied unless we have knowledge of the facts. We need to know the nature of human beings in order to decide on the best political structure. So it becomes an important question, for the utilitarian, how to acquire this knowledge.

The most sensitive point here is the principle that everyone pursues their own interests. For this looks (as Macaulay also pointed out) either trivial or false; either as just meaning that whatever people do is to be called their interests (trivial), or as that everyone acts in an selfish manner (false). Yet Bentham, at least, was perfectly prepared to allow that there were cases of altruistic action. He accepted that people showed sympathy for, and cared for, others. His use of the principle depended more on the idea that people should not be trusted to act otherwise, particularly when they were in power. As regards finding out what interests were, he compiled long lists of motives, such as in his *Springs of Actions* tables. In fact, the utilitarians can fairly be presented as more open-minded and more empirical in their approach than it would seem from the deductive procedure of Mill's *Essay* or Macaulay's criticism. Part of Bentham's resistance to entrenched constitutional provisions, for example, was to keep an openness towards the future. This was also his prime objection to the balanced constitution: balance meant that things did not move and 'know you not that, as in the case of the body *natural*, so in the case of the body *politic*, when motion ceases, the body dies?' (*Plan* 450). For him the good polity was always experimenting, always finding out more, always changing its provisions in order to improve them. And as regards democracy, for Bentham this was not just some utopian or a priori deduction. He frequently cites the United States as an example (or examples, since he is thinking of the separate states) of democracy at work, and successfully at work, even though with its balancing elements, it is not his preferred form of democracy. (And, of course, just as with the earlier use of classical Athens, in calling it a democracy at all some idealisation is at work; women and slaves are again excluded.)

Bentham was confident. He had seen the future and it worked. It was only his fellow countrymen, subject to all sorts of prejudice manufactured by the ruling classes in their own interests, who were resistant. And clearly, whether prejudiced or not, people were nervous about democracy in Britain, and continued to be as the century progressed. We shall shortly see the nervousness in J. S. Mill. But, before then, it is interesting to compare differing reasons why nervousness might not be in place. If democracy worked, the question was why it worked. The question, asked by intellectuals to intellectuals, writing their political theory in books, tracts and journals, was why the unintellectual should be trusted. Just as in

Plato the question was how the unlearned, the unwashed, could deliver good government. This is a question about the political judgment of (the greatest number of) the people, and why it should be supposed, on the whole, to be correct.

To this question two answers were possible: deference and virtue. The idea of deference was the sociological claim that the great mass of the people would follow (defer to) their betters; so as long as these betters had the right ideas, allowing everyone the vote would still give good government. James Mill goes this route in the end, claiming that the people at large would follow the middle class, and that this provident, frugal, industrious class had the right views about society. Even if Mill were right about the middle class, this amounts to a great breach in his principles since, as Macaulay pointed out, there would be no need in that case for universal suffrage. Also, the sociological generalisation was at best shaky: even if the lower orders started deferential, given political power they might well have other ideas about goodness (such as the goodness of expropriating the accumulated property of the middle classes). So James Mill is caught in a dilemma here: if his sociological claim is correct, he has no reason for enfranchising the lower orders. Whereas, if his claim is false, there is indeed a reason for their enfranchisement, in terms of their interest, but no reason why they should come up with the right answer.

The other route to take was virtue. This is the assumption that the great mass of people knows about the good and so is likely to get the right answer. This is the way that Bentham went (and, at times, James Mill). This is the use of the claim that, if everyone cannot be a skilled cobbler or tailor, everyone can tell if shoes are badly made, or clothes do not fit. The assumption about virtue is no longer any view about people, or some people, having a special moral intuition into the nature of the good or a special disposition to behave altruistically. Instead, everyone is supposed to be self-interested, in both thought and action. But this is just the point. It is supposed that judgment follows interest. The interest of the people as a whole is in good government, because good government just means what is in the interest of (the greatest number of) the people. Since they have no interest in getting anything but a correct judgment about their interest, on the whole they will do so. 'The people?', as Bentham asked, 'what interest have they in being governed badly?' (*Plan* 445).

Just after his remarks about the tailor, Bentham wrote in his manuscripts that 'the surest visible sign and immediate evidence of general utility is general consent' (Box 127, sheet 3). There is no claim that the coincidence of public opinion with truth is perfect; just that this is the best sign that we have got. As Bentham put it, at about that time, when accepting his honorary citizenship of the new French Republic, 'the general will is everywhere, and for every one, the sole external index by which [whether a particular proposal leads to the general good] can be decided' (*Correspondence* IV 401). It is an external index. It is the best evidence, even if it is not perfect. As the Revolution progressed, Bentham unsurprisingly lost confidence for a while in this index. Yet he returned to it. By the time of the *Code* he held that, for the Public Opinion Tribunal, 'even at the present stage in the career of civilisation, its dictates coincide, on most points, with those of the *greatest happiness principle*' (36).

This returns us to Bentham's great interest in publicity. Communication was crucial between governed and governors. The people had to know what was going on. About the only restriction on suffrage which he consistently proposes is a reading qualification. This was not a covert way of restricting the vote to a class, or classes, who might on other grounds be thought to have the right answers. For anyone who is sufficiently interested can teach himself to read, or so at least Bentham thought. So, as a restriction, it excludes nobody (anyone who wants can meet the condition). However, what it does ensure is that voters are in a position to be informed. By reading what goes on, they are in a position to be able to exercise good judgment. Their interest is meant to be able to take good care of that.

Hence we gain the solution to the problem of government, whereby democracy puts the interests of the government in line with that of the people; hence ensuring that the people are governed as they ought to be. We reach an alternative solution to the problem of checks and balances; of securities against misrule. Or as Bentham puts it in his *Plan for Parliamentary Reform*:

> At present the cause of *misrule* is this: viz. the *rule* is completely in the hands of those whose interest it is . . . that the misrule should continue: – the thing required is . . . so to order matters, that the controuling part of the government shall be in the hands of those whose interest it is that good government shall take place of misrule.
>
> (447)

When we get to James Mill's better known son, J. S. Mill, such utilitarian thought is worn with a difference. J. S. Mill (1806–73) famously underwent a terrifying educational programme of his father's, watched benignly by Bentham, who was a sort of secular godfather. Their joint hope was that the boy would be worthy of them. And so, in a sense, he was. However he, also famously, reacted against his education and his father. At times, in utilitarian terms, he was no better than a semi-detached Benthamite. All his life he was inclined to see the positive points in opposing views. So, in his late and chief work on democracy, the *Considerations on Representative Government* (1861), he tried to combine his utilitarian inheritance with opposing influences.

In particular, J. S. Mill was clearly influenced (or shaken) by Macaulay's criticism of his father. Partly this was methodological: he wanted to give more scope for empirical results and to be less purely a priori, or deductive, in treatment. But partly it was because he was more interested in history and sociology. He had a temperamental inclination to think that, intellectually speaking, things were better done in France. So he kept importing the latest French views to improve the British public, usually under the by-line that this was the thought of the nineteenth century (organic, developmental, observational) to correct the thought of the eighteenth century (mechanical, static, deductive). In fact, many of these ideas, with respect to progress and the development of society, had started in Britain and in the eighteenth century, with the developmental theories of civil society produced by the Scots.

Part of the younger Mill's claim, therefore, as against his father, was that different kinds of government were suitable for different kinds of society. Society can be taken as developing, and it is only when it reaches a certain level of development that democratic representative government is either possible or desirable. In the earliest stages, the important thing is that people learn to obey; hence they are better suited to a despotic regime. J. S. Mill says in the *Considerations* that

> institutions need to be radically different, according to the stage of advancement already reached. The recognition of this truth, though for the most part empirically rather than philosophically, may be regarded as the main point of superiority in the political theories of the present above those of the last age;

in which it was customary to claim representative democracy for England or France by arguments which would equally have proved it the only fit form of government for Bedouins or Malays.

(393–4)

A deductive argument will prove the superiority of the same kind of government for all; J. S. Mill's more empirical, more developmental and more sociological approach will find differences. The theory 'of the last age' he has in mind seems clearly to be that of his father.

His interest in different natures of people, or peoples, meant that J. S. Mill had a fuller view of the point of good government. All the utilitarians thought that the point of good government was the goodness of the people, for the criterion of good government was people's welfare. But, with a more developed view of the difference between people, J. S. Mill was able to spell out more completely the nature of this goodness. People were developing, and it was good for them to develop. The point of government was the goodness of the people. Hence good government was precisely that government which helped the people in their development, which aided them on their progress up to the next stage on the ladder.

This gives J. S. Mill extra arguments for the goodness of democracy. For it is not now sufficient that the people have good laws. These could be provided by a benevolent despot; and, indeed, we have seen how Bentham commenced by appealing to such. Nor is it merely that we have to move away from this position to democracy because of a problem about who was going to control the controllers and therefore a need to provide checks to the despot. J. S. Mill agreed with this. But the need for the move to democracy for him depended more upon the need for the positive goodness of the citizen than the need for his protection against the malevolent use of power. It was by being given freedom, by being given control over himself, that he was able to develop and learn. Government, for J. S. Mill, was primarily an instrument of education, and representative democracy provided the best kind of education.

On the other hand, the problem of guarding the guards did not disappear. J. S. Mill saw, that once the prescriptions of his father and Bentham had been put into effect, there might well remain a serious problem of protection. Even with democracy, people would still need to be protected against the power of government. 'One of the greatest dangers of democracy', he says, 'as of all other forms of government, lies in the sinister interest of the holders of power' (446). In a democracy the ultimate power lies with the people. But the holders of this power are not the people as a whole, but rather a majority of them. Against this majority other people, the minority, needed protection. Therefore, as J. S. Mill puts it, 'it is an essential part of democracy that minorities should be adequately represented' (452). Taking the phrase from de Tocqueville, in his *On Liberty* he talks of the 'tyranny of the majority' (Chapter 1). Earlier, in his 1838 essay on Bentham, he had asked rhetorically, 'is it, at all times and places, good for mankind to be under the absolute authority of a majority of themselves?' (*Collated Works* X 106). His answer is no. 'To give', he says,

> any one set of partialities, passions, and prejudices, absolute power, without counter-balance from partialities, passions, and prejudices of a different sort; is to render the correction of any of these imperfections hopeless; to make one narrow, mean type of human nature universal and perpetual.
>
> (107)

In his more specific proposals in the *Considerations* J. S. Mill therefore spends considerable effort disconnecting the idea that everyone should be represented from the idea that they all ought to have equal representation. 'But though every one ought to have a voice – that every one should have an equal voice is a totally different proposition' is one way he puts it (473). He wants some elements, in particular the more educated elements, to have a greater representation. Only then, as a minority, could he feel that they were protected against the uneducated majority. As he puts it, 'the distinction in favour of education, right in itself, is further and strongly recommended by its preserving the educated from the class legislation of the uneducated' (476).

When criticising his opponents in his *Plan of Parliamentary Reform*, Bentham says 'on this occasion, as on all others, before you put yourself to any expense in the article of *argument*, look first to *the state of interests*' (507). In considering any set of proposals, his recipe was that we should look for the interests they represented. Following this, we would expect that aristocrats might extol the great virtues of a hereditary House of Lords in terms of the special virtues of people with leisure; and we might think that this

107

was what they would say, given their interests. Similarly, in the 1820s we might expect the new middle class to press for inclusion in the suffrage on the basis of the particular virtues of the middle classes (thrift, foresight, responsibility and such-like). Again, we might think, this is just what they would say. The talk, particularly the talk by the aristocrats, is of the dangers of class-based legislation (that is, legislation in the interests of other classes than their own); the reality is a defence of interests. This, following Bentham's recipe, we might expect. What is slightly startling is to find J. S. Mill doing exactly the same thing. The claims of a particular class, the intellectuals, are here promoted. It is promoted because of its particular virtues, which should therefore be given special weight in representation. Yet, again, the class promoted is the class to which the promoter just happens to belong. Again, the objection is to that class being at the mercy of 'class legislation'. The deeply moral prescriptions may, in the end, be no more than the prescriber's interest.

Certainly this is a divergence from Bentham. For Bentham, there was to be not only virtual universality of suffrage; but also equal suffrage. The balances and compromises of J. S. Mill show, in these terms, a loss of confidence in democracy. On the other hand, J. S. Mill does force a distinction between common utility and greatest utility. When his father said that 'the community cannot have an interest opposed to its interest' (10), this seems like the merest tautology; an appropriately trivial axiom from which to commence the deduction. However, if it is remembered that the community is a collection of persons, and that these persons have different interests, then it can be seen that the greatest interest of the community, in the sense of the greatest welfare, may be very much against the welfare of certain individuals. The community may be divided into different classes, races or religions. Parts have different interests from other parts. One of these, a larger part, may sacrifice the interests of another of these, a smaller part. The greatest interest is served, but not the common interest. Even people for whom happiness, or welfare, is the sole criterion of value might have two views about the rightness of such sacrifice of the welfare of the minority to the welfare of the majority.

J. S. Mill resists such sacrifice from the standpoint of equality. The minority, equally citizens, are not equally represented. The minorities are effectively disenfranchised, and this is 'contrary to the principle of democracy, which professes equality as its very root and foundation' (449). He does not mean by this that, in the final analysis, the majority should not win out over the minority, but he wants to provide mechanisms (such as plural voting for the educated) to give the minority a say. 'In a really equal democracy', he says 'every or any section would be represented, not disproportionately, but proportionately' (449).

There are two points of interest about J. S. Mill's use of equality here. First, the Benthamite position could also claim that it was regarding people equally. For everyone, equally, is to be given the vote. Not allowing some people to have more votes than others is precisely to treat them equally; whereas J. S. Mill could be said to be giving unequal preference to the intellectuals. There are obvious problems here about the relationship between democracy and equality which will have to be teased apart later in the book. The second immediate point of interest is that an appeal to equality seems to be an appeal to a source of value outside utility. Yet the utilitarian position is that utility is the only (ultimate) source of value. However this merely illustrates J. S. Mill's semi-detached position. In *Considerations on Representative Government* there are very few explicit appeals to welfare or utility. A moralised language invoking notions like duty, justice, equality, does most of the work. This is another way that he runs beyond (or regresses behind) his fathers. His thought cannot be taken as a full representation of utilitarian thought about democracy, since J. S. Mill was not fully a utilitarian.

Another example of J. S. Mill's use of moral language is with respect to voting. He treats the voter as a person in a position of trust. The voter is a public official who acts on behalf of the whole community. 'His vote is not a thing in which he has an option', he says, 'it has no more to do with his personal wishes than the verdict of a juryman. It is strictly a matter of duty; he is bound to give it according to his best and most conscientious opinion of the public good' (489). So, whereas the elder utilitarians based their philosophy of government on the basis that everyone acted in their interests, J. S. Mill seems to allow that everyone is capable of being motivated by a higher morality; by their duty. Of course this would not amount to much practical difference if the citizen's interest coincided in most cases with his duty. And in the Bentham/James Mill view of democracy, this is indeed the case. But the different stress by the younger Mill is not just a difference in flavour; it is a recognition that interest and duty may diverge. For it has been seen how Mill brings out the difference between narrow or sectional interests and the general interest. The citizen has a duty to vote for the general interest. But, if interest and duty diverge, then we get again to the problem of why the citizen should be expected to do his duty. Both Bentham and James Mill thought that it was not safe to assume that he would.

There is a problem, therefore, about whether the voting citizen will do his duty. But there is also a question about whether he even ought to, from a utilitarian point of view. Talk of a general interest sounds rather like Rousseau, although J. S. Mill in these stretches of the *Considerations* does not mention Rousseau (Rousseau wrote in the right language, but in the wrong century). Bentham's thought can, however, be reconstructed without any such notion as the general will. Of course, what the legislator wills he wills generally. In that sense the people exhibit a general will. If a law against theft is enacted, it applies generally against all potential thieves. However, these laws, even though they apply generally, might still advantage certain groups rather than others. And, if the advantage they gave to the advantaged group was greater than the disadvantage to the disadvantaged group (for example, because the advantaged group was larger), then these laws would be quite appropriate from a utilitarian point of view.

For Bentham we just have a sum of interests. If some give way to others; if the minority are to be sacrificed to the majority; that is just the way of getting the maximum welfare. (It would usually be less, for example, if the majority were to be sacrificed to the minority.) A common interest is just an interest that individuals happen to share, not a special kind of interest; and the democratic process will work as successfully as a revealer of people's interests, and hence will allow maximisation, if it reveals interests which people do not happen to share.

There is an important point about information here, of which J. S. Mill was conscious at the beginning of the *Considerations*. The benevolent despot would not in fact be a good promoter of utility because it is hard for him to know how his proposed legislation might affect people. So, even with the best utilitarian will in the world, he is liable to make mistakes in his construction of a perfect code of law. But, if people themselves are able to reveal their interests, then no such centralisation of information is required. If people reveal their interests by their votes, then the vote will reveal what is in the greatest interest, and so will discover the right sort of legislation. But this will only happen if people vote in their interests. So there is a good utilitarian reason why people should not be trying to engage in an attempt at duty, as opposed to interest, when they are voting. The utilitarian does not want their views about rightness. That is not important information to him; and he knows the answer to this question already (rightness is what gives the greatest happiness). What he needs is information on happiness. On the assumption that people understand their own happiness better than they do the happiness of other people, he needs people to tell him what will make them, individually, happy. He needs people to vote in their interest.

Nor will this situation change if certain interests are, in fact, common. The utilitarians as a whole thought that people had a common interest in having law. They thought that people had a common interest in not being attacked. They thought that the legal protection of property was in everyone's interest. Supposing that this is a common (and in that sense a general) interest, the question is what effect this should have on theory. One reaction might be to give these things (life, property etc.) a particular moral status, calling them natural rights, and then use this as a reason for giving them a particular constitutional status, entrenched in a written declaration of rights and defended by an independent judiciary. However this was not Bentham's way. Bentham famously fulminated against natural rights. For him, utility was the only ultimate criterion of value. For him parliament was sovereign and there should be no splitting of powers or supreme court over against parliament. For him there should be no entrenched legislation; everything was open for revision and development in the light of experience. So there was no check on the majority. But if on the whole people can be expected to act in their interest, and if something is in everyone's interest, then it can be expected that people will see this and defend it. After all, it is supposed that it is in everyone's interest, and only a majority needs to see this.

Property is the particular problem. Ever since Aristotle it has been thought to be a problem in democracy that the more numerous have-nots will expropriate the property of the haves. Both Bentham and J. S. Mill thought that this was not actually in the interest of the have-nots. The legal defence of property was in everyone's interest. The question, then, is whether the majority can be trusted with the defence of their interest. Contemplating the enfranchisement of the working classes, J. S. Mill did not think that they could; even if property was in the long-term interest of the newly enfranchised working class, he foresaw them taxing it away in pursuit of their apparent short-term interest. Bentham (not so immediately faced with this problem) thought that they could; in the present age public opinion was a reasonable guide to utility, and most people could be expected to defend the general interest.

Utilitarianism is a simple moral theory, but its application demands complex and complete information. Purely factual assumptions or guesses have to be made. Among these are ones about how well people understand their interests. Bentham was, on the whole, optimistic. J. S. Mill was, on the whole, pessimistic. There is nothing in utilitarian theory to say who was right. But who was right makes an enormous difference to the application of utilitarianism to democratic theory.

CHAPTER VII

Reason in History: Hegel and Marx

In 1831, one year before Bentham died in London, Hegel died in Berlin. As Hegel died, the Great Reform Bill was being vigorously discussed in England: as Bentham died, it was being given the royal assent. This bill, which radically extended the English franchise, was strongly supported by Bentham and his followers. Yet the last thing which Hegel wrote was a long critical commentary on the bill. This was only one of many contrasts between Bentham and Hegel; but they did not contrast in every respect. For example, they both attacked English common (or traditional) law, both calling it an 'Augean stable', and both wishing to replace it by a rationally formulated, comprehensive code. Both supported their own local reform movements. Both thought, as Hegel put it when writing about the English Reform Bill, that 'the right way to pursue improvement is not by the moral route of using ideas . . . but by the alteration of institutions' (*Political Writings* 287). However, at a fundamental level they were very different, and had very different attitudes to democracy. Bentham, it will be remembered, wanted to have a 'Public Opinion Tribunal' acting as a check on the power of the government. Hegel declared in his main political work, the *Elements of the Philosophy of Right* of 1821 that 'the first formal condition of achieving anything great or rational, either in actuality or science, is to be independent of public opinion' (*Phil. Right* §318; 355). Clearly someone with such views about the people will have a different attitude about, and so will set different questions for, democracy. These questions will be the topic of the present chapter, the last of the historical chapters, which will also deal briefly with Hegel's heretical follower, Karl Marx. Hegel and Marx may not be comfortable companions for the democratically minded; but they are thoughtful ones.

113

The value which has been most closely examined in the last four chapters is freedom. So what, if anything, can be learned about freedom from Hegel? Let us try a few remarks to get the flavour of the man. 'The state is the actuality of concrete freedom', he says (*Phil. Right* §260; 282). This may sound hopeful; except that that 'concrete' is a shade disturbing. We are clearly in another new world: not the old balancing of powers world; nor yet the bright new world of utility. (All that is concrete for the utilitarians are people's sensations, and freedom, like anything else, is only to be valued by the quantity of pleasant sensations produced.) We are in a new world. Listen to this: 'the state', says Hegel, 'is the actuality of the ethical Idea – the ethical spirit as substantial will, *manifest* and clear to itself, which thinks and knows itself and implements what it knows in so far as it knows it' (*Phil. Right* §257; 275). This may sound exciting, or it may sound repulsive; but it is certainly baffling. 'Society and state', he says in his *Lectures on the Philosophy of World History* 'are the only situations in which freedom can be realised' (99). That is more comprehensible. It gives a target; a target for understanding the state and for understanding freedom; perhaps also a target for understanding more about democracy.

We have seen how a writer on constitutions and liberty such as Constant had to come to terms with the initially invigorating and ultimately threatening unfolding of the French Revolution. So also did Bentham. So also did Hegel. He was initially an admirer, and continued to think that much could be learned from it. Writing a commentary on a proposed constitution for his own native state of Wurtemberg after the defeat of Napoleon, he notes at the start that

> the intellectual development of the age has afforded the *idea* of
> a state and therewith of its essential unity. Twenty-five years of
> past and mostly terrible history have given us a sight of the
> numerous attempts to grasp this idea.
>
> (*Pol. Writings* 160)

Later in the work he says, more positively, that 'there could have hardly been a more frightful pestle for pulverizing false concepts of law and prejudices about political constitutions than the tribunal of these twenty-five years' (199).

Liberty is what we are tracking in Hegel; and inscribed on the banners of revolution was certainly the word 'liberty'. Also inscribed there was 'equality'. It is true that 'utility' was not so inscribed. But the earlier American revolutionaries, in their Declaration of Independence, had substituted for the expected 'life, liberty, and property', 'life, liberty, and the pursuit of happiness', making utility (or happiness) a fundamental natural right. The French in their Declaration of the Rights of Man and the Citizen had said in the first article that 'Social distinctions shall be based solely on public utility'. Utility, happiness, was in the air. Yet more central than happiness for Hegel was the third member of the famous trinity which was actually inscribed on the French banners, fraternity.

Fraternity, or community, seems to be one of those things from the ancient world which the busy commercial world of large modern states has left behind. Fine for the small classical Greek *polis*, it seems to go with what Constant, writing at about the same time as Hegel made the remarks just quoted, called the liberty of the ancients, rather than that of the moderns. Liberty for the modern age is the liberty of individuals, with their separate welfare, rights, commercial relations. In the last two chapters we have looked at politics in general, and democracy in particular, from the point of view of the individual. The individual has to have his liberty preserved, in different versions of balanced constitutional thought, or he was to have his welfare promoted, as in different versions of utilitarianism.

The state, since Locke and Hobbes, has been looked at as something into which such individuals might enter, in defence of their individual rights or properties. The state has been looked at from the point of view of the individual; an individual who was supposed to be free in his natural, pre-political, condition. Yet here we have Hegel saying that freedom is only possible in states and societies. It is only with fraternity, it is only with state or society, that freedom is supposed to be possible at all. For Locke, people contracted into the state; yet, as Hegel put it in one of his occasional political writings, a contract between government and people 'is essentially distinct from a political bond which is a tie objective, necessary, and independent of choice or whim' (*Pol. Writings* 197). Rather than thinking of independently choosing individuals, we should think of people gaining their individuality from the society in which they are placed; we should think of them as created and determined by what Hegel called the 'ethical life' (*Sittlichkeit*) of such communities.

Just like the revolutionaries, Hegel admires the Greeks. They had a full ethical life, so that participation in the life of the polis determined the life of the citizens. This might just seem the sort of misplaced nostalgia which Constant condemned. However Hegel was not nostalgic. In his outline history, this Greek stage had been succeeded by first a Roman and then a Germanic stage. This last stage had produced Martin Luther, individual conscience; an inner side to set against the outer side of a socially determined 'ethical life'. He wished to synthesise these two moments, or elements, so that the modern, post-revolutionary state, would determine the roles of the citizens just as the Greek state had; but these citizens would wish, in full individual conscience, to play these roles. With this synthesis would come proper freedom.

Thus the state forms a context in which people may give expression to their will. They can make their will rational (and so free) by willing the rational actions laid down by the state. The dictates of the state have an inner side, in that they can be willed by the citizens, as well as an outer side, in that they are laid down independently of the wishes of particular citizens. This doubleness is important for Hegel in the cases of ethical substance which fill up the modern world. I have got to be able to discover my duties in an ethical life which exists independently of me as an individual. On the other hand, if it is to be my duty, it has also got to be something which I can will myself into, so that I take on its own commands as being my own will. Only then will I find perfect freedom. I will have subjected my 'volition to discipline so as to elevate it to free obedience' (*Phil. Right* §270; 294).

Another historic change in Hegel's account is in his use of the idea of civil society. Locke had talked of people contracting into civil society; that is, deciding to leave the state of nature, or pre-political society. One of the many things which Hegel achieved was a change in the meaning of 'civil society' (*bürgerliche Gesellschaft*). He distinguished between what he called civil society and what he called the state. Marx, following, made the distinction even more pronounced. In Hegel's *Philosophy of Right*, 'civil society' and 'the state' are, together with 'the family', the three separate sections of the third and main part of the work, the part which deals with 'ethical life'. They are three different forms of communal life. For Hegel, 'civil society' is understood as the kind of community which develops out of individual people seeking economic advantage and being concerned to defend their property. This produces a system of law, or something like law, which protects these individuals, and aids their economic activities. In this structure '*subjective selfishness* turns into a *contribution towards the satisfaction of the needs of everyone else*' (*Phil. Right* §199; 233). As Hegel says,

> the concrete person who, as a *particular* person . . . is his own end, is *one principle* of civil society. But this particular person stands essentially in *relation* to other similar particulars, and their relation is such that each asserts itself and gains satisfaction through the others.
>
> (§182; 220)

The social system produces practice of regulation, laws promoting welfare. In civil society, we gain 'the tranquillity of civil law and the secure satisfaction of needs' (§203; 235). In this sense of 'civil society', 'the creation of civil society belongs to the modern world' (§182; 220).

However, for Hegel, beyond this lies the state. The state is a world of community, of rights and duties, that lies beyond such individual advantage. It is the state, for example, which summons people to war. These people have a duty to help the survival of their state. If this duty were merely a self-interested calculation in terms of protection of their property or lives (their liberty in that sense), they quite likely would not fight. Yet, for Hegel, they do and they should. They should because there are other kinds of duties than merely economically self-interested ones arising from the state; that they do shows that people recognise this.

Let us now return to freedom. Freedom is the central theme of Hegel's *Philosophy of Right*. Explicitly, of course, it is about what Hegel calls *right*. However in the first section he notes that 'the Idea of right is freedom' (26), and soon he is saying that 'the system of right is the realm of actualized freedom, the world of spirit produced from within itself as a second nature' (§4; 35). By the end, when we reach the full account of the state, it is again freedom which is in the foreground. 'The state', says Hegel in §260, 'is the actualization of freedom not in accordance with subjective caprice, but in accordance with the concept of the will, i.e. in accordance with its universality and divinity' (282). Notice that this is not just 'freedom', but an explicit contrast between real freedom, where there is universality, and mere arbitrariness. To act capriciously is not to act freely, so not all unconstrained actions, or fulfilments of desire, are

117

going to count as genuinely free. As with Rousseau, freedom is central to the account, but 'freedom' turns out not to mean quite what we might expect. For Hegel, 'it is only as *thinking* intelligence that the will is truly itself and free'. It is only rational action which is free action. But Hegel also thinks that the supreme expression of rationality is the state. The state 'is the *rational* in and for itself' (§258; 275) and hence 'one should expect nothing from the state except what is an expression of rationality' (§272; 307). Because the state is rational, following its dictates gives its citizens freedom. Living in it, following its instructions, they partake of its ethical substance.

So much for freedom. Now we have to look at the consequences for democratic theory. The reversal of the order of community and individual obviously is important. Rather than taking individuals as given, as in liberal political theory, and then seeing what happens when they vote in parties or government, we have here to start with state and society. So if the theory is to be democratic at all, it will be in a quite different way. Yet Hegel is not simply authoritarian. He does not just want a ruler (a Prussian king) with the people acting as obedient subjects. As seen at the beginning, he does not have confidence in the wisdom of the people. But neither does he have confidence in the wisdom of a king. Thinking that a king was necessary to give unity to a state, his ideal king merely expresses this idea of unity, or unified law, but does not create it. 'In a fully organized state', says Hegel, 'all that is required in a monarch is someone to say 'yes' and to dot the 'i'; for the supreme office should be such that the particular character of its occupant is of no significance' (§280; 323). Wisdom, policy, come not from the monarch, nor from the people, but from the 'universal class', the specially trained civil service.

However, Hegel also thinks that the people should be represented in the governmental process, and this is where we get nearer to democracy. This is not because of their wisdom, but because they also have to think of the actions of the state as expressing their will (it is because of the importance of the inner side; of the growth of individual conscience in a Protestant, 'Germanic' age). So there has to be representation. But this is just where the other kinds of social organisation (fraternity, ethical life) become important, and make Hegel's thought distinctive. For him, this representation should not be of individuals as such, but rather of these other elements of ethical life, into which individuals enter, and which compose their being. Central among these are what he calls corporations. These care for the individual, and the individual understands himself as a member of them. He is a certain kind of person, a carpenter or a merchant or whatever. Out of this is formed his estate. So Hegel can say that 'a human being with no estate is merely a private person and does not possess actual universality' (§207; 239). His estate gives him ethical life, just like the family; indeed Hegel says that 'the *family* is the first *ethical* root of the state; the *corporation* is the second, and it is based in civil society' (§255; 272). So we should see the state as growing out of these lesser spheres, which lay down the duties of people's lives, and in which they have honour.

So, for Hegel, when we reach the question of representation, we should not lose sight of the position of the corporation or the estate. Indeed the same word *estate*, or *Stand* in German, can stand loosely for a certain order of society and also more precisely for a particular part of the representative process, as with the French Third Estate. So, unlike in liberal political theory, Hegel does not conceive of political order as the state on the one hand and a mass of individual citizens on the other. In so far as we have representation, representation is not to be just of such individuals. That is a mere mass, without coherence or order. Yet, for Hegel,

> it is extremely important that the masses should be organized, because only then do they constitute a power or force; otherwise they are merely an aggregate, a collection of scattered atoms. Legitimate power is to be found only when the particular spheres are organized.
>
> (§290; 331)

Organisation is required. 'The state', says Hegel, 'is not a mechanism but the rational life of self-conscious freedom' (§270; 297). The analogies he uses are all organic. He says that 'predicates, principles, and the like get us nowhere in assessing the state, which must be apprehended as an organism' (§269; 290). The state is an organism, but so also are the families, corporations, and estates, within which the people have their ethical life. The last thing we want is a 'formless mass'; so we need organisation, articulation, structure. We need organic relationships, where

> in an organic relationship, the units in question are not parts but members, and each maintains the others while fulfilling *its*

own function; the substantial end and product of each is to maintain the *other* members while simultaneously maintaining *itself*.

(§286; 328)

'The idea that *all* individuals ought to participate in deliberations and decisions on the universal concerns of the state', says Hegel, 'seeks to implant in the organism of the state a *democratic* element *devoid of rational form*, although it is only by virtue of its rational form that the state is an organism' (§308; 347). So it might seem that the people should be kept completely out of government, as possessing no form; and democracy is just a bad thing. However, it is not as simple as this. As a mere terrifying 'formless mass', the people, or 'the many' can indeed do no good:

> *the many* as single individuals – and this is the favourite interpretation of 'the people' – do indeed live *together*, but only as a *crowd*, i.e. a formless mass whose movement can only be elemental, irrational, barbarous, and terrifying.
>
> (§303; 344)

But the people, or at least most of them, belong to corporations, estates. As members of estates they have form and organisation. As members of estates they can therefore properly enter as elements of the state into the political life of the country. The estates can be represented in Estates, and the Estates 'ensure that individuals do not present themselves as a *crowd* or *aggregate*, unorganized in their opinions or volition, and do not become a massive power in opposition to the organic state' (§302; 342). They become part of the organism, and 'when it becomes part of the organism, the mass attains its interests in a legitimate and orderly manner' (§302; 343).

This is the theoretical solution, but it also fits with Hegel's more particular commentary on actual practice, as in his commentary on the English Reform Bill or the proposed Wurtemberg constitution. Writing on the English Bill, he agrees with the utilitarians in the desire to sweep aside entrenched privileges. He talks of

> the deep insight of princes in making the guiding stars of their legislative activity . . . such principles as the state's well-being, the happiness of their subjects, and the general welfare . . . and giving them reality in face of merely positive privileges,

traditional private interest, and the stupidity of the masses.
(Pol. Writings 289)

This sweeping aside of traditional private rights is what he takes, in the work on Wurtemberg, to be one of the great lessons of the French Revolution 'as the struggle of rational constitutional law against the mass of positive law and privileges by which it had been stifled' (198). Yet, in both cases, this should not be replaced by the representation of abstract individuals as such. Removing such entrenched rights or privileges is normally a prelude to increasing democracy; but for Hegel it will be no advance if this just leads to greater scope for the 'stupidity of the masses'.

Writing about England, Hegel notes that 'experience teaches that elections are not in general attended by many' (311) or 'what seems to prevail in the electorate is great indifference' (308). When individuals are treated as mere atoms, it is barely worth their while participating. Hegel thinks that we will understand this 'if we ponder what must obviously contribute to such lukewarmness: namely, the sense that amongst the many thousands of votes cast at an election a single vote is actually insignificant' (309). This is the kind of paradox examined by later political theorists; how it could ever be in any individual's interest, in a large constituency, to vote. Hegel's solution, of course, is to reach for the corporation. It is not the individual as such which should be represented, but the corporation in which he has honour; honour, local solidarity, will make him participate in the life of his corporation, and his corporation will be represented in the Estates.

Hegel's fullest statement of this is in his commentary on the proposed Wurtemberg constitution, which is worth quoting at length. He first makes an historical observation, noting that

> the great beginning of internal legal relationships in Germany which presaged the formal construction of the state are to be found in that passage of history where, after the decline of the old royal executive power in the Middle Ages and the dissolution of the whole into atoms, the knights, freemen, monasteries, nobility, merchants, and tradesmen formed themselves into societies and corporations to counteract this state of disorganization.
>
> (176)

With this ethical life in place, it could be utilised in a good constitution. As Hegel recommends:

> Now, however, it would surely be time, after concentrating hitherto mainly on introducing organization into the circles of higher state authority, to bring the lower spheres back again into respect and political significance, and, purged of privileges and wrongs, to incorporate them as an organic structure in the state. A living relationship exists only in an articulated whole whose parts themselves form particular subordinate spheres. But, if this is to be achieved, the French abstractions of mere numbers and quanta of property must be finally discarded. . . . Atomistic principles of that sort spell, in science as in politics, death to every rational concept, organization, and life.
>
> (176–7)

On the alternative view 'the citizens come on the scene as isolated atoms, and electoral assemblies as unordered inorganic aggregates; the people as a whole is dissolved into a heap' (176); and we have seen what Hegel thinks of heaps and atoms.

Thinkers, like Hegel, who wish to represent the present as the culmination of a process of education are liable to think of it metaphorically, as being like the development of a person. If so, the present stage might be expected to be one of fully developed mature manhood. Not so for Hegel. For him the present (his present) was a state of old age. The 'world historical' states which started in the East, with the sunrise, progressed, as we have seen, through Greek adolescence and Roman maturity before they reached Germanic old age. Similarly with the famous owl of Minerva taking flight with the coming of the dusk, who appears in the Preface to the *Philosophy of Right*. It is not just that things can only be understood once they are over (finished, completed, perfected). It is that we are already late in the day. This makes it difficult to extrapolate from Hegel towards his future; and indeed he himself rigorously eschewed prophecy. There is a sense in his writing that the United States is 'the country of the future' but, just because of that, 'it is of no interest to us here, for prophecy is not the business of the philosopher' (*World History* 170; 171). There is a sense of history having ended; and, indeed, so far as the Prussian constitutional monarchy seemed to be the ultimate development of the concept, there seemed to be nowhere left to go.

So the ending of this historical section with Hegel seems to be appropriate, even though it ends, as it began, with a major political thinker who was not a democrat. The thought turns back to the beginning. It turns back to Greek thought. It turns back to wholeness, ethical life, the co-ordination of individual desire and the life of the community. It turns to the small societies in which democracy was the substance of people's lives. However, this is a look with the perspective of history. Seeing things historically, seeing things in terms of development, means that there is no point trying to recapture these periods. This is a much deeper point than the question of the mere size of states. It is that all the learning in between, in particular for Hegel the development of individual subjectivity, means that the modern situation must be different from the ancient one. At most, the Greeks (like the Romans) can be incorporated as a moment in the final product. At most, there are similarities in the final, developed, perfected state and its Greek form. They both have a co-ordination between individual will and communally laid down duties; but it is for different reasons in each case. It is the final perspective, the Owl of Minerva taking flight, from which we can survey and understand the past, but there is no way in which we can restore it. As Hegel says, 'no lessons can be drawn from history for the framing of constitutions in the present' (*World History* 120).

Of course history, whether it is the march of states which Hegel describes in *The Philosophy of World History*, or the march of ideas he describes elsewhere, does not come to an end. With Owl of Minervan hindsight we can see various developments implicit in Hegel in which his thought as well can be surpassed, overcome, preserved and transformed. We can see him reach on to Marx; we can see him reach on to Nietzsche. And we can, unfortunately, see what happens when optimism becomes pessimism. Hegel was a perfectibilist. Logically, history has to produce the perfect. Imperfection is a contradiction (an incompatibility between the concept and its realisation); hence it will be eventually overcome; hence the Idea (the realised concept) will be incorporated; and history will have produced perfection, that final form which can be understood by the philosopher looking at history. Here we have the motor of history. 'The spirit, as it advances towards its realisation, towards self-satisfaction and self-knowledge, is the sole motive force behind all the deeds and aspirations of the nation' (*World History* 56). Here we have the idea 'that reason governs the world, and that world history is therefore a rational process' (27). The 'investigation can be seen as a theodicy, a justification of the ways of God' (42). It advances towards its final perfection in the 'Gothic cathedral' of 'rational freedom' (121).

However, suppose that the contemporary Prussian state is not thought to be the march of God in the world, or heaven on earth. Then there is room for development, or at least disaffection. Then we might think, like the young Nietzsche in his *Untimely Meditations*, that

> the belief that one is a latecomer of the ages is, in any case, paralysing and depressing: but it must appear dreadful and devastating when such a belief by a bold inversion raises this latecomer to godhood as the true meaning and goal of all previous events, when his miserable condition is equated with the completion of world-history.
>
> (104)

Or we might, like the young Marx in his *Critique of Hegel's Doctrine of the State* note: 'that the *rational* is the real is contradicted by the *irrational reality* which at every point shows itself to be the opposite of what it asserts, and to assert the opposite of what it is' (127).

For Marx then, the present situation is not perfect. As with Nietzsche we have inversion. As with Nietzsche, there is no longer Hegelian optimism about the present. However, unlike Nietzsche, there is optimism about the future. All these contradictions in the present situation lead somewhere. We have in Marx a different mechanism, a different motor of history. This motor leads somewhere, and so there is still development. However, once we have a different mechanism, there is no longer an intrinsic reason to think that the future will be better; if Marx has mistaken the mechanism, it may well be worse. Certainly the optimism can no longer be sustained by theodicy. If, in Hegel, God comes down to earth, for Marx he is dead, even if the people do not see their opium. Marx adopted and adapted the theological criticism of such Young Hegelians as Feuerbach. The idols we bow down before are idols which we ourselves have created.

The real mechanism for Marx, the real motor of history, is technological or economic. It is not the development of the Hegelian Idea which does the work but the development of the steam engine.

It is changes in the economic structure of society which such developments produce which move history on. It is this economic base which explains ideas (politics, ethics, philosophy), rather than vice versa. Hence Marx's long devotion to the study of the economics of contemporary, capitalist, society. However, before he wrote any of this economics, and before he had even fully developed his materialist view of history, Marx wrote, in 1843, the long manuscript criticism of Hegel's *Philosophy of Right* which has already been quoted.

In this *Critique* Hegel is constantly criticised for getting things the wrong way round. Hegel explains or justifies everything else by the development of the Idea; for Marx ideas are to be explained by developments elsewhere. More specifically, Marx reverses the order of explanation of state and civil society. For him the real economic relations of civil society explain the ideal relations of the state. If reality is at the level of civil society, then the state, or more generally political affairs, becomes its imaginary heaven. Marx makes extensive use of this metaphor to explain and criticise political conceptions then current. The contemporary world is marked by the new power of the bourgeoisie, of industrial capital. This real power, in the area of civil society, leads to fantasised political ideas in the separate political heaven of the state. Shortly after his criticism of Hegel, Marx wrote, with Engels, *The German Ideology*. In it they wrote that 'the ideas of the ruling class are in every epoch the ruling ideas, i.e. the class which is the ruling *material* force of society, is at the same time its ruling *intellectual* force' (64). If the ruling class is the bourgeois class, then the ruling ideas will be bourgeois ideas. Here they specifically mention 'the concepts freedom, equality, etc.' (65). It is precisely these concepts, and the way they feature in the political heaven, which are criticised in the earlier work.

Bourgeois society replaced aristocratic society as the dominant force. In aristocratic society the dominant ideas were ideas like honour and loyalty. In aristocratic society people were locked into preordained positions (or estates) and people gained their political positions by birth. So, in his earlier *Critique*, Marx noted that Hegel gave a special role to the landed aristocracy. His idea of representation by Estates harked back to the past, was nostalgic. In present conditions Hegel's invocation of the Estates was a Romantic fantasy, and a misleading or dangerous one. 'The Estates', Marx writes, 'are the illusory existence of state affairs conceived as the affairs of the people' (*Critique of Hegel* 125). It is an illusion to think that they represent people's will; for, if they do so, they do so only symbolically or formally. As he put it, 'the *Estates* are *the political illusion of civil society. Subjective* freedom is purely *formal* for Hegel' (126).

Looking at more modern countries, thinks Marx, like France to some extent, and pre-eminently America, the special position of Estates had been abolished. There was a division between the private and the public; between state and civil society. Distinctions were abolished in the political society, so that it was a society of (political) liberty and equality. It was indeed a fraternity, a political community. All was as inscribed on the banners of the revolution. The French Revolution, in other words, represents for Marx both the accession to power of the bourgeoisie, and the way in which liberty and equality are inscribed on the political banners of the bourgeoisie.

This was heaven; but the fictional heaven of the bourgeoisie; the idols which, like Feuerbach's god, we first made and then worshipped. In the *Critique of Hegel* Marx says that

> it was a definite advance in history when the *Estates* were transformed into social classes so that, just as the Christians are *equal* in heaven though unequal on earth, the individual members of the people become equal in the heaven of their political world, although they are unequal in their earthly existence in *society*.
>
> (146)

As a political citizen, a person thinks of himself as free or equal (he is no longer, for example, bound by birth into a position of subservience such as serfdom). However, this political equality masks inequality where it counts, in the real world of civil society. Here people have vastly different property and control; they have vastly different real liberty; they are really unequal.

This criticism is taken further in a work which Marx wrote shortly after his criticism of Hegel, his article 'On the Jewish question', which was published in 1843. Here Marx returns to examination of the rights of man. 'The first point that we should note is that the so-called *rights of man*, as distinct from the *rights of the citizen*, are quite simply the rights of the *member of civil society*, i.e. of egoistic man' (229). These rights allow the war of all against all which constitutes bourgeois society. 'The practical application', he writes, 'of man to freedom is the right of man to *private property*' (229); which 'leads each man to see in other men not the *realization* but the *limitation* of his own freedom' (230). So we only have freedom in heaven, not real freedom.

The situation would be different with a different social and economic structure. Marx says little about communism in his voluminous writings, which are mainly concerned with criticism of the current society; that is with capitalism and bourgeois ideology. However his brief glances forward show that different freedom would be possible with a different economic and social order. 'In a real community', he writes in the *German Ideology*, 'the individuals obtain their freedom in and through their association' (83). This is where there is communism, that is, communal ownership of property. 'Only in community', he writes, has each individual 'the means of cultivating his gifts in all directions; only in the community, therefore, is personal freedom possible' (83).

This is a lyrical passage, from the work which contains the famous interlude about how, in the communist society, people will be able to hunt in the morning, fish in the afternoon, rear cattle in the evening and criticise after dinner (which also comes from the *German Ideology* (53)). However, in the present context the point is that in this putative future society, the split between public and private, between civil society and state, has been healed. Economic and political society have been joined together again, just as they were in feudalism and the city-state; only now in a much more perfect way with no outsiders (serfs, slaves). No longer do we have freedom and equality in heaven to compensate for their lack on earth. We have real liberty and real equality in the everyday life that is actually being lived. Or that, at least, is the theory.

The relevance of this for democracy is that it provides a powerful critique of freedom and equality, which are precisely the two terms which have been used, since the Greeks, to justify democracy. Marx makes us ask whether, when freedom and equality are involved, we are considering real freedom and real equality. He wants to know what is really happening. He wants to know whether people really have political equality when they have very different wealth and very different control over resources and their lives. If different economic power gives different (real) political power, then the supposed formal equality of the bourgeois democratic state (symbolised by everyone equally having a vote) does not amount to real equality.

Similarly for the political form of society. As Marx's thought developed, he analysed contemporary movements, such as the various revolutions in France, or the changing party structure in England, in terms of the changing relationships between the different economic classes, such as aristocracy, big bourgeois, small bourgeois, peasants and workers. He saw the state as an instrument of domination in the service of the economically strongest class. So it did not really matter what the form of this state was. The transition from constitutional monarchy to republic (or formal democracy), for example, might be just a change in the form of control exercised by the ruling classes. It did not amount to real control by the people, to real democracy, any more than it amounted to real liberty or equality.

Hence much of Marx's practical political writing consists of distinguishing between communism and the so-called democratic parties. Alliances could be struck for particular purposes, or warnings could be issued about the dangers of such alliances. But Marx was not just simply out to promote what he called in a late work 'the old democratic litany familiar to all: universal suffrage, direct legislation, popular rights, a people's militia, etc.' This was in a warning about alliance, the *Critique of the Gotha Programme* of 1875. Such surface changes would not give Marx what he wanted, because this depended upon the real control of the conditions of production. As long as capital was in private hands, things like universal suffrage or people's militias were decoration.

Marx was a democrat, but he was cautious about describing himself as such, at least after the period of his early criticism of Hegel. Back at that time, if Hegel reversed the real order of explanation, it was partly because he tried to explain society in accordance with the idea of the state, rather than explaining the state by the nature of society. It is because we start with real human beings, rather than the Idea of the state that 'democracy is the solution to the *riddle* of every constitution. In it we find the constitution founded on its true ground: *real human beings* and the *real people*'. So 'the constitution is thus posited as the people's *own* creation. The constitution is in appearance what it is in reality: the free creation of man' (*Critique of Hegel* 87). Starting from the people, the idea is to bring it back to the people. The future communist society will hence be, for Marx, a real democracy. Power will have returned to the people. They will rule themselves.

There is thus a Marxist kind of democracy. But most of what is called democracy, both in Marx's time and today, is different from this. It is explained and justified in terms of precisely that set of ideas which Marx criticises, led by the notions of freedom and equality. If it is called democracy therefore, it should at least be seen as a subspecies of the genus. It is liberal democracy. Even as liberal democracy, it has to be asked whether it practises what it preaches, or delivers what it promises. Treating men as selfish, individual, atomistic men in the way that Marx diagnoses, it has to meet the charge of why it does not reduce people to an Hegelian rabble; or, more prosaically, why people have any incentive to participate in its practice. Since its community is merely ideal, in heaven, it is a question of what incentive it gives real individuals on earth. For both Marx and Hegel, there is a lack of that kind of real political community typified by the life of the Greek city-state.

Another question which Marx sets is to what extent the consideration of democracy is a useful philosophical activity. It has been seen that, for Marx, the motor of history is not in the development of the Idea, and hence not in the criticism of ideas, but somewhere else. It is in economic and technological developments. So, on this view, someone tracking where things are really happening should not be doing philosophy, or exploring the internal structure of bourgeois concepts like freedom and equality, but rather should be doing sociology or economics. Ever since Aristotle so-called philosophers have also been interested in the description and understanding of actual society; in working out the practical possibilities and limitations of different forms of government. They have been interested in economic restraints and class structure. They have observed that the rule of the majority may just be an excuse for the more numerous propertyless class to remove the assets of the propertied classes.

These are thoughts about actual practice. Questions about practical possibility and opportunity are another set of problems about democracy. These are real problems: relevant, difficult to solve, important in their implications. However they are not philosophical problems. Marx reminds us of this, but anyone taking this reminder seriously has, like Marx but unlike Hegel, to pass beyond philosophy to another subject. In this book we stay inside the perimeter of the camp, but that there is life outside the wire is, no doubt, a suitable reflection with which to end this sequence of historical chapters.

One reflection philosophy does permit about life beyond the wire is whether there are any necessary reasons why we should be optimistic about it. It was noted above that Marx's thought is like Hegel's in being optimistic, although in a different way. However, once reason is removed as a motor of history, there are grounds for becoming much more pessimistic. The question is whether the developments predicted by economic theory are liable to be beneficial. Adam Smith influenced Marx and Hegel, just as he (and the developmental historians of the Scottish Enlightenment) was a hidden presence behind many of the thinkers of the last two chapters. The paradigm is that of the hidden hand: how social processes may produce results unintended by the individual actors. Hegel describes this at length, and gives examples, in *World History*. Marx analyses Smith's thought carefully in his *Economic and Philosophical Manuscripts* of 1844. As he puts it there, 'the motive of those engaged in exchange is not *humanity* but *egoism*' (373). In the hidden hand, and in classical economics more generally, the results are supposed to be beneficial. The butcher and the baker are greedy and egoistic; but it is through their greed that I get fed and clothed. For Hegel, this is the 'cunning of reason' (*World History* 89). The possibly entirely selfish designs of 'world historical individuals' advance the development of the idea.

However, if the motor of the machine has descended to economical processes, whether described in a classical or in a Marxist manner, the question is what right we have to be so cheerful. In the classical mode the question is by what right we think that the unintended consequences of the actions of selfish economic man are liable to be beneficial. Of course, if the hidden hand is the hand of God, that provides an answer. But if God is dead or forgotten, then more work has to be done. This is done by the abstract models of classical theory. On certain highly unrealistic assumptions, it can be shown that unimpeded market forces produce the best results. But it is also the case, in terms of such abstract modelling, that individuals independently seeking their best (or 'rational') ends can produce results which would not be wanted by any of them. The unintended consequences are worse, not better, than intended ones would be. Reason may, perhaps, be cunning, but collective rationality leaves a lot to be desired, if it is just understood as the sum of a set of individual rationalities. (The famous 'Prisoner's dilemma' is only the best known of such paradoxes.) So, looking well forward from

Marx, it is not obvious that the disappearance of the state, and the unimpeded progression of civil society, tends towards the good. Man, merely as economic man, may not satisfy even economic man. More is needed for collective rationality than a collection of rational people. So there would still seem to be a need for political or communal decision-making, which still raises the question of democracy. This is the question which will be considered more analytically in the rest of this book.

CHAPTER VIII

Foundations

In the first chapter it was remarked that throughout most of human history democracy has not been thought to be of value. Even the selected group of philosophers discussed in the succeeding historical chapters turned out to be equivocal about it. Bentham approved of it, at least towards the end of his life. Rousseau and Madison supported quite different versions of what we would today call democracy, yet they did not want to call it by that name. Marx supported yet another kind of democracy, but not the movements called democratic in his day. For the rest, they criticised and disapproved. This is true even of the leading philosophers from classical Athens, where democracy flourished. They may, of course, have meant different things by 'democracy'; and it is important that history reveals a variety of conceptions. It is important that these conceptions have been subjected to trenchant criticism by leading thinkers. Yet something else noted in the first chapter is also important. This is that democracy is almost universally felt to be of value today. Criticised in history, it is the flavour of the century. So, as we now move to the present, and to the second, more analytical, part of this book, the chief task is to find out whether this near universal agreement about the goodness of democracy is justified. In so doing, we want to find out not so much whether democracy is of value but rather why it is. For even if we all agree that our ancestors were wrong and that we, by contrast, are right, we do not agree why they were wrong or why we are right. We must therefore now investigate the foundations of this supposedly valuable thing, democracy. If we can discover why it is of value, we should also discover what its actual value is.

To put the question in this way may already seem to beg an important question. For it presupposes that democracy does have foundations, even if it may be difficult to find them. Yet foundations are not as fashionable today as they once were. It is often thought that knowledge does not have any foundations. So democracy might not have any either. It might be that there just was not any other thing which provided a ground or reason for the goodness of democracy. Democracy might instead be a simple final value, which was good in itself and not good for any further reasons. That it was good might be all that it was possible to know about it, and so in agreeing on that we would already be in the position of knowing all that there was to be known. If democracy were like this, then its goodness would just be known by simple intuition, and this would be an intuition which we, unlike our ancestors, just fortunately happened to possess.

Yet, without taking any general view on the availability of foundations, I think that this is implausible in the case of democracy. As well as a fairly widespread agreement that democracy is of value, there is also a fairly widespread assumption that it is of value for some further reason. People disagree about the reason but they think that there is one. They think that democracy is of value because it promotes or incorporates some further thing. Of course people may be wrong. But the view that democracy is not so much good in itself as good for what it represents, incorporates, produces or replaces is not a surprising one. For democracy is a fairly complicated object of value. Being complicated, if it is thought to be a good, it is likely that this judgment is based on some of its aspects rather than others. So some facts about it may provide reasons for its worth in a way that other facts about it may not. Yet if some facts provide reasons rather than others, we have reasons why democracy is of value, reasons which depend upon other, separately named, things. It is about these separately named things that people who agree about the overall value of democracy may argue; and so it is on the question of what these separately named things are that the discussion should focus.

To describe the general problem as a search for the evaluative foundations of democracy may be felt to make another presumption. This is that there is some one thing, democracy, whose foundations we are seeking. Yet, as has been seen from the historical chapters, there have been many kinds of democracy. As we come to the present there is no particular reason to suppose that there is one single thing which people have in mind when they talk about democracy. Democracy, at least at present, is supposed to be a good thing. So it is quite plausible to suppose that people take various things which they approve of and call these quite different things by the single word 'democracy', hoping thereby to confer on them some extra validity. However, if they are all quite different, then there is in fact no more real agreement about the goodness of democracy than there is about the reasons for its goodness.

This objection has a sound basis. It is obviously possible, given that apparently quite different political systems are all called democratic, that the word means several different things. Yet this is not in fact an objection to the present project of looking for foundations. For this project does not need to presuppose that there is a single meaning to the term. The point of finding out the reasons why democracy is a good thing is to find out what about it is good and therefore, in this sense, what it is (as a good thing). If there is ineliminable disagreement about the reasons for the goodness of democracy, there will be ineliminable disagreement about the nature of democracy itself. The whole point of investigating the reasons, the foundations, is to go under or behind democracy's mask. If there cannot be agreement about the reasons, or if proper reasons cannot be found, then there will be nothing supporting or validating the mask, and the agreement will indeed have been found to be illusory. There may be different things behind the mask, or there may be nothing at all. Indeed, it is the idea that it might be such an illusion which is one further thing pressing us to look for reasons or foundations. Although we start with agreement, we do not have to treat it as sacrosanct.

So we shall now investigate the foundations of democracy, that is, the problem of seeing how democracy can be derived, as a secondary good, from another source of value. Inevitably we immediately run into the problem of what this source should be. Ideally there should be an agreed value, or values, which we can adopt and deploy. However, instead of agreement, we get a babble of different tongues; we get competing evaluative discourses. We could look for our source in everyday moral judgment. We could look for it in the more general and theoretical expressions of official ethics, political philosophy or value theory. Yet whether we seek our source in everyday or more theoretical discourse we are liable to come up with members of two great families of sources of value. In the one family the ultimate source of values derives from what is of good to human beings. Values are then of the generally consequentialist form that they assume in utilitarian political thought. Something is taken to be a good because it promotes human happiness or welfare. We saw in Chapter VI how this type of reason operates, when looking at Bentham and the Mills. In the other great family of sources of value, people are thought to possess inalienable moral value as individuals. They are thought to possess moral properties which it would be wrong to remove from them and which give them entitlement to certain respect or certain services from others. We then ascribe rights to them. We saw in Chapter III how this type of source of value worked with Locke.

Quite different kinds of justification are available, depending upon which kind of source of value we adopt. If we are justifying things in terms of consequences, our justification is future-directed, aiming at the best future state of affairs. If our justification is in terms of rights, then it respects present realities, taking people as they are and respecting historical facts about what they have or have not done. For example, justifications of the existence and authority of the state will come out in quite different ways. If they are based on utility, the state is justified because it increases human happiness. If it is based on rights, justification must show not only that the state supports rights, but that having a state does not infringe them. Hence the importance of the idea of original contract. If people, already possessing rights, freely contract to have a state, then the state can be taken to respect those rights which were freely exercised in its formation. In the one case the justification is future-directed, towards future happiness. In the other case the justification looks backwards, to a past history of actual agreements.

If these are the available fundamental justifications on offer and if they seem to be in sharp disagreement, then we seem to have a problem. We seem to have to choose between them to get started on the task of justification without anything on which to base the choice. We cannot do it by invoking either everyday or theoretical discourse, which just repeats the confusion. On the other hand, we need a foundation. We can no longer cite, criticise or examine other philosophers. We have finished the historical part of the book, and come out from the relatively comfortable business of describing and commenting on other thinkers. We now have to make a fresh start. We need a fresh support. Yet it may seem that we are looking into a void. Vertigo threatens. Once we leave the comforts of history, nothing may support us. Of course, we can look for the supports in our own contemporary thought, just as the past philosophers did in theirs. However, contemporary thought comes up with mixed voices. Contemporary authorities are confused and conflicting. If we have the advantages of a pluralist culture, we also have the defects, and studying history just adds to the pluralism of possibilities.

Things, however, are not so serious. We do not have to resolve a horror of an evaluative vacuum by mere plumping in the void for rights or utilities. In spite of the differences, the conflict between these two sources of value is not as extreme as it seems, nor as fatal for our justificatory purposes. The rest of this chapter is devoted to supporting this proposition, and working out a strategy whereby we may reasonably seek foundations for democracy without finally taking sides on the question of whether everything is ultimately founded on rights or whether everything is ultimately founded on utilities.

The first reason why we do not need to take sides between rights and utilities is that there are advantages in keeping both types of justification in play; indeed also the rival accounts or what utility or rights amount to. This is not because it is hoped that some synthesis will emerge from the incompatibilities, but because the rivals provide various alternative resources of justification. The justification provided by one particular view is hypothetical justification. It appeals only to someone who holds that view. Up to a point, therefore, the more justifications we can use, the more people to whom we can appeal. If we assemble a mix of alternative sources of value, we increase our chances of being able to appeal to any particular person. However, this cannot be the main justification for keeping rival accounts in play. Eclecticism can be overdone, and if we try any or all arguments just because they happen to be available, we stand the danger of getting into the trouble the Greek philosophers did when they first went to Rome. One day they argued in favour of democracy and the next day they argued against it. This did not increase the Romans' interest in democracy so much as give both Greeks and argument a bad name. He who can adopt any argument loves argument not wisely but too well and may like Othello end up by strangling the thing he loves. To seek to be everyone's friend is to end up as no one's.

We need, therefore, a better defence for keeping both families in play than the mere advantages of variety. I shall now attempt to give two further reasons for doing this, both based on trying to show that the opposition between rights and utilities may not be direct as has been supposed. The first is that the central difference between them is more to do with form or structure than it is to do with content. It relates not so much to which particular things are taken to be of value but, rather, to how these values should be thought about or treated once we have them. For the important difference between these two general lines of approach cannot just be whether the ultimate goods are to be called utilities or are to be called rights. After all, a right is normally thought of as a good, or utility, to someone and, alternatively, the most important goods for that person (life, liberty, the pursuit of happiness . . .) may be called their rights. Rights are goods and fundamental goods may be called rights. So I think that the important difference, and one which is therefore only accidentally picked up in the language of rights or utilities, is the difference to do with how one person's good relates to someone else's. When these are taken as utilities, they are considered as comparable and additive. Twice as much good can be produced by doing the same good thing to twice as many people. Analogously, a course of action can be seen to be preferable when it does a great good to someone at the cost of a little harm to someone else. On the other hand, if people's goods are taken to be rights, then the possibility of eitlier such addition or comparison becomes meaningless. It is never right to deprive one person of their rights however much good might accrue to someone else. Calling something a right takes it out of the area of calculation and places non-negotiable constraints on action.

Describing rights and utilities in this way, of course, is to treat them as ideal types placed in sharp contrast. But as they are used in actual description or argument, they are used in a myriad of different ways, and much current evaluative theory or political philosophy depends upon trying to ameliorate the sharpness of the distinction and marry elements of each. Some utilities may be regarded as more important, not comparable with others, and referred to as rights. Or institutions which confer rights on people are justified, as institutions, in terms of utilities. Or it is allowed, after all, to trade off things called rights against each other so that infringement with one person's rights is justified in terms of the benefits of rights to others. This naturally produces tangles and complexities. Furthermore, rights themselves can be looked at in two different ways, either as representing the benefits secured to people by duties imposed on others, or as representing protected areas over which someone has the full power of choice.

These tangles mean that the whole language of rights and utilities, being deeply contested, is a difficult terrain in which to search for secure foundations. The great variety of discourse may be useful for charging up argumentative resources, as noted above, yet it tends to smudge the sharpness of points which depend upon distinctions between rights and utilities. So, to make the claim that I just have that the distinction is more formal than material does depend upon looking at simplified varieties, or ideal types. Still, I think that it does give us a guide as to how we should treat some of these more luxurious forms of interbreeding or variety. For example, if form is centrally important, then the so-called utilitarianism of rights, whereby we act to maximise the prevalence of a right such as liberty, is much more to do with utilities than rights. This is because its form is that of a utility, maximising and additive, rather than that of a right, whereby the goods are secured inalienably to every individual. With the utilitarianism of rights we are allowed to trade in one person's liberty in order to get greater liberty for several others; and it is precisely deals like this which the form of (simplified, ideal type) rights theory prevents.

If we think that the contrast between rights and utilities is more formal than material, then this is a reason for keeping them both in play. For the particular content of moral evaluation will then originate elsewhere. And when we have a particular content, we can then ask whether it should be treated more like a right or more like a utility. In other words, we can ask how this good should be distributed: whether it can be maximised, or whether it has to be secured to every individual as such. So keeping both families in play is keeping a resource with which we can discipline and order suggestions about content.

The second reason why I think that the contrast between rights and utilities may be overdrawn is because I think that the two opposing rival conceptions of value can themselves be seen as different, partial, conceptions of a yet more fundamental value. Let me try to make this point by returning to simplified ideal types of rights and goods, where we either have a good which can be maximised, as in the utilitarian tradition, or a right which forms what Robert Nozick calls a 'side constraint' on action, that is, a moral boundary which no one is permitted to cross, however good the consequences. Opposed as these two conceptions are, we need not take them as primitive, but rather as two alternative ways of understanding a central and highly important moral value, that of impartiality. A natural, or at least normal, constraint on value judgments is that it ought to be possible to make them from many different points of view. They are not just held because of the special or peculiar circumstances that someone happens to occupy at the time at which they are making the judgment. Yet if we consider all positions or points of view impartially, that is we give them all equal consideration (at least in some sense), this can still be interpreted in two quite different ways. Giving all positions equal consideration may be understood to mean that we should support those moral positions which are acceptable from most of the positions, or it may be understood to mean that we should support those positions which are acceptable from all positions. On both these ways of understanding, all positions are treated equally; but in the former case, this means that they are given equal weighting, and hence the majority wins out, while in the latter case we treat each position as having an equal veto.

Another way of considering this difference is by trying to think about how we would feel if we were in other people's positions. By imagining what something looks like from other people's points of view, we do something to give these other points of view equal consideration with our own. With such imaginative access, we clearly gain extra information. There still remains the question, however, of how the extra information is to be treated. Again, we have the two cases. We can think that it gives us a basic input of data about how something affects people, weight the effects on everyone equally, achieve impartiality by considering ourselves no more or no less than anyone else, and then sum up the different outcomes of different courses of action. This amounts to the first case treated above, where (for equally strong feelings) treating people equally involves following the majority. It is also very like the utilitarian moral position in which equal weight is given to all the affected parties so that, for equally severe effects, what affects the majority becomes therefore more important in value. By using our imagination to see how we would feel in that position, we may realise that something harms the minority. Nevertheless we can also see or imagine what it feels like to be one of the majority, and summing all these feelings equally means that the majority wins out.

There is, however, another way in which we can treat the

information we gain by such imaginative access, for example, our understanding of the harm done to a minority. In this way, once we have thought ourselves into such a position, we feel that it would be intolerable for these interests or desires of ours to be sacrificed for the sake of someone else. If we think of it in this way, then we are thinking of it in the second manner mentioned above, in which treating people equally is to give everyone a veto. We would now think that, however many other people there are, and however pleased it may make them, this is something which should not be done to us. So instead of this distaste being treated as an input into a calculation in which everyone's desires are weighed up and this one happens to be outweighed, we now think of it as something that cannot be traded off against any amount of happiness for others. It is non-negotiable and we have, or would like to possess, a veto. This position is similar to rights-based theories of evaluation in which, to use Ronald Dworkin's metaphor, rights form a sort of trumps so that something which affects an individual's rights is always considered to be more important than anything else. On this view sacrificing the basic rights of a single individual would never be justified however much good might come to others from such a sacrifice.

This presentation of the rival fundamental positions puts them both in terms of the possibility of trade-offs so that the central difference is whether or not it is permitted to sacrifice the happiness (or anything else of central value) of one person for the sake of the greater good of someone else. It brings out two very important points, both of which will feature in what follows. First, both positions have been developed from an idea of equality or impartiality, and it will be argued in Chapter II that this basis in equality is a potent source of democracy's value. Second, although both positions grant an equality of respect to individuals, in one of them this respect takes the form of granting them certain moral properties which would seem to give them an absolute veto on the action of others. Yet if such trumping, or vetoing, is an essential part of rights, it seems hard to see how any kind of state at all could be legitimate. A state involves the use of power over its individual citizens, so that they can be made, on occasion, to do what the state wishes rather than what they independently desire. Yet if the individuals possess a veto then it does not seem that a supposed state, or form of government, could have any such power or, therefore, how any real state or form of government might legitimately exist at all. So, although the two positions may be symmetrical in the value they assign to equality of respect (or impartiality of treatment), they are highly asymmetrical in the way that they may give a foundation to the value of a political system (such as democracy). For while a utilitarian theory will justify a political system, just like anything else, if it has good enough consequences, it is not clear that a rights-based system can justify any political system at all.

This asymmetry means that there is also an asymmetry about how much more needs to be said about utilities and rights at this stage. Utilities may not in fact be promoted by democracy, but the question of whether this is so is reasonably well formed. By contrast it is much less clear what it would mean to found democracy on rights. At least in the simple primitive way in which we have been handling rights, no such foundation would seem to be available. Indeed, if rights are treated as some kind of absolute trumps, little argument seems to be possible about this. Either one believes in absolute inalienable rights or one does not. If one does not, the question of this foundation does not arise. If one does, the question seems to be insoluble. For if individuals really possess rights upon which no other person or body may legitimately encroach, then it seems that there cannot be any legitimate form of absolute, or sovereign, power. For whether this power be a democracy or a dictatorship, there are still going to be certain things which it may now not legitimately do. Hence it would seem that it is not an absolute power at all; hence the question arises of whether it could be a government. This reinforces the worries expressed in Chapters III and V about whether, or how far, a theory of rights could be used as a basis for democracy.

So far we have only considered rights in terms of the possibility of one person trading off what is a good for them against what is a good for someone else. However, this still leaves various options open about the status of these rights. The invocation of rights is clearly meant to protect individuals from external threat, whether by the state itself or by other citizens, but this leaves quite open what essential or central human quality is to be so protected. It could be that certain features are thought to be part of human good, to be protected for all humans whether they like it or not. Or it could be that what is protected is the human being as sovereign, so that the power of others is held back to allow an individual an area of petty sovereignty to him or herself. In other words, it has so far been left open whether the point of invoking rights is to protect human goods

141

or to protect human will or authority. The difference may be dramatically significant as can be seen from treating the fundamental right to life on the alternative interpretations. As a human good, the right to life names a good (life itself) which no one may legitimately take away from anyone. Put like this, the 'no one' here includes the person whose life it is; he or she is also protected against him or herself, and the point of using rights in this way is to put the question of life beyond all reach of utilitarian calculation, even calculation by the person whose life it is (such as the calculation that their life contains more pain than pleasure and so is not worth living). On the other hand, if the right is taken to protect an area of petty sovereignty, of human will and decision, then the right to life names an area which should be subject only to the will of the person whose life it is. No one but he or she has the right to say whether he or she will live or die; however, on this version they are fully entitled to take such a decision. Suicide on this view infringes no one's rights.

Just as these two different ways of understanding the nature of rights have dramatic differences in the way that they protect life, so also have they dramatic differences in the way that they might legitimate particular forms of government. If rights are taken as an absolute over which even the right-holder has no say, then the only questions are what these rights are, and whether they can possibly be compatible with government. If, on the contrary, the right-holder is taken to have a say over the exercise or operation of his or her rights, then no kind of activity is blocked a priori by the mere existence of rights. The important question now becomes what the right-holder wishes to do. Having the right in this latter way of understanding it gives the right-holder status, authority and power; but as long as this status is preserved, anything else may happen. It is this latter way of understanding rights which is obviously of most interest in considering democracy. The equality of respect (or impartiality) involved in the notion of rights comes from respecting everyone as having authority in their own area; a kind of petty sovereignty. This respect is due to everyone and is preserved against all possibility of trading it off against a greater good for someone else. In this sense it is a genuine right. Yet once this respect, or sovereignty, has been granted, it is then free for the individuals to use it as they think fit.

One way in which they could use it is to create a political system. Suppose that everyone agrees about how to do this, as in some versions of the original contract story. Then, if their rights are not only taken to allow them choice but also to allow them to alienate their choice, then they could choose to give up their independent rights and put themselves under a government. This would solve the problem about how government might be compatible with rights, but at considerable cost. For, although the original decision might be democratic in the sense that everyone was engaged in it and agreed about it, once the decision had been made the resultant government which was set up might be anything but democratic. And although the people started with rights, in the sense of powers of choice, what they end up with are no rights at all, in that they are not allowed to make any further choices. As the original Hobbesian story shows only too well, the sort of consideration which might encourage individual independently contracting citizens to relinquish their rights could very well lead them to install some sort of absolute government which paid them no further respect. If the only alternatives were a nasty anarchy and a nasty authority which nevertheless provided some measure of security, then the contractors might well opt for the nasty authority. A use of rights which might at first seem to provide a foundation for democracy turns into an argument for abolishing it in favour of strong government.

This shows how, after all, it is possible to start with a theory of rights and use it as a foundation for government. Of course, it is only a possibility. The question of a deep antimony between all kinds of government, including democracy, and certain basic rights remains. Rousseau's question, the question of how we may both have government and be free, is one which I hope to solve in a later chapter. For the moment this example is only an illustration. It shows how understanding the formal structure of rights in different ways can help us to discipline and present alternative accounts. It also shows just how tangled and contested this area is. Only some supporters of rights will understand them in terms of choices, and only a few of these will also allow choice about relinquishing one's rights. For other supporters of rights, they will be inalienable, not just by others but also by the right-holder. So, to return to the particular example, at best these are useful alternative ideas about foundations which provide hypothetical justification for those people who happen to share the starting points. Others, without a basis of rights, or without this particular kind of basis of rights, will not be moved.

I said above that assembling hypothetical justifications may well be a useful exercise, and that the different accounts of rights may help to discipline it. However I also said that we can do much better. For I do not think that we are in fact reduced to offering a disparate mixture of possibilities and alternatives, hoping rather forlornly that one will appeal to someone, which is what the strategy of alternatives may sound like. We should take seriously the idea, particularly with rights, that the alternatives are more about form than content. What the alternatives do is explain the formal connections which rights have with other rights, duties, the right-holder and so on. They say whether the right-holders can trade their rights, whether it is possible to add rights together, whether rights always have correlative duties and so on.

At first sight this may just seem to make the problem worse. For if there is this much disagreement at the formal level, it would only seem to get worse when we come down to content and try to decide, for example, whether people have a right to property, a right to be offended and so on. The disagreements about form would be multiplied by disagreements about content, providing a bewildering myriad of alternatives. However, things are not this bad. The points about form allow us an array of possibilities, which provide alternatives about how we can discipline our talk about content. But I do not think that we need to multiply them by another set of disputes about content. In fact, I think that here we have the key to the right approach to the problem of foundations. The final, and most important, reason for thinking that we can keep both rights and utilities in play is that it is possible to search for foundations without having to take sides between them.

We do not have to take sides either on disputes about the nature of rights or on disputes about whether the ultimate basis is rights or utilities. This is because, whatever the ultimate basis, there will still be a large measure of agreement about the intermediate values which are supposed to be founded on this basis. People who argue about the nature of rights and utilities agree about the value of other things. One of these, of course, is democracy, which is what sets the problem. But there are other such intermediate values. The attractions of a theory of rights, particularly in its choice version, is related to the importance of our feeling that people should be allowed to make choices, that they should have freedom, control over their lives, autonomy. Freedom or autonomy are values, whether or not we spell out their foundations in the language of utilities or in the language of rights. So, without taking sides on particular issues about utilities or rights, we can ask how a political system is possible in which such autonomy is protected. Or, taking autonomy as a good, we can ask what political system should therefore be favoured. Or, concentrating on democracy, we can ask whether it can solve the problem of the preservation of autonomy.

This strategy can be extended. Autonomy and freedom are goods, but they are not the only ones. There is also welfare. Whether or not we ultimately base all value on utility, people will generally agree that human welfare has some value. So also for (some kinds) of equity, justice, equality. So also for knowledge or efficiency. It is possible, therefore, to adopt an intermediate range of agreed values, whatever their ultimate foundations might be, and then see how these other values relate to the one we are hoping to explain, namely democracy.

It was seen in the previous chapters that it is precisely these kinds of values which seem to create problems for democracy. We have the Platonic problem about how democracy can provide knowledge. We have Rousseau's problem about how any political society can leave people free. We had in Chapters I, II, and V the worry that democracy treats the minority unequally or unfairly. I shall, therefore, in the rest of this book consider these sorts of goods; goods like knowledge, autonomy, freedom, fairness and equality. The prime question now becomes how, or whether, these values are promoted by democracy. This provides, as the historical chapters have shown, a series of problems to be solved. With luck, the historical chapters may have enabled us to gain a fuller insight into some of these values. In any case, they are agreed to be of value. So if democracy promotes one of these undoubted values, then it will itself have been given some derived value, or foundation.

We can therefore provide foundations without taking sides in the battle between rights and utilities. While doing this, however, we may keep the analytical structure of the differences between rights and utilities as a guide. The content can come from these more specific values, but, for any of these intermediate goods which we wish to adopt or consider, it can be asked whether it is to be treated in a maximising way or with side constraints; who has the power of decision over whether it applies; whether it protects a choice which may be alienated by the choice-holder and so on.

Another way in which we can simplify our problems, at least in the first instance, is by considering decisions in much smaller units than contemporary nation-states. The historical chapters were inevitably principally concerned with political procedures at the level of states. With the vast difference in the size of typical political units between ancient Greece and the modern world we get, as was seen in Chapters V to VII, very different kinds of democracies. Democracy was first adopted in Greece, in a face-to-face society in which people could be individually known and in which it was possible to gather all the citizens together in a single assembly. Modern political units, by contrast, need and have produced different theories, in which representation plays a central role. This was why Madison, for example, arguing for a large state, did not call his preferred system a democracy. For us now, in the modern world, democracy at the state level is representative democracy rather than direct democracy.

However, the concept of representation, problematic enough as it is, is not the only philosophically difficult thing about democracy. Most of the problems arise independently of it, and apply whether or not we are thinking of representative democracy. Conversely, as was pointed out in Chapter I, some of the problems of representation apply at all scales, and will arise even in small face-to-face political units. Since the problems of democracy do not stand or fall on the problems of large states, it seems easier to begin by considering these problems in the context of small units; first seeing whether these problems can be solved if direct democracy is used as a decision procedure. We may consider a corporate decision which has to be made by a relatively small number of people and decide whether or not it is appropriate to make such a decision democratically, with the understanding that, if it is decided democratically, everyone has the option of being directly involved. In this way it is easier to control the question of the relation between democracy and the intermediate values just identified, such as equality, liberty and knowledge. These questions can still be meaningfully asked at the level of small political units; and it is easier to control the answer.

Deciding to work mainly with small political units might seem to be just a philosophical fiction; an ideal case or desert island example; something which never happens but is produced in an attempt to simplify or clarify thought. Or it might seem to be a mere piece of historical romanticism; a retreat to the Greeks; an improper Rousseauean return to the Ancients. On the contrary, however, it is perfectly realistic. Very many of the corporate decisions with which we are actually involved are of this character. We all belong to relatively small social entities who have to make corporate decisions: families, clubs, colleges, perhaps streets or neighbourhoods. The decisions made in these units may well have more effect on our lives than the decisions made in nation states. Yet they are all of a size where direct democracy would be perfectly feasible, if it were thought desirable. Conclusions reached about small political units are concrete, contemporary and applicable.

At least initially, therefore, I will have small units in mind while considering whether or not democracy is desirable or when trying to decide on the nature of its foundations. In doing this, as I said, the best strategy is to attempt to solve a series of problems, rather than to construct one single argument designed to demonstrate to anyone the goodness of democracy. The problems have partly been posed already in the more historical parts of the book. So I shall start with knowledge, Plato's problem. Then, given the great importance of freedom and autonomy, and the great problem which it seems to provide for all forms of government, I shall move on to this. It was, in different forms, Locke's, Rousseau's and Hegel's problem. So here are two problems: whether democracy can deliver knowledge and whether it can deliver freedom. Alternatively put, the problems are whether a government with a distributed power of decision can come up with the right answer and whether, even if decision-making is so distributed, it can promote or preserve the freedom of these decision-makers. Two such problems might be quite enough for one book to resolve. However, this is only the start. For I shall move on to problems created by the positive valuation which most of us give to welfare, equality and the respect for other moral agents. Even that does not complete the agenda. There are problems of practicality. Even if democracy is fully vindicated in theory, it may not be possible to combine individual decisions in one overall social decision; even if we can do this, the procedure may not be thought practical in a world peopled with apathetic or non-political citizens. At this point problems about representation return. A rich diet of problems here: quite enough to provide sustenance for the rest of the book.

CHAPTER IX

Knowledge

In the last chapter it was proposed that we should examine the philosophical foundations of democracy by attempting to solve a series of problems. These problems are posed by the relations between democracy and other things of value. Each of these intermediate values, as they were called in the last chapter, will be considered in turn. Each poses its own problem. The problem with which we begin goes right back to the first thought about democracy, as described in Chapter II. Knowledge is clearly something we take to be of value. We want our political decisions to be informed. If one answer is better than another for a community making a decision, then that answer is the one which the community ought to reach. Therefore, it would seem that the right form of decision procedure for that community should be the one which produces that answer. Yet this does not reliably happen with democratic decision procedures.

The problems which knowledge poses for democracy go back at least as far as Plato. Plato was particularly concerned with knowledge about the good, and in how to discover the good for the community. His arguments were described in Chapter 2. However, their heart could perhaps be put as follows. Suppose that values are objective, so that what ought to happen in a state is a matter of fact independent of any particular individual's thoughts about it. Suppose further that, although independent, it is something about which human beings can have knowledge. Then it is certainly possible (and, indeed, although contingent, highly likely) that some people will know more about what ought to happen in the state than others. So: some people are better judges than others. Now, suppose that we are trying to decide the best thing to do in a society, that is, what ought to be done in a state, and we are considering whose views should count. Clearly, or so this argument runs, it would be absurd to consider everyone equally and give them all equal weight. For surely we gain more of the truth, a closer approach to the right answer, if we give greater weight to those who know more about it. So the views of some, preferably those people specially trained to make better judgments about the good, should count more than others. The famous analogy for this in the *Republic* is that it would be crazy to get all the sailors to vote on where the ship should go rather than following the trained person, the pilot. Therefore democracy, which pays no particular attention to the knowledgeable and instead counts the views of all equally, is a mistaken theory about how to make decisions in politics.

Here then, we have a simple argument which connects knowledge with the appropriateness of democracy as a method of political decision-making. If there can be knowledge about political values, then democracy is inappropriate. Now today we are much more favourable to the idea of democracy than Plato himself was. So it seems that we should find something wrong in the Platonic argument. Luckily, or so it seems, this is not difficult. The argument may indeed be perfectly valid, but it would be quite natural today to assume that it has a false premiss. We cannot, or so it is normally thought today, find out moral facts just like natural facts; nor can we train a group of people in this area whose answers will be better than those of others. So, although the inference that if there were moral knowledge democracy would be inappropriate may be perfectly correct, this need not worry us. For there is no moral knowledge, and lacking moral knowledge, the inference need not get started.

Indeed, the present tendency is to go further in assuming a connection between the lack of knowledge and democracy. Because there is no moral knowledge, it is often supposed, it follows that any one person's views are as good as any other. Hence the current support (at least in more gentle, reflective circles) for toleration, democracy, sensitivity to other people or cultures or ethnic groups. Instead of the desire to learn the good we have the rejection of cultural imperialism; instead of the state being led by the beautiful and the best we have non-dictatorship taken as an axiom in social choice theory. Contemporary thought is inclined to think that it is precisely because there is no moral knowledge that democracy is the right form of decision-making. We have, nowadays, abolished moral or philosophical knowledge and, with it, the philosopher kings. We can all, equally, have a go at thinking; so we should also all, equally, have a go at ruling.

It seems, therefore, that there is a close connection in some current thought between scepticism and democracy. Each is taken to imply the other. On the one hand, if nothing can be known, then one person's views are as good as another's; hence we ought to treat them all equally and decide democratically. On the other hand, if some people's views are better, then democracy is an absurd way of proceeding. Thus (it seems), scepticism implies democracy and democracy implies scepticism. I say 'it seems' because what I want to show in this chapter is that the implication does not hold in either direction. It is not that I am adverse to the conclusions about toleration, cultural sensitivity and so on which are derived from moral scepticism. It is just that I am adverse to this way of deriving them, because it is a bad argument, it is an unsound basis, however good the conclusions.

I want therefore to show that democracy does not imply scepticism, nor scepticism democracy. Let us begin with the latter. The first thing to notice is that this implication does not follow from the Platonic argument given at the beginning. That argument held that, if there is moral knowledge, then democracy is inappropriate. Nothing at all follows from this about the case in which there is not moral knowledge. The Platonic argument, if it works, shows that scepticism is a necessary condition for democracy, not a sufficient one. So the claim that a commitment to scepticism implies a commitment to democracy does not follow from Plato's argument. Furthermore, the claim itself is easy to refute. For, if scepticism is true, such that any one moral opinion is as good as any other, then any evaluation about procedures of decision-making is as good as any other. Hence there would be nothing to prevent me, as a moral sceptic, espousing any sort of decision theory I like. If no view is better than another, and no one can show anyone else that their view is wrong, then I might just as easily opt for dictatorship and say that everyone should do what I say. My view would be as good as any other; in particular, as good as any weak-kneed democratic view.

Scepticism, therefore, does not imply democracy. The argument that it did depended upon trying to show that a particular evaluation, namely the appropriateness of democracy, was a correct evaluation because of a particular truth about evaluations, namely that questions about correctness do not arise for evaluations. This is obviously self-defeating. Evaluation of democracy is evaluation of how to use people's judgments in arriving at a decision. This makes it different in that it is a second-order evaluation rather than a first-order one. It is a judgment about judgments; an evaluation about evaluations. However it is still an evaluation. So if no evaluation is better than any other, it itself falls prey to the sceptical premiss of the argument that was meant to establish it. If there is no right answer about what people should think, then there is no right answer about what they should think about democracy.

I have just argued this in terms of scepticism, but I think in fact that similar points hold also for many other views about the nature of evaluative judgment. The key idea in the argument just discussed is that evaluative judgments are equally good (or bad) in a particular respect, and hence that the appropriate second order evaluation to make of these evaluations is that they should be treated equally, as happens in democratic decision-making. The refutation of the argument consists in saying that the second-order evaluation is also an evaluation; but is not itself being treated equally by the argument. Equality of esteem is both applied and denied; hence the argument is self-defeating. This structure of possible argument and refutation will also apply to many other grounds for considering evaluations equally. It also works, I think, for various kinds of emotivism or projectivism and also for relativism. In scepticism, I take it, it is held that there is, or at least may be, a moral truth, but it is not such that anyone can know it. So the equality consists in everyone being equally bad at knowing it (that is, totally hopeless). By contrast, in emotivism, projectivism and relativism the truth, or supposed truth, is created by ourselves, or depends upon us. However, we again get a sort of equality. There are as many truths as there are opinions, and there is no way of deciding whether one of these opinions is better than another. Again, since the opinions are equally good, the same argument would seem to go through. Since there is nothing to choose between them, the right procedure to adopt might seem be one which treated them equally. Thus we should decide democratically. However, the same objection applies. If this argument really did provide a positive foundation for democracy, then this positive evaluation of democracy would not itself have been treated in the way in which the argument assumes that evaluations should be treated. If the original assumption is relativism, this conclusion is not being treated in a

151

relativistic way; if it is emotivism, this conclusion is not being treated emotively and so on.

This is not to say that there could not be a good argument for democracy based on the equality of judgments. Such an argument would have to distinguish between first-order judgments, which should be treated equally, and second-order judgments, which should not. The utilitarian argument for democracy discussed in Chapter VI does something like this. It assumes that everyone is equally good at expressing their preferences at the first-order level, and then concludes that the most efficient way to find the greatest happiness of the greatest number is to let everyone vote, count everyone equally, and do what the majority decides. This utilitarian argument, however, avoids the present problem by not treating the first-order judgments as moral judgments. Moral judgments only arise with the application of utilitarianism itself at the second-order level. The utilitarians (except, as was seen, for the deviant J. S. Mill), treat the first-order judgments fed into the voting machine as being mere expressions of preference rather than as being full moral evaluations.

What I have tried to show so far is that scepticism does not imply democracy. This implication does not follow from Plato's original argument and the most natural independent argument to establish it is self-defeating. The case, however, seems to be more hopeful for the converse implication, namely that democracy implies scepticism. This time, at least, the implication does follow from Plato's original argument. In Plato's argument we get the proposition that, if we have knowledge, then we do not have democracy. So, if his argument is right and we do have democracy (that is the negation of the consequent) then it follows that we do not have knowledge (the negation of the antecedent). Or, to put it more briefly, if knowledge implies no democracy, then democracy implies no knowledge. Or, to put it more informally, if we adopt a democratic decision procedure, then we are committed to the view that anyone's views count equally with anyone else's; that is, any old view is as good as another; that is, there is no moral knowledge. So even if, by the earlier arguments, democracy does not follow from scepticism, once we happen to have adopted democracy, whether for good reasons or for no reasons at all, we would seem to be committed to scepticism.

I do not think, however, that this argument works. It depends upon assessing the goodness of a particular means for a particular end.

The end is doing what is best for society, and therefore the means picked out is to follow the views of those who know best what this is. It is because the end is the discovery and application of knowledge (finding the right answer for society) that the analogy of the pilot in the ship works so well. However, if this is not the end, or not the only end, then the argument is not so convincing. If, for example, we wished to flatter, woo or mollify people, or give them some feeling that they were vaguely in control of their lives, or prevent their anger or questions, or give them the feeling that they counted, then other procedures might well be more appropriate. Methods which gave less good results with respect to truth might well do better by some of these goals, and some lack of truth would therefore not be an appropriate criticism of these methods, unless truth were immeasurably more important than these other goals. Whether this was so or not would depend upon what, overall, we were trying to achieve.

So one problem about the Platonic argument is that there are more than epistemological goods. The Platonic argument just assumes that doing the best in society involves using the procedure which is best at producing knowledge about this. But there are other ways of achieving the best than finding out about it. So, even if Plato is right about its lack of connection with knowledge, democracy may nevertheless be the best decision procedure. If there are other values, which might on certain occasions outrank knowledge, then this means that democracy might still be the best form of decision procedure, even if knowledge is available about the right answer. This is so even if the knowledge is knowledge about values. Thus knowledge and democracy would be compatible, and so any argument, such as Plato's, designed to show their essential incompatibity must be wrong. I shall come back to this.

In any case, even if we ignore the possibility of other values, more than just the possibility of knowledge is needed to get Plato's argument to work. It is also necessary that the people who do know can be identified in order that they can be given the task of government. To save a regress of justification, this means that they have to be able to be identified as the people who know independently of the content of their knowledge. It is no good saying that there are people who know more, if we cannot tell who they are. It is also no good if the only way that we can say that they know more is because we already possess the knowledge ourselves. We have to be able to tell in advance who is more likely to know, so that we can then put those people into power. We need, therefore, principles about learning, or the acquisition of knowledge, so that we can tell in advance who is going to be in the know. This, of course, does happen in Plato, but in his account it illustrates the importance of the education of a specially selected political class. In other words, his conclusions don't flow just from the possession of knowledge by some people rather than others; so the mere differential possession of knowledge by itself will not show that democracy is inappropriate.

This argument shows that, even if there is no other good than knowledge, it still does not follow that another form of decision-making is superior to democracy. More is required, and it is worth recapping the argument. We start the Platonic argument with the questionable assumption that there is a truth about moral values. This alone, however, will not determine one form of decision-making rather than another; for we need some kind of access to this truth in order to reach the right decisions. Hence we also need knowledge; that is, we also have to assume that this truth is accessible to human beings. However this is still not enough to discountenance democracy as a form of decision-making procedure for a community. If people have knowledge, or access to the truth, this does not by itself tell us who to put in charge. We need also to assume that people have differential knowledge; that the access of some of the people is better than the access of others. Then we should put those with most knowledge in charge. Even this, however, is not enough. To put those with most knowledge in charge, we have to be able to identify them, and be able to do so independently of knowing what they know. So we need a method of training, or at least principles of learning, so that we can educate, or at least identify, our special ruling group. That was the argument. Recapping it shows that it depends upon several strong conditions. These conditions all have to be met for the Platonic argument to go through. Even then it would only work if there was no other good than knowledge. Plato himself might have believed this; but it is another very strong condition. What this all adds up to is that there is no simple argument just from the existence of moral truth, or the existence of moral knowledge, to the badness of democracy.

This conclusion can be reinforced by considering the alternative position in which it is still assumed that there is both truth and knowledge, but in which it cannot be told independently which people possess the knowledge. Suppose, further, that this is a case in which no one is infallible, but in which each person is more likely than not to be right. Then the best method of finding the right answer would be to take what the majority believe. That is, if we can assume that the average judgment of the average person is more likely to be right than not, then there are epistemological advantages in democratic decision-making. For if this is the case on each judgment, then the judgments of most people on a particular question are even more likely to be right, and the probability increases both with the number of the people and also with the relative size of the majority. So, if we can assume in any area that people are generally reasonably good judges, then democracy is an efficient method of decision-making for that area. Notice that this is true even if we are uninterested in anything else than epistemology (that is, if our only interest is to get the right answer). Even if the only good is knowledge, democracy may be the best way of gaining it. Hence democracy and knowledge are not necessarily incompatible.

In response to the Platonic argument, therefore, we have two lines of reply. First, there are more goods than epistemic goods, and this means that on particular occasions it might still be right to use a democratic decision procedure even if it is agreed that some other method was epistemologically more efficient. Second, democracy is only epistemologically inefficient on certain further assumptions and these, again, may not hold for the cases we are interested in. Both answers not only defend the goodness of democracy against Plato; they also show that democracy may still be the right method to use even if there is knowledge about the good, as Plato supposed. Neither, that is, relies on attacking Plato's optimism about the possibility of possessing (moral) knowledge.

So far I have been arguing relatively abstractly. What I would now like to do is to try and make the points more concrete by considering particular cases of decision-making. These will inevitably be simplified examples, but at least, in contrast to the above, they will have a more specific subject matter. As suggested in the last chapter, I shall consider examples of small group decision-making. In these something has to be decided for the group as a whole, and the question is what the best method is of reaching this decision. In each case we need to see what happens when the decision is arrived at by taking everyone's opinion, considering them equally, and following the majority view when they diverge. That is, we want in these cases to see when a democratic decision procedure would be appropriate, and when not.

Suppose that the group's first task is finding the answer to relatively simple arithmetical calculations. Here it might well be the most efficient procedure for everyone to do the calculations independently, vote on the outcomes, and take the majority view as being the group decision. That is, with roughly equal competence and no one infallible, it may well be best to treat the views equally, assuming that the randomness of error means that convergence in each case will be on the correct answer. We can assume that what is aimed at here is truth, which may be for some practical purpose of the group, such as to stop bridges falling down or to win a competition. So this is a case in which there is a clear, hard-edged, truth. There is a right answer, and the group either gets it or it does not. The group also has access to this truth; people possess knowledge. Individuals make mistakes; the knowledge is differential. So this is a clear case in which there is truth and differential knowledge. Yet, unlike Plato's views with the pilot and the ship, it is still efficient to have everyone treated equally and vote on the answer. With truth and knowledge available, democracy still turns out to be the best decision procedure.

However, suppose we change this by taking, as a second case, a situation in which people are not (roughly) equally competent. Suppose that the mathematics is more difficult so that only some people understand it. Suppose that these experts can be identified on the basis of their earlier successes. Then it would seem that we are back with Plato's answer. Fewer bridges will fall down if the answers of these few competent mathematicians are taken as the views of the group. The differential possession of knowledge here counts against the efficiency of democracy as a decision procedure.

Let us test this out by comparing it with a contrasting case in which neither truth nor knowledge is available. Suppose, for example, that the task is to choose the colour of the uniform which the group as a whole has to wear, and that there are no grounds for thinking that any answer to this question is better or worse in itself than any other. It is not that it is important that members of the group can be easily noticed, that they induce restful feelings in their clients, or anything like that. Here there is no right answer. Here no one can know. Here, with nothing else to go on, it might well seem that voting was the right method. One colour is as good as another. So there would seem to be no better reason for choosing, say green over blue, than that more people preferred green. This might seem to be further support of the Platonic point. With no knowledge, democracy comes through.

However, it was seen above that Plato's argument merely permitted, but did not positively recommend, democracy where there is no knowledge. If, therefore, we feel that voting is appropriate in cases like the choice of colour, this must be for some other, more positive, reason. Such a reason might be that this procedure was likely to maximise the satisfaction of the members of the group; following the majority view will mean that more of them get what they want. This might also reduce conflict inside the group, and produce other beneficial effects. Now, if such things are goods, they are also goods in areas in which there is a right answer. So, let us take another case, in which what the group should do no longer seems to be a mere question of taste, but in which it can meaningfully be said that some answers are better than others. Suppose, for example, that the group has to decide on the best way to deal with a particular threat. They have to decide whether or not to pre-empt an attack from another group. There may well be a right answer to this question, which depends upon prediction of the behaviour of other people. Furthermore, it might well be better known to some of the group than others, and the group that are more likely to know might be able to be identified independently of their views on this particular question. They might, for example, be the group with more experience of the other group.

So, it seems, this is a case which, with detectable differential knowledge, ought to follow the Platonic prescription precisely. It would seem, therefore, that just as with the competent mathematicians and the bridge, the views of the experts should be followed, even if they are in a minority. As the particular case has been set up, this must be the best strategy if all that is being aimed at is the truth. If some know better than others, and we can probably tell who they are, and if all we want is the truth, then we do best to follow these supposed experts. However, if there are other goods relevant to social decision-making, which the example of the choice of uniform colour indicates, then these other goods have to be considered as well as truth. So, in a particular case, it might be better to promote more of these other goods at the cost of a lower probability of achieving the right answer. The lack of agreement or satisfaction, or the greater conflict which might arise if the views of the expert minority were followed, might be sufficient to outweigh the greater chance of getting the right answer. It all depends upon the relative importance of the gains and losses got through the best or sub-optimal strategies for reaching the truth on the one hand against the gains and losses inflicted by the decision-making process itself on the other. As well as the goodness of the end (the final judgment arrived at) there is also the goodness of the means (the method by which this judgment is reached). Something which would be, in itself, the best solution might impose too high costs *en route*. Something which might get more truth could leave us worse off by the time we got there.

We started with examples, like the one about the simple sums, which showed that the Platonic conclusion about the incompatibility of democracy and knowledge was not necessarily true. Even if we are only aiming at truth, democracy might still be an efficient decision procedure. Sometimes democracy is epistemologically superior. However the last example suggests something even more interesting. Even when democracy is epistemologically inferior, it may still be the appropriate decision procedure. This is because there are more than epistemological goods. Choice and putting into effect particular decisions each have costs. These costs may outweigh the benefits of what would be, in itself, the best decision.

The costs of putting a decision into effect, in particular, may be important for democracy. For if the costs of policing a decision, that is of making it happen, are roughly proportional to the numbers that have to be policed, then there is a clear advantage in adopting the decisions of the majority. For some decisions literal policing, that is, the direct threat of harm or punishment for non-compliance, is impossible or unavailable or inappropriate. Then it is likely to be particularly important to adopt as a group those decisions which most people would independently be most happy to adopt; or at least would be prepared to adopt because of their intrinsic merits rather than through the threat of punishment.

Let us test this by taking another case of a small group decision, rather like the last one. Suppose, again, that there has to be a group decision about how to respond to a particular threat. This time the group has to decide which of two positions to defend against the attack of another group. The group may disagree about which is the better position but what is certain that, whichever position is chosen, the group must stick together in its defence and be committed to it. Now, as before, there might be an intrinsically right answer; that is, it might be true that one of the positions was easier to defend than the other. Also, as before, this might be something which an independently identifiable minority was in a better position to judge than people generally; they might, for example, have more experience of this kind of thing. So, we have a right answer and independently identifiable military experts (who form a minority of the group); and the problem is the best method of reaching the decision about which position to defend. If, of course, the experts can persuade the majority, there is no problem (and the majority, with an equal interest in survival, have just as much interest in discovering the truth as the minority has, so they should be favourable to expert advice). However, suppose that on this occasion the majority are not persuaded. Then we have a genuine conflict, not just of people, but also of goods. One answer is epistemologically superior. The view of the expert minority is more likely to be right. But the view of the majority may be much easier to enforce. For what is crucial is that, whichever position is chosen, people will stick to it. And it will be more likely that more people will stick to the position preferred by the majority. It may be better to defend a worse position with three-quarters of an army than a better position with one-quarter of an army.

I am not saying that the right answer in this case is one way or the other. It depends upon many more details about the situation; such as how different the two positions are, or how the citizen army is disciplined. All that is important is that the right answer could go either way, depending upon the particular circumstances. For this means that, even if all the Platonic conditions of differential knowledge and an independently identifiable epistemologically superior group are fulfilled, it might still be right in certain circumstances to adopt the majority's views as the decision of the group. Democracy might still be the best procedure. Furthermore, this result was achieved by looking at only one further value in addition to knowledge, the advantage of group solidarity. Obviously this forms a pattern by which, by considering more values, more examples could be constructed. However, one value and one example is enough to make the general point.

So democracy seems to survive the Platonic assault. That the main argument depends upon introducing other values than knowledge might seem to weaken it. But the central point is that in terms of the connection between democracy and knowledge, democracy may still be the best method even if knowledge is available. This merely depends upon knowledge sometimes being trumped by other values. So there is no essential incompatibility between democracy and the availability of knowledge. Also, it should be remembered that this was not the whole argument. Even if (perhaps like Plato himself) we think that knowledge is the only good, democracy might still be the most efficient method. It all depends upon how differentially spread the knowledge is, and how easily the experts can be independently identified. If we think, like Plato, that there is moral truth, but that knowledge of this is potentially more widely spread than Plato thought, so that by and large one person's intuition is as good as another's, then a democratic procedure might well be the best way of gaining these epistemological goods. As was seen, all that is necessary for this is that the average person is more likely to be right than wrong. Then convergence will be beneficent, and majority decision will be efficient.

The concentration on moral, or evaluative, knowledge in most of this chapter may also be felt to weaken the argument. Most knowledge is not knowledge about values. Indeed, unlike Plato, we may be sceptical about whether there is knowledge about values. However, the concentration on moral knowledge is not, in fact, a defect. The same points as were made above go through for other kinds of knowledge. In the particular examples discussed there was normally no problem about the values being promoted, or hence about knowledge of value. It was quite clear what was good for the group in each case; or, at least, how they understood their good. What they wanted was such things as that their bridges did not fall down or that they survived assault from another group. It was here that knowledge featured and was important. It was here that there were disagreements about what was the case, showing that there was differential knowledge. Yet this knowledge was straightforward hard-edged knowledge about such things as mathematics, the behaviour of the physical world, the behaviour of other people and suchlike. These are areas in which we can all agree that knowledge is available. Yet it has been seen that nevertheless it may sometimes be best to operate democratically.

These arguments are not arguments against the possibility or importance of experts. The question is only about how experts should be selected and expert advice used. In many circumstances the people as a whole will form as good a control on expert advice as some smaller group. Even dictators have to choose experts and the best method of choice available to them is one also available to the people at large. This is to choose experts by their success. The people want to be fed; they want their bridges not to fall down; they want to survive the attack. Generally speaking, the best experts to choose are the ones which have produced food; whose bridges have not fallen down; whose past advice has been successful (or would have been successful, if followed). In this the more views about what is actually happening, or has happened, the better. Dictators or oligarchies are more insulated from what is going on than the people at large. To find out whether the people have actually been fed, the best people to consult are the people themselves.

These last points in favour of democracy would hold even if knowledge were the only good. Yet, as has been seen in the course of this chapter, knowledge is not the only good. Some of the other goods I have at times traded it off against in this chapter have been utilitarian in character; they have been concerned with the value of survival, or the benefits of satisfying people's preferences. These may well not be the sort of moral foundation to which someone wishes to appeal. If another value is to be set against knowledge, then people may be happier with a value which they think has intrinsic value and is connected in no way with pleasure or advantage. One such possibility is freedom, or autonomy, and this is the value to which I shall turn in the next chapter.

CHAPTER X

Autonomy

It was seen in the last chapter that values other than knowledge mean that the route by which a decision is reached may in some circumstances be as important as the decision itself. It is not enough to get the right answer. It must also be got in the right way. Sometimes it may be preferable to have a less good answer reached by a better route. However the constraints imposed by the route may be tighter than was there suggested. Sometimes, however good the answer, there is no permissible means by which it may be reached. Sometimes only one route, or a tightly constrained group of routes, is morally permissible. A natural candidate for such a constraint is that permissible routes should respect the value of autonomy, the principle that people should have control of their own lives.

I say that autonomy is a natural moral value, because it is normally thought to be a good thing for people to have control of their own lives. It is a moral basis which it is plausible to assume; or at least is worth investigating hypothetically. Furthermore, as well as being a frequently assumed value, autonomy also looks to be a useful one on which to found democracy. For both democracy and autonomy value self-rule. If I am autonomous, I rule myself. I give myself my own laws. Yet the central idea of democracy is also self-rule. In democracy the people rule themselves. So, with this common content of valuing self-rule, autonomy might seem to be the right sort of foundation for democracy.

This is one reason why autonomy might seem to be a natural basis for democracy. Another is that since it concentrates on the means by which a decision is reached rather than the content of the decision itself, autonomy would seem to be exactly the kind of value needed to solve the problem of the last chapter: that in democracy, people are likely to reach the wrong answers. In the last chapter I suggested instrumental reasons why democracy might nevertheless be a good thing. But such instrumentalism may well seem both indirect and morally rather grubby. The shortest and morally most satisfactory answer would surely be to discover a moral basis which claimed that it is intrinsically justifiable for people to reach wrong answers. Yet this is just what a belief in autonomy provides. To adopt autonomy as a value is to hold that people are to be perfectly entitled to damn themselves. It is thought better for people to choose the worst than have the best thrust on to them. With autonomy, therefore, reaching the wrong answer is sometimes morally appropriate. So with autonomy, it seems that the problems of the last chapter, which stemmed from this, should disappear.

However, even if this is so, adopting autonomy as a value seems to lead to a new, and even worse problem. For if the goodness of the proposed means is that individual people should rule themselves, it is not clear how this can be compatible with any form of government. For with government, even with democracies, laws come to someone from the outside. The individual citizens have to do things because they are the law, even if it is a law which they helped in creating. Surely, so the problem runs, once people engage in a community and are bound by that community's decisions, then to that extent they lose their autonomy. They are each like one-time little independent republics now merged into a larger common-wealth. Formerly they gave themselves their own laws, now they must take it from elsewhere. They have ceased to be autonomous.

This problem first emerged in Chapter VIII when it was considered whether there might not be a fundamental kind of antipathy between an individual's possession of rights and the power of a government. Autonomy can be treated as a right. It seems that it is in the same kind of conflict. In that chapter I said that whether there was indeed such a conflict depended upon how we understood rights. I also said that I thought that the important thing about varying views about rights was the alternative structural moves they permitted. It was not so much what the values initially were but how they were sub-sequently to be treated which marked the important distinctions. For example rights might just be a name which some people gave to certain fundamental goods. This would give them a content, but what is more important is the way such content would then naturally be treated. For understood in this way, rights would be things of value which could be traded off against, or compared with, other things of value. The natural aim would be to maximise the value, or right, so that we got as much of it as possible. So a course of action which interfered with the rights of one person in order to secure the rights of several others would be recommended. This, however, is an unusual way in which to treat rights. More normally such trading is not permitted. Rights are thought of as being constraints rather than goals. They are something absolute, connected with each individual right-holder, and which it is not permissible to maximise or trade. This is the ideal type with which I operated in that chapter. One person's so-called rights may not be interfered with for the greater good of someone else's so-called rights.

Now treating rights in such an absolute, or non-trading, way is fine for the autonomy of individuals. For their own individual decisions, they can be regarded, either literally or metaphorically, as having their own piece of territory protected from any say or control of others. In their own individual garden they can say and do what they will. It is like a one-person state and they are in charge, with dominion over their land. However, precisely because of this, there are profound problems about trying to preserve this idea in any kind of social decision-making, including democracy. I said above that autonomy, with its mutual idea of self-rule, might be a natural foundation for democracy. But consider what the most straight-forward argument basing democracy on autonomy would be like. Presumably it would say that control of your situation is a good (autonomy) and that more people control their situation in a democracy than they do in rival systems. In a monarchy or an oligarchy only one or a few people have control. In democracy the majority do. However, this argument does not work once we think of autonomy in terms of side constraints. For in this argument autonomy is being traded, or maximised. It is not the case that everybody's autonomy is being treated as a non-tradeable absolute. For the minority are not so treated. They do not have control of the decision and so their autonomy is not respected. The autonomy of the minority is being sacrificed for the sake of the majority.

The argument is strengthened if we consider what might lie behind this claim of a right to autonomy. It is natural to think that it is the Kantian picture in which people should, autonomously, choose their moral law. It is an important part of this Kantian picture that people should be treated as ends rather than as means; that is, we are not allowed to do things to people for the sake of the good of others, however much this good might be. It is this that forbids maximising. Yet in democracy we seem to be doing exactly this, treating the minority as means to the greater good of the majority, sacrificing their autonomy for the greater autonomy of other people.

If autonomy is treated as a right, therefore, and rights are treated in the normal manner as constraints rather than goals, there are severe difficulties about making autonomy compatible with democracy. The natural argument basing democracy on autonomy as a foundation does not work. In Chapter VIII another, more heroic, solution was sketched whereby rights were still treated as side constraints, but side constraints which right-holders themselves were allowed to alienate. People exercise their rights by giving them away. Put in terms of autonomy this solution would be that people have one autonomous decision, namely whether or not to put themselves under government. If we suppose that they have so chosen, then we can say that the decision was indeed autonomous, but now they have a duty to obey. So we have both individual autonomy and justified governmental power. The individuals freely chose to allow the government into their private gardens and so are not now allowed to complain about the municipal planting. This kind of argument normally applies to the original foundation of states, as in the original contract tradition. We might, it is supposed, get a unanimous autonomous decision at this stage, setting up a decision procedure for the future which would then bind everyone. Everyone, for example, might decide to institute majoritarian democracy. Then the minority could not claim that their autonomy was not being defended, or was being sacrificed. For it could be said that they also had autonomously participated in the unanimous decision whereby this procedure was instituted, and so they were also bound by its results as a consequence of their own free autonomous choices.

This familiar kind of justification is highly sensitive to the actual historical facts. It will not sustain any kind of hypothetical contract treatment, where we consider what people would have decided, if they had had the chance. Hypothetical contracts may be a good device for finding what is in people's interests, or what they might rationally be prepared to defend. But if we take people to be bound because of what they have actually promised, then it is important that the promises are indeed actual rather than merely hypothetical. Similarly for a justification which depends upon autonomy or free

165

choice. If something is to be justified because it was freely chosen, then it is important that it was actually chosen, not just that it would have been chosen. So the historical facts are important. Yet, notoriously, although such coming together and unanimous construction of a decision procedure is possible, it is not frequently actual. Hence, even if it did provide justification, it is not a justification which would actually apply.

This may be thought not to be a particularly severe criticism. Perhaps possibilities are of most philosophical significance. It is important to discover whether democracy can be justified, whether or not the justifications apply to many actual situations. Also, once it is remembered how many small-scale units people are actually involved in, the conscious unanimous construction of a decision procedure whereby everybody accepts the majority vote is probably more common than this familiar objection to the historical contract argument allows. It is sometimes also thought that voting is itself some kind of contract. Everyone who votes thereby, autonomously, declares themselves ready to abide by the result. So the act of voting can itself be construed as the unanimous adoption of a decision procedure by all those who vote. This would not justify application of the decision to non-voters, but it would to all the voters and, in particular, to the minority of the actual voters who have had their wishes rejected. They have no basis for complaint on the grounds that their autonomy has been sacrificed or overrun.

These particular suggestions about why the autonomy of the minority may not be sacrificed would, no doubt, benefit from particular detailed treatment. It has always seemed puzzling to me, for example, why we are entitled to construe an act of voting as if it were like making a promise or signing a declaration when this is not how it is understood by many people doing it and when this is not any explicit, or independently observable, part of the ceremony. However, I shall abstain from further treatment of these particular responses, because I think that there are serious problems with the underlying idea of autonomy on which they are all based. Autonomy here is being treated in the way which I said in Chapter 8 might resolve the problem of how we could have both individuals with rights and governments with power. The central idea there was that the rights were alienable. Having a right means also having the power to relinquish that right. So, for example, a right to life is to be construed as including a right to commit suicide, preventing subsequent exercises of that right. Or a right to liberty is to be construed as including a right to sell oneself into slavery, preventing subsequent exercise of that right. So the key question with autonomy is whether it can be thought of in the same way, so that it could be an exercise of someone's autonomy for them to make decisions which mean that they have no further autonomy. Supporters of autonomy would normally think that it may not be thought of in this way. J.S. Mill, for example, faces this problem in his paradigmatic text *On Liberty*. When discussing whether someone should be permitted to choose slavery, he says: 'The principle of freedom cannot require that he should be free not to be free. It is not freedom to be allowed to alienate his freedom.'

This may well be thought to be a sufficient difficulty. However, there is also a quite separate problem about trying to use autonomy as the basis of an argument for democracy. Autonomy is having control over one's situation. We have just seen that, in a democracy, the minority do not seem to have such control. However, at least in one sense, the individual members of the majority do not have control either. It is true that their wishes come about, whereas the wishes of the minority do not. But people are not autonomous just because their wishes are fulfilled. It also has to be the case that their wishes are fulfilled because they themselves choose that they should be. In a democracy it is true that the individual members of the majority do choose the result which in fact happens. But it does not happen just because they individually choose it. It only happens because a certain number of other people want it as well. Of course each person does have an input into the decision procedure. But so, in this sense, do the individual members of the minority.

It might be objected to this that all action presupposes background conditions and that one's intended action only has a particular effect because of the way things are. I can hit a target I am throwing a stone at, for example, only because of certain general background conditions (stones have mass, we are in a gravitational field and so on) and because of certain particular contingencies (I happen to have a stone, the target is within range and so on). So, it might be said, my decision as a member of the majority only results in action because of both background standing conditions (we are operating in a democratic system) and particular contingencies (most of the others happen to have voted the same way as me). In terms of Kantian morality, however, this would be a mistaken assimilation. It makes all the difference whether the causal route to action operates through another person or merely through unthinking things. This can be thought of in terms of responsibility. If I persuade someone to be nasty to a third person, I am of course responsible. But not wholly. The nasty result is also the responsibility of the person whom I persuaded. More than one person's will is involved, and this necessarily makes a difference. So also in the democratic case. Unless considerably more than one person's will had been involved, I would not be on the winning side. My decision has the effect it does only because of the separate decisions of many other people.

So the high moral ground of autonomy looks to be rather harder to occupy in defence of democracy than more mundane or grubby utilitarianism. However, I think that in fact we can mount a better argument for democracy based on autonomy than has so far been suggested, and this is what I shall attempt for the rest of this chapter. The key moves, obviously, will be to decide why it is of value and what sort of value it is. With regard to the latter, the earlier argument which I described as the natural argument from autonomy to democracy shows that it has to be a value which it makes sense to maximise, trading one possession of value against another. With that we would be able to start with autonomy and then produce an argument for democracy as being the decision procedure in which we got most of this value. The possibility of trading or maximising, therefore, is something which we would hope to retrieve from considering why autonomy is of value.

Let me start with the Kantian background, since this seemed to provide the complete block to maximising; the minority were not to be treated as means for the greater good of the majority. However, in spite of appearances, I do not think that normal democratic decision-making does fall foul of Kantian principles. For moral judgment in Kant is related to possibility. As the famous slogan has it, *ought implies can*. This is why Kantian morality is a morality of intention rather than result; for it is supposed that it is always possible to try even if it is not always possible to succeed. Now even if the minority do not control what happens, they can still try to influence it. They can decide what ought to be the case and attempt, as far as they can, to promote it. This is also what the individual members of the majority do. It is these moral decisions which in both cases they should make autonomously on Kantian principles. Yet, in both cases, this is something which they are able to do. The point about no individual being in control cuts both ways. All any individual can do, whether they are of the majority or minority, is try.

The Kantian background does not therefore automatically produce the side constraints view. However something fuller than Kantian moral autonomy is normally taken to be involved in autonomy when this is taken as a value for practical or political purposes, something more like real control over one's situation rather than the mere ability to control one's intention. The next question, therefore, is what this extra is; why autonomy is of value. Presumably the value is the value of freedom; autonomy is a kind of freedom and freedom is thought to be a good thing. One reason for this might be instrumental; we get more welfare if we are free. This would lead, of course, immediately to a maximising conception and a possible defence of democracy. However we are not at present using utilitarian defences. So autonomy, or freedom, needs another defence. Perhaps the best is the simplest. Freedom is a good thing because it is intrinsically good for people to be able to have control of their lives.

So now we have the value as a basis, even if rather imprecisely. The value is freedom. The next question is whether this value has to be looked at as a constraint or as a goal. That is, whether every individual's freedom is a complete block to action by others; or whether, by contrast, freedom is a value which it is permissible to trade and maximise. To try and answer this we need to unpack the concept of freedom a little. Freedom is a notoriously tangled concept, whether we are thinking of political freedom or the more general metaphysical question of free choice. We have seen in the historical chapters many different versions of political freedom. As in Chapter I, we may again simplify the options to whether freedom should be understood as a negative or a positive concept. The basic idea is whether freedom should be understood in a *free from* or a *free to* sense. It is whether freedom is centrally to be understood in terms of being free from the external interference of others or in terms of being free to exercise some power of one's own.

As well as these ways of understanding political freedom, which were more fully worked out in the historical chapters, I think that it is also helpful to keep in mind freedom as discussed in contemporary metaphysics. Here it is asked whether, or in what sense, human beings have free will. The chief options in this metaphysical debate are whether freedom is ultimately to be understood in terms of satisfaction of desire or in terms of exercise of choice. If we think about how these metaphysical options might correspond with the options usually discussed in political theory, then both these options are more of the positive *free to* kind. People can neither exercise their choice nor satisfy their desires unless certain facilities are provided. If, for example, the government, or other stronger powers, leaves them alone to starve, then they are free from external interference. But they can neither realise their desire for food, nor choose to eat if they wish. In other words, they are not free to eat; and since eating is a prerequisite of life and so of any other activity, they are not free to do anything else either. Free to starve, they might be thought to be free in one of the political senses, the negative one; however it is plausible that they are free in neither of the metaphysical senses.

This is but one small point in favour of positive freedom but, in general, the many facets of freedom means that the problem of how it is possible to have on the one hand free people and on the other hand government may after all be capable of solution. As long as freedom is just thought of in terms of people being free from interference, then it seems that government and freedom must be contraries: the more government, the less freedom; with the only full freedom to be found in the so-called state of nature, without or prior to government. However, if freedom is power, and if government can increase rather than decrease the power of individuals, then more government may mean more freedom. Returning to the freedom to starve example, a government which provides food may free people rather than constraining them. So more government in this case means more freedom. We may, therefore, justify government by citing freedom. We do not have to think that they are necessarily inimical. This forms a solution to the original problem and it is a solution which, unlike the heroic possibility discussed as an example in Chapter VIII, does not depend upon people using their autonomy to surrender their autonomy.

Notice that this is a solution because it allows maximising. It shows that freedom is a value which we can meaningfully have more or less of. Provision of food makes people more free; it gives them more of this value. The solution not only shows that there is no direct antipathy between individual freedom and government, but also opens the way again to the natural argument from autonomy to democracy. For if individual autonomy is not a complete block to action but something which we can have more or less of, then we can ask whether it is something which we would have more or less of in a particular political system such as democracy. The answer, in line with the simple argument given above, would seem to be that we would have more. We should have more choice, because more people are involved in choice, in democracy than in rival systems such as oligarchy or dictatorship.

We can come at this in another way. The block which autonomy seemed to provide to every sort of government, including democracy, depended upon treating it as an absolute. Nothing at all was to be allowed that interfered in any way with this autonomy. So if anything was considered which would depend on any other will than the will of the individual in question, it was forbidden as interfering with their autonomy. Autonomy could not be compromised and any decisions affecting an individual had to flow only from the will of that individual and no one else. In such circumstances it is indeed difficult to get beyond single individuals, willing for themselves, about things which concern only themselves. If we ask, however, whether this is the value we really want or have in mind when we think of autonomy, the attractiveness of this picture is liable to fade. Such an absolute value would be very hard to maintain in harmony with other values, or with normal social interaction. Consider, for example, promising, which is a means we have of moralising or controlling our social actions. Autonomy, thought of in the absolute sort of way, would forbid any such promises. For even though the promise is freely made, some of the will of the person making the promise has been handed over into the control of someone else. For example, a person might have promised her friends that she would come to a meeting at five. When five o'clock comes, therefore, she can do no more about it. She cannot unwill the normative situation she herself has created any more than those people placing themselves, Hobbes-style, under absolute government in the original contract can remove that government. She depends upon the will of her friends, of the people to whom she made the promise, to undo or modify her obligation. So, if she is taken to possess absolute autonomy, she could make no promises. Yet the ability to make promises would normally be thought to be an increase of freedom rather than a limitation of it. If we have an institution of promises and promise-keeping, we have a resource which helps us to plan the future and which individuals can choose to use for their advantage. Again, freedom is increased rather than diminished; but, again, this

171

has the effect that the will of individuals is sometimes bound by something outside themselves. Again, the key notion is that of maximising, of there being more or less freedom, rather than freedom being taken as an absolute which is either possessed completely or not possessed at all.

It is on these lines, I think, that we cannot only clear the way to the simple natural argument from autonomy to democracy but also see better what was wrong and what was right in the original picture whereby it was thought that the autonomy of every individual had to be protected, come what may. It now seems that to treat it in this absolute way leaves in fact very little value in what is thus trenchantly protected. The way is therefore open for some trading, so that more of what is really of value can be produced by some sacrifice of the autonomy of particular individuals. Understanding the value of freedom in a perfectly natural way, whereby it can be seen why it is of value, we can trade one person's autonomy with someone else's as a way of maximising freedom. Democracy will, other things being equal, get more of such autonomy than other systems. Autonomy is a good. So democracy is a good thing, and its promotion of autonomy is why it is a good thing.

This argument depends upon maximisation. However it does not follow from this argument that all protection may be discarded. There may be other rights which may only be treated in an absolute way. Even if we get democracy out of this argument, therefore, it may still be subject to the constraints of certain absolute rights. Whatever the majority wish, it does not follow that they are allowed to kill, enslave or maim the minority. Just because we engage in some maximising, or trading, does not mean that everything can be counted or that anything goes. The point about maximising is restricted to freedom itself. Working with the choice conception of freedom, as we have been so far, then it is reasonable to suppose that someone's freedom is increased if their choices are increased. Starving, they have no choice at all. Having to work incessantly for food, they still have no choice. If, however, they come into a situation of slight surplus, then they have a little spare time and energy and can make a few choices. A system of government may increase their choices, just as we saw could happen with an institution of promise-keeping. A law of property protects some of their choices, thereby increasing them. A law of contract, the legal corollary to the institution of promising, allows them more control over this and other property in the future. A law about wills and testaments allows them to control their property after their deaths, increasing their choice yet further. And so on. This is not to say that government will necessarily increase choice, but shows how it is possible for it to do so.

These are the possible general benefits of government. The next question is what, if anything, is specifically added if that government is democratic. After all, the rule of law, and law about property, contract or testaments also feature in rival systems of government. The short answer, as has just been seen, is that with other things being equal, democracy as a method of decision-making will increase every individual's choice, since, more often than not, this system will allow an individual's choices to be effective. The longer answer is more complex. Obviously one important consideration here is the composition of the majority and the minority. If this varies on the issues, so that any particular individual is as likely to be in the majority as any other, then through time this system will allow any individual to increase their choice or control. The situation here is similar to having a system of promise-keeping. With the system in place, each individual can use it for their own advantage and do things which they would not have been able to do if there had been no such system. So, if we have democracy, no individual can decide whether or not to have it on a case-by-case basis but, overall, it will give them more choice than if there had been no such system. Things are very different, however, if the majority and minority on any issue does not change but is known in advance, so that one side (one class, one race, one religion, say) always has the advantage. Then it is not the case that having a democratic system would increase the choice, or potential control, of any arbitrarily selected individual. From the point of view of members of this permanent minority, this democracy gives them no more control than an oligarchy would. So whether or not democracy increases choice does depend upon the actual facts of the situation. The above general argument was just meant to show that it could, not that it necessarily would; that there was nothing intrinsic about autonomy which necessarily blocked an argument to democracy.

This has all been put in terms of freedom as a value, where freedom has been thought of as exercising choice. It is time to see what the effect would be if the other metaphysical view of freedom were adopted, namely freedom understood in terms of satisfaction of desire. If someone's freedom consists in the satisfaction of their desire, then what is important is that the desire is satisfied, not how it is. If a person's desires are satisfied, that person is free, whatever part they themselves have had on the process. The question of whether democracy frees people would then become the question of whether it fulfils their desires. This is practically the question of whether it increases human happiness or satisfaction; that is, utility. So on this way of understanding it, the question of whether democracy is justified because of the support it provides to human freedom becomes the question of whether democracy can be justified on utilitarian grounds.

As was seen in Chapter I, on more extreme versions of the approach that freedom consists in desire satisfaction, people are allowed to be mistaken about what they desire. They are supposed to have real interests of which they are unaware. It then becomes permissible for governments to fulfil these wants or interests, even in the teeth of the apparent or expressed desires of the people whose supposed interests these are. They are, in Rousseau's phrase, to be forced to be free. Now if we understand freedom in terms of desire satisfaction, whether of the modest or more extreme version, then we lose one of these ways in which autonomy was supposed to put constraints on means to balance against goodness of ends. The end point of the greatest satisfaction of the interests of the community is the sole element of importance. So it will not matter how the end point is reached, providing that it is. If a minority group, if the aristocracy or guardians, have a better idea of how to achieve the welfare or interests of the people than the people have themselves, then it would be appropriate for them to make decisions. And not just appropriate in the sense of a more efficient means of reaching the right answer (assuming that this is the right answer), but also more appropriate in the sense of maximising the people's freedom. For if freedom consists in getting what you (really) want, and this is what people (really) want, then reaching the right answer will also make people free, whether they want it or not. There will then be no distinction between the goodness of the end and the goodness of the means by which it is reached, and so neither the problems nor the democratic solutions of the last chapter.

However, as was seen in Chapter IV, it is exactly because this way of understanding freedom seems to be unnatural or dangerous that the problem is in fact still in play. People do not normally think that they are free if they are being forced into getting something, even if it is something which satisfies their interests. It is not what they get, it is also how they get it which matters. They think that they are free only if they get things as a result of their own choices. That is, they get those things not just which happen to satisfy their desires; nor even because they satisfy their desires; but because they choose to have that desire satisfied. It is not only important for people that the right result is reached but also that they reach it themselves. This has obvious democratic results, in terms of the way in which the question was put in the last chapter. For, from the standpoint of ordinary members of the community, even if an aristocracy can provide better answers, these answers will be decisions made by those individual members, not decisions made by the members of the community themselves. Even if the right result is reached, they have not reached it. So if freedom is understood in terms of choice, we have a valuation of the goodness of the means by which an end is reached which can be set over against the goodness of the end itself.

This is why I have chosen in this chapter to put the problem in terms of autonomy rather than in terms of freedom. Just how freedom can be understood in widely different ways comes through clearly from the historical chapters, where this was the most discussed value. Yet further options could have been considered. *Autonomy*, I think, is a more specific term, which picks up one (or at least a smaller set) of the many different things which are valued in the name of freedom. Autonomy, which literally means self-rule, or giving oneself one's own laws, picks up those aspects of freedom which concentrate on choice or exercise of will, rather than those aspects of freedom which concentrate on satisfaction of desire. It therefore focuses better on how a decision is reached rather than the content of the decision itself. Concentrating on means rather than ends, it helps with the solution of the problem of the last chapter.

So suppose that power is the value behind autonomy, the possibility of controlling one's situation. This means that it is a good that people have effective choice; that they have things between which they can choose and that they are able to choose between them. As we have just seen, this is a good which may be increased or decreased. It may, for example, be increased by government. So this is a value which can be treated in a maximising way. The consideration of why autonomy is a good thing has shown, in more formal terms, what sort of good it is. It allows trading. So the main block it provided to democracy has been removed. Also, although it is not necessarily the case that individual power will be increased in a democracy, it is certainly normally the case that it will be. So here is one way of backing power, defending democracy and reaching the result that it may sometimes be right to have a decision procedure which reaches what is, intrinsically, not the best result.

CHAPTER XI

Equality

Ever since the Greeks, liberty and equality have been taken to be the central marks of democracy. In Chapter II it was shown how the citizens of classical Athens were said to have increased in liberty and equality as they became increasingly democratic. In the later historical chapters liberty was more prominent than equality. However in Chapter IV Rousseau was seen to have granted it a central place. Even J. S. Mill, who was seen in Chapter VI to have sponsored inegalitarian voting schemes, quoted with approval 'Bentham's dictum, "everybody to count for one, nobody for more than one"', which he said 'might be written under the principle of utility as an explanatory commentary'. The drive towards democracy, in his day and after, has been marked by increasing equality in political power. If the eighteenth century tried to preserve liberty by the mixed constitution, as described in Chapter V, this was partly as a way of controlling democracy; when democracy, by contrast, came to take over, things were not so much mixed as levelled. Each successive increase of the franchise marked a growth of equality, rendering different groups of society more equal in their political power.

Whatever the history, equality is usually today taken to be something of value. As such, just like liberty, it is a contested political concept. Both have been understood in various ways. But both are prime candidates, in one or another of these interpretations, for being a foundation for democracy. In the last chapter I tried to solve the problem of whether, or in what sense, liberty might be a foundation for democracy. Now it is the turn of equality. We have to see whether democracy may be regarded as a good thing because it promotes equality, or whether it is a bad thing because it prevents equality; or whether, under different interpretations, it might be both of these. In other words, equality may provide a foundation for democracy, or it may provide a problem for democracy, or it may provide both.

At first sight it may seem that, although equality may provide a foundation for democracy, it could not provide a problem for it. For it seems that democracy must be egalitarian, as compared with other political systems. The very name suggests that it, is the rule by everyone, as opposed to rule by one person (monarchy) or by a few (oligarchy). If everyone rules, it seems that this respects everyone equally. On rival systems some people have more power than others. Democracy, by contrast, seems necessarily and essentially to give everyone equal power. If equality is a good thing, therefore, so it would seem is democracy. No more, it might be thought, needs to be said; equality practically follows from the very meaning of the term.

However, the obvious and essential nature of a connection between democracy and equality disappears once we consider how democracy works in practice. It needs a decision procedure when people do not unanimously agree. This is standardly majority rule. But when it is considered how majority rule operates, it seems that democracy may work very unequally. The people whose decisions get accepted, that is the majority, have the effective power. The others, the minority, do not. The majority and the minority are not treated equally. Hence the problem, which worried people like de Tocqueville and J. S. Mill, of the dictatorship of the majority. What looks egalitarian ends up in practice as dictatorship. Rather than equality being a simple and natural foundation for democracy, it starts to pose a problem.

Mill's own partial solution to this problem was to propose certain conditions, protecting individual liberty, which should hold on all governments, whether democratic or otherwise. There was to be a protected private sphere over which no government should legislate; the majority might dictate what should happened to murderers, but not what should happen to people with unusual sexual tastes. This is, in effect, to propose a set of rights protecting individual liberty against central government power. As such it seems to have nothing particular to do with democracy. Many people do indeed talk of democratic rights. But, at least at first sight, there is no reason why the theory supporting Mill's liberty rights should be any different in a democracy. A theory which supported the liberty of individuals against government (such as Mill's own) might well work against all, or at least many, kinds of government. In other words, it has yet to be shown that there is anything particularly democratic about a theory of rights, or the idea of individual protection against government. I shall return to this question in Chapter XIII. For present purposes the point is that, in so far as rights are introduced, they may equally well be working against democracy as in its favour.

So, suppose that we accept equality as an intermediate value. The democratic procedure of voting and majority decision seems at first sight particularly to emphasise equality. It allows equal participation in the vote to all. Everyone is equal in the vote. Therefore, accepting equality as a good, democracy is a good thing. However, majority voting turns out to have inegalitarian implications. The result of the vote is that some people impose their will on the rest. So it seems to be very unequal. Accepting equality as a good, therefore, it seems that democracy is a bad thing. Perhaps this could be countered with a theory of rights. It may be claimed that there are some rights (or protections) which all, equally, ought to have. These rights stop the minority being exploited by the majority. But these rights, it seems, trench on democratic power by constraining majority decision-making. So, unless they themselves have a democratic basis, these egalitarian rights will be something outside democracy, limiting it in the name of equality.

That equality may count both for and against a particular course of action is not, in itself, surprising. There are many examples where equal treatment produces unequal results; or equal results are produced by unequal treatment. Indeed, this is the normal state of affairs. For example, a mother, wishing to treat her children equally tries to decide what pocket money to give them. Her first thought might be to give them equal sums of money. Nothing, it would seem, could be more equal than to give them each a pound. But Henry, who is thrifty, has already saved five pounds while Charles has only got one pound in his piggy bank. If she gives them each the same, then one of them will end up with three times the other. Perhaps, she might think, this does not matter. Henry should get the credit for his past thrift; and applying equal treatment to an unequal world is bound to end up with unequal results. Indeed, perhaps, it is the improvident Charles to whom she is really giving more. For the pound will double his holdings, whereas it only amounts to a sixth of Henry's vaster possessions.

She thinks on. If her two children had exactly the same desires, or needs, then she would be doing more for Charles. The second pound is bound to be more important than the sixth. However, as she knows, they do not in fact want the same things. Henry's whole fascination is with a game which costs twenty pounds; a toy costing two pounds would equally satisfy Charles. If she gives them both a pound, she will be fully satisfying Charles while Henry will be nearly as far from his dream as before. At this rate he will not be satisfied until Christmas. She would, she might think, be treating them very unequally if she were to give them equal sums of money. Particularly when it is Henry that is so thrifty; it seems funny to pour money into Charles so that he can immediately satisfy his desires. Perhaps the best, or most equal, treatment is to give neither of them anything. She goes to the shop and buys something for herself.

This everyday tale could obviously happily run through several soap serial episodes, playing the variations. But the overall problem is clear. Doing, or supplying, exactly the same thing in different circumstances may produce very unequal results. We have to distinguish between equal procedures and equal outcomes. Equal procedures may not lead to equal outcomes. Conversely, equal outcomes may be the result of quite unequal procedures. The notion of equality applied to the goal, or outcome, seems to be quite different from equality applied to the method, or procedure. As a goal, the requirement is that whatever procedures are adopted, people should end up in similar positions. They should end up, that is, with the same amount of wealth, esteem, power, or whatever it is that is valued. Achieving this may involve treating people in very unequal ways, for example taxing some people harshly in order to redistribute wealth to others who are less well off.

Something like this distinction between equality of procedure and equality of result was behind the conflict between rights and utilities described in Chapter VIII. There it was seen that both these warring partners could be taken as being supported by different applications of equality. Both depended on awareness of all other positions and on treating them equally. In utilitarianism, the equally treated utilities of all are maximised so that the possibility is selected which produces most utility. In rights theory, such maximisation is prevented. But this is by giving everyone, equally, fundamental rights which may not be traded away.

We have already seen both of these applications of equality. The utilitarian dictum 'everybody to count for one, nobody for more than one' has been quoted. All utilities are equal. As was seen in Chapter 6 this naturally leads to a majority voting procedure. We produce the greatest happiness of the greatest number by doing what the greatest number declare themselves (by voting) to want. All utilities are equal. All votes are equal. These equally treated votes lead to the control of the majority. Yet, as we have also just seen, it is precisely to prevent such majority tyranny that we may introduce rights. The sacrifice of individuals by the majority is commonly taken to be one of the chief criticisms of utilitarianism. Equal treatment in voting may lead to very unequal results. Equally regarded utilities, or wills, may lead to the domination of some of these wills over others. An equal input of votes may lead to an unequal output of power or satisfaction.

So such conflicts involving equality are familiar. That equality can be brought in both for and against democracy does not distinguish democracy from other areas. It does not mean that there is a fundamental contradiction in equality, or in democracy. It does mean, however, that we have to look at both equality and its application to democracy more carefully. I said before that equality, like liberty, was a highly contested concept. In fact, it is in an even more difficult position than liberty. Liberty is almost universally thought to be a good; so the contest comes through the attempts to use different conceptions of this agreed positive value in particular applications. With equality, by contrast, not everyone agrees that it is a good. The first thing which people probably take to be meant by equality is equal distribution of property. Yet this is a highly contentious matter; indeed, most people are against it. To say that something would produce equal distribution of property only provides, at best, weak support. To say that something promotes liberty always provides support, to say that it promotes equality may not. Some people in political discussion think that it is a good; some a harm. So to find that democracy does or does not exemplify or promote equality may or may not be taken as a support for it, or as a problem for it.

One answer to this may be to unpick the different uses. In some of its senses or uses, equality may be agreed to be a good; others are more contentious. Another answer is to treat the question in the hypothetical spirit discussed in Chapter VIII. We might assume for the sake of argument that equality is a good, and see whether this provides a support or a problem for democracy. In fact, the two procedures can be combined. Some uses of the concept are much more approved of than others. So it is reasonably safe to assume that these are a positive measure of value. Once they have been applied, then other uses can be examined in a more self-consciously hypothetical or provisional spirit.

The conception of equality which has most support is that of equality of treatment, closely connected with the idea of fairness. The root idea here is that it is right to treat the same kind of case in the same kind of way. That this is a natural, or naturally attractive, idea can be brought out in two interrelated ways. The first is that it follows logically from the idea of giving reasons for a particular course of action. If a reason can be given, justifying a particular course of action, this will be because of some feature of the action itself, or of the situation in which it occurs. (I gave her bread because she was starving; I went back because he was upset; and so on.) Yet if these features serve as a reason, justifying this particular action, they will also serve as reasons justifying the same kind of action wherever else they apply. If we get the same features again, we get the same reason. Of course, other features may differ between the two cases, providing other, countervailing reasons. But, as far as it goes, if our actions are to have reasons and be justified, then we are committed by the sheer nature of reasons to treating the same kind of case in the same kind of way.

This can also be brought out by the kind of objection made by people who think that they are in a similar position to someone else, but have not been treated in a similar kind of way. They naturally feel resentment. Resentment is a moralised emotion. It is a good index for a lack of morality or justification in the action. The particular content of the resentment is best elicited by considering the question which the people so treated might ask the people treating them. This is the question why, since something has been done for someone else, it hasn't also been done for them. Here the logic of giving reasons takes over. If there really was a reason why the thing was done for the other person, and the cases really were similar, then this question is unanswerable. *Ex hypothesi*, no reason distinguishing the cases is available.

This is only a sketch of an account, but I hope that it is sufficient to show how the idea of treating the same kind of case in the same kind of way is rationally defensible; indeed may be taken as axiomatically correct. Yet this is already to endorse one use of equality. It is to say that people in the same position should be treated equally. People who feel resentment when this is not done might say that it was not fair, or they might say that they had not been treated equally. So here is one use of equality which we can use with confidence as a means of criticism or justification. The problem is how, if at all, it applies to democracy.

The problem we found with the question of whether democracy was equal or not was that a method of decision in which people equally participate can lead to very unequal results. We distinguished above between equality of procedure and equality of result, or outcome. Democracy scores on the basis of equality of procedure. It is a procedure which treats everyone equally. Yet it does not score on equality of result. The majority get what they want; the minority do not. An equal procedure of voting may lead to unequal results. Alternatively, more egalitarian results might be achieved by a less egalitarian procedure. For example, a benevolent dictator or oligarchy might force through an equal distribution of property. The people would not have participated equally in the decision, but it is a decision which in its result produces equality. We seem here to have a very sharp distinction between two ways of treating equality. It can be treated as evaluating a method of decision, or procedure; or it can be treated as evaluating a result or outcome. In the first way equality forms a support for democracy; in the second it does not.

We now need to return to the different conceptions of equality, discussed above, and see how they might be applied to these two different applications. In particular we want to see whether the approved, uncontroversial conception of equality, which followed from the idea of giving a reason, can be applied. At first sight it may look as if we have a remarkably good fit, providing an exciting basis for the goodness of democracy. Reasoning is a process, a way of reaching results. Therefore the uncontentious kind of equality which flows from the use of reasons would seem to apply more naturally to process than to results. So, it might seem, it should be especially suitable for supporting procedural equality. On the other hand, the more contentious notion of equality discussed above is one concerned with substantial outcomes, such as the equalisation of wealth. Therefore, it might seem, we have a perfect fit. The kind of equality we can all support, connected with the use of reasons, works in support of egalitarian procedures; hence of democracy. By contrast, the kind of equality which is concerned with the equalisation of goods is not promoted by democracy, but this would not provide a problem because it is a conception which is highly contentious. If this works, it forms a perfect argument relating democracy and equality. We would have a snappy, albeit sophisticated, solution.

Unfortunately, this proposed solution is not so much sophisticated as sophistical. The problem is that the requirement that the same kind of cases should be treated in the same kind of way is purely formal. It does not have sufficient content to arbitrate even between different kinds of procedure. Therefore it cannot be identified with, or taken to provide automatic support for, procedural equality. With democracy the idea is that everyone involved should be equally able to participate in the decision-making. This already goes a long way beyond the merely formal idea of treating the same kind of case in the same kind of way. To extract it from the merely formal idea, it has also to be stipulated that each person, different as they may be in insight, concern, age, knowledge, sex, height, or whatever, are really the same kind of case from the point of view of their appropriate political power. Yet this is precisely the central point that needs to be proved. If they are the same, then of course the provisions of rationality say that they should be treated in the same kind of way. That is, they all should be given the vote. But this is a trivial, uninteresting or automatic, application of the central principle. The work was all done when it was decided that these varying people were, for this purpose, all the same.

The requirement of rationality merely means that anything (or anyone) having the relevant characteristics should be treated equally, at least unless there are other relevant differences. So, to take a democratic example, if it is thought appropriate that the voting age is 18, then anyone over 18 should equally be entitled to vote. But this is only if there are no other relevant features distinguishing them. They are equally entitled to vote; until they are found to be an alien, or insane, or a criminal or whatever. The possibility of such differences shows how easily the requirement can be evaded. All that is required is to find another relevant feature distinguishing between two people. They may then properly be treated differently. The formal notion of equality ceases to have power, and any objection to this in the name of equality must depend upon the substantial notion. This is the hard work, and it is only when this hard work has been done that the purely formal notion can come into play again, silently applying the results so that similar cases are treated in similar ways. The substantial notion says what is a similar case; the formal notion then merely treats similar cases in similar ways.

These perfectly general considerations about reasons and formal equality do not apply any more particularly to democracy than to any other political system. It means that once the appropriate democratic system has been worked out, it will be applied equally in this way; but then this is also true of non-democratic systems. In a democracy, all those fulfilling the requirements of participation will be equally entitled to participate; but this is also true in an oligarchy. All those belonging to the oligarchical class are entitled to participate in an oligarchy. In a monarchy, anyone who is a king has power. In the latter two systems the conditions are drawn more tightly than in a democracy, but argument between the systems is over these conditions, not over the formal equality of their application.

Arguments in favour of procedural equality and democracy, therefore, cannot be directly derived from the mere idea of rationality. However I think that a more indirect approach may be possible, using rationality to give some support to procedural equality, although it is a support which falls well short of conclusive demonstration. The condition that similar cases should be treated in similar ways is not completely without effect. It means, at the very least, that the onus is on someone wishing to treat two cases differently to find a relevant feature which distinguishes them. If there is no such relevant feature, then the two cases should be treated in the same way. So, even though it can be evaded, being the default position gives equality some power.

The kind of more substantive argument that a defender of democracy wishes to use can then be built on the idea of equality as the default. The onus is on the opponent to find a relevant difference. The strongest argument for democracy is that no differences are relevant. Merely being a human being gives the qualification for entry to political rights and power, and no further distinctions are justified. Of course, any proponent of an actual system will in fact propose additional requirements, such as have just been given: age, sanity, nationality; perhaps morality; perhaps sex; and so on. Add property (a stake in the country) and we have quintessential oligarchy. But perhaps this is right: the distinction is one of degree, not kind. What the democrat is proposing is that things should be nearer the end of including people. What the oligarch is proposing is that things should be nearer the end of excluding people. The argument between them, therefore, is about how far along this continuous line one should be. But if it is put like this, then the default idea of treating people equally until relevant differences are established seems to help the democrat. It means that the argument should start at the democratic end. Every distinction between people that takes the system in the direction of oligarchy has to be separately argued for and justified. If distinctions based on age can be justified, then there will be a minimum age requirement for full participation; if distinctions based on sex cannot, then there will be no sex bar on participation. Of course, it may well be possible to make such arguments. But because democracy is the default or initial position, the final position may end up not too far from it.

So far this concerns the arguments for and against political participation. There still remains the problem that equal participation can lead to unequal results, and that equal results could be achieved by systems of unequal participation. We distinguished above between equality of procedure and equality of result or outcome. An argument has just been sketched by which particular kinds of procedure might be easier to justify than others, merely starting from the formal idea of treating the same kind of case in the same kind of way. However, this sort of argument does not just distinguish between the two applications of equality. It can also be applied to results or outcomes. Here as well we can start with the default position that two cases should be treated in the same way until it has been shown that there is a relevant distinction between them. If there is a reason for a particular person having a particular amount of property, then there is a reason for everyone else having the same amount of property, until it is shown that there is a relevant difference between them. Equal property becomes the default state. Having equal property does not need to be further justified; having unequal property does. Of course, such justification may be easy. Differences between two people may be rightfully based on the claim that it is appropriate that one should have more than another. But there being a default state, departure from which needs to be justified, seems to be common to both the procedural and the outcome cases. We not only get an (admittedly weak) argument in favour of equal participation; we also get an (admittedly equally weak) argument in favour of equal distribution of goods. The one works in favour of democracy, the other works against it, and we seem to be back where we started.

This attempt to try and make something of the giving reasons argument, moving it beyond its merely formal or trivial base, therefore, seems to move into the problem that it delivers too much or too little. Either the argument is too weak to be any use or else it delivers implausibly strong conclusions about the desirability of equality of outcomes. So perhaps we should try another approach. Perhaps we have got unnecessarily fixated by the distinction between procedure and outcome. Perhaps this distinction is not as important as has been assumed. After all, states of affairs have many different features. So if two states of affairs are compared, they may well be similar with respect to one feature and not with respect to another. But we need a separate argument to show that any one particular similarity or difference is of any importance. For any two states of affairs, there will be millions of such comparisons which could be made, most of which must be trivial. So, for any particular communal or social decision, different things can be said about it. It can be said what it produces (for example, how wealth in the society is to be divided). It can be said how it was arrived at (for example, by voting and taking a majority). These can both be regarded as features of the decision. But there are numerous other features on which we could concentrate; it is artificial to isolate these two.

It cannot be denied that every state of affairs has many features. So, if we were aiming at some kind of overall evaluation such as happens in utilitarianism, we should compare any two situations by considering all these different features. We would score each feature for utility or whatever, add them up and choose the alternative which provides the most attractive total. In one circumstance a procedure might be outranked by results; in another the procedure would win; in others a quite different kind of feature might be preferred, and nothing systematic could be said about it. However the point at present is not to try and apply utilitarianism, in which equality, like anything else, would be a mere means to an end. The present concern is to isolate and evaluate the importance of equality in its connections with democracy. So we are engaged on a kind of factor analysis, distinguishing different factors and analysing them separately. We want to examine the features which are particularly connected with democracy and see how they rate for equality. Among these is clearly the majority voting procedure. This feature is intrinsically connected with our normal familiar type of democracy.

This is the justification for considering procedure. As regards output, or consequences, the position is less clear. Obviously consequences which are necessarily connected with the democratic method should be considered. But the looser the connection is, the less important it is to consider them. We talked above of unequal outcomes arising from different people having different power. But it is important to distinguish between different ways in which they may have unequal power. We might be saying that the majority have more power than the minority because they gain more wealth, property, prestige or whatever. These are distinguishable consequences which are only, at best, contingently connected with the democratic process. Or we could be saying that the majority has more power because it is their will, rather than the minority's, which is put into effect. This latter consequence is an essential outcome of majoritarian democracy.

So while we may allow that there are many different features of any social situation, only a few of them are closely connected with the operations of democracy. We have a close, intrinsic connection with a particular kind of procedure. We have an intimate connection with outcomes described in a highly specific manner. There may also be looser, and therefore in this context less important, connections with such goods as wealth or prestige. But this keeps the situation under control. It would seem also to show that the concentration on the distinction between procedure and result is not a mistake. However concentration on this distinction could now come under attack from a different direction. Rather than it being claimed that this distinction is not important because there are so many distinctions, it might be claimed that this distinction is not important because, when we are considering equality, no distinction is important. For it could be argued that equalities are strongly correlated, so that inequality in one dimension goes with inequality in another. Hence the argument would be that if we are considering equality, it does not matter which feature we consider. For it may very well be held, as in Rousseau, that democratic procedures will not work properly if there are too great inequalities of power. Different equalities may be connected. People with very unequal wealth may not be able to enjoy equality of participation. They may formally all have a vote; but what this means will be very unequal in terms of political power. We saw, in Chapter VII, Marx's description of this, by which people pretend equality in a political heaven to disguise their real inequality on earth. With different property, they have different control over people's lives, they have different power. With different power, they have different political power. So even if the system allows equal formal participation, this is not really equal participation as long as there are other inequalities. Therefore, the contrast between equality of procedure and equality of outcome when considering democracy is not significant.

In fact, if we consider the distribution of wealth, then democracy probably does not score too badly. The points made by Rousseau and Marx are about what happens when we use standard democratic procedures in a world which already has greatly unequal amounts of property, and so of power. But, as was seen from the tale of Henry and his mother, doing equal things in an unequal world naturally produces unequal results. Also, we are only concerned at present with the effects of particular factors. We want to know what effects democracy might have, in itself, on wealth distribution. So far as this goes, its effects will generally be egalitarian. Of course, as has just been pointed out, the connection with any wealth distribution is at best contingent, and quite likely loose. Also, equality of wealth was the more doubtfully supported application of equality with which we started. So even if democracy, loosely and generally, leads to equalisation of wealth, this may at best only form some kind of hypothetical support. Yet, as far as it goes, democracy is likely to remove great disparities. It is likely to score better on standard measures of inequality. A small group of the very rich is less likely to survive with all its assets intact.

The majority are more likely to have some wealth in a democracy, for obvious reasons. Indeed it will be remembered that the worries about democracy from people as diverse as Aristotle and J. S. Mill were that it would lead to an attack on property, rather than that it would promote the property of the wealthy. Of course, if it is a minority who are (relatively) badly off, then it does not have such an equalising tendency. The unemployed or dispossessed, as long as they form a relatively small minority, may well be ignored.

The reply to these arguments, therefore, is as follows. There may be some correlation between equalities. However, this doesn't necessarily mean that democracy has inegalitarian implications in its product, or output. For, first, any output in terms of wealth is only loosely correlated with the decision procedure. Second, the equality of the decision procedure is likely to have a tendency towards an equality of outcome, a tendency which is masked if we start with situations of great inequality. Third, and most importantly, we should distinguish between outcomes. Some of these are much more closely connected to the actual process of democracy than others. The inequality of power that may result from some wills being put into effect rather than others is more immediately connected with the nature of democracy than any inequality of power resulting from an uneven distribution of wealth.

So the general theme of this chapter, concentrating on procedure and outcome, can be defended. The original problem, which arose from distinguishing between these two features, and seeing how they are connected in different ways with equality, remains a genuine one. This can be shown by demonstrating that it can arise even if there are no great inequalities of wealth or antecedent power. The problem does not just arise through trying to apply an equal procedure to an unequal world, as with Henry's mother and his pocket money. For in the sort of small face-to-face examples used in the previous chapters we need not have any such inequality of property or power. We, of roughly equal wealth (or other sorts of power), may have to decide on what to do with our street or club. Suppose that we do this democratically, giving people equal say. The question can still be asked whether this is really an egalitarian procedure given that some people will get what they want using this method and some will not.

For example, Henry and Charles, still under the expert tutelage of their mother, have now reached their teens. They belong to the same tennis club. They both now have sufficient wealth easily to pay their subscriptions and buy their equipment. So differential wealth is irrelevant. The club is running a league competition which they both badly want to win, and it has to decide how many sets should be played in each match. Some members are in favour of matches being decided by the best of three sets; some are in favour of a single set. (The former is felt to be more testing; the latter allows more matches to be played.) The club is a democratic club in which all the teenagers equally take part, and matters are decided by majority decision. Now Henry, as a tennis player, is a good starter. He normally wins the first set, but then he gets tired. Charles, by contrast, is a stayer. The matches he wins he usually wins in the third set. The club votes. The single set party has the majority. So Henry gets what he wants and Charles does not. Both of them featured equally in the vote. They had equal participation. But Henry is now likely to finish much higher in the league than Charles. Their mother contemplates again. Henry has got much more out of the vote than Charles. With equal inputs, and no background differences of power, the result is unequal. She doubts whether this is right. She wonders about buying something for the unfortunate Charles to compensate him. But, on the other hand, it is also not clear that the decision was wrong. And Henry has won a handsome trophy. She goes back to the shop but decides, again, to buy something for herself.

This shows that the basic question is real. It continues to be real even when we move to questions more directly concerned with the distribution of wealth. Suppose, to finish the saga before it is finally taken off the air in response to adverse audience reaction, that we return to Charles and Henry. They are now grown up and released from mother. They are ready to participate in national decision-making. This time we might compare their position in two different systems for making such decisions. Under the first they both vote. That is, they participate equally in elections. However, lucky Henry again belongs to the majority; the vote is about a particular type of taxation; and the result leaves him considerably better off than Charles. The condition they are in in the end is unequal. It is even worse than the episode of the pocket money (which, for those just joining the story, they did not get). Alternatively, they might be in a system in which, mother having departed, the state takes over her role. It decides for them. They do not participate, let alone participate equally. But the good state does even better than mother did. It manages to distribute burdens and goods between them so that they end up in positions of roughly equal satisfaction. Here are two systems, with different features. Just as with the pocket money, which system is egalitarian depends upon which feature is important.

So we still have the original problem. It is not trivial. The question of which of the two systems just discussed should be preferred seems to be a genuine question. If mother had still been around, she would have had problems. Wanting nothing but the best for her children and wanting to act equally between them, she might still be stuck comparing a system which treated them all equally in procedure and one which did even better than a mother with respect to equality of outcomes. The question between procedural and outcome features is genuine and difficult. Of course, which feature is preferred may depend upon the particular circumstances. We might use a general consequential method, such as utilitarianism, for comparison of all features. We can still meaningfully concentrate on the two features of intrinsic procedure and inevitable outcome, and ask how they compare. Our problem remains. To solve it, it seems, we would have to be able to say which of procedure or outcome was more important.

Putting the question in this way may now make it look as if it no longer has anything to do with equality. Once we have decided whether procedure or outcome is the more important good, that will be the end of the matter. Once it has been found to be a good, equal distribution of that good would be recommended, and democracy accordingly either justified or criticised. Equality might now seem to have become invisible. All the work is done elsewhere, deciding which goods there are, and which are more important. If participation is important, we might go one way; if outcome, another. In neither case, it seems, has this anything to do with equality. So equality seems to be invisible.

This, however, is only partially right. It is right that an argument comparing procedures with outcomes need have nothing directly to do with equality. But it is wrong to think that this makes equality invisible. There are questions about equality as well as about other goods. For it is not that, once we have found what is important, equality silently takes over and tells us how it should be supplied. This is because once we have decided that something is a good, we still have to decide how that good should be distributed. Equality of distribution is only one among many distributions, and we need further reasons telling us which one to adopt. This can be seen clearly for wealth and other private property. These are normally thought to be goods. It is better to have them than not to have them; and having more of them is better than having less. Yet, as remarked above, it may not be thought better to have an equal than an unequal distribution of them. So something may be agreed to be a good without agreeing that equality is the best way of distributing it. There is still work, therefore, for arguments for equality to do. In the present context, with respect to democracy, it can be agreed that participation is a good, without agreeing that equal participation is a good; or it can be agreed that wealth is a good, without being agreed that equal wealth is a good. Equality may apply differently in these two cases; which, in turn, means that it may still be possible to distinguish procedural from outcome equality.

This locates the default argument more precisely. If nothing else is known, then equal distribution of the good is appropriate. For no reasons are, *ex hypothesi*, available in favour of any other distri-bution. Other things being equal, as the phrase goes, we should also be equal with these things. However, this now means that we can tell when this breaks down and we have cases in which something is a good without equal distribution of it also being a good. One example is when there is another good, so that we get more of what we want of the other good by unequal distribution of this one. This is the obvious example, and the one we have been concerned with through-out. However, there are other examples. One of these concerns nothing but the good itself. If we enquire into its condition of production, we may discover that we get more of the good if it is produced in a way which leads to uneven distribution. Since more of the good is generally better than less, we may well think that this greater unequal distribution is better than a lesser equal distribution. This is normally, for example, why people may favour unequal distributions of wealth; they think that this arises in circumstances in which there is greater total wealth; or, if they are more squeamish, in which there is more wealth for everyone. There are other examples. There are positional goods, which cannot exist at all unless they are unequally distributed. I may want to be the best swimmer in the city; but being the best swimmer is not a good to me if everyone else in the city is an equally good swimmer. I may want the last house in the town before the country starts. This is undoubtedly a good, with marvellous country views and convenient access to the town. But, again, it is not a good which can be equally distributed to everyone. Once we have decided on what is a good, therefore, we need to go on and examine whether this good should or should not be equally distributed. Equality will not be the automatic answer.

We can now return to the question of procedure and outcome. There are now three problems to solve if equality is to work as a support for democracy. First, it has to be shown that the democratic procedure is a good. Second, the goodness of the procedure has to be such that equality is the appropriate distribution, rather than one of the other kinds just mentioned. Third, this has to be compared with the goodness of democratic outcomes, which includes consideration of the best form of distribution for these outcomes. The first problem has already been solved. In the last chapter it was shown that participation in the processes of government is a good to the participants because it is an exercise of liberty. Power, as exercised in liberty or autonomy, is a good. It helps people to get what they want. Someone who participates in government exercises such power or autonomy.

So we can take it that the democratic procedure, which involves participation, is a good. The next question is why it should follow from this that it is a good which ought to be equally distributed. The default argument says that, other things being equal, it should be. So we need to look at the kinds of cases in which other things are not equal, as these were sketched above, and see whether any of them applies to participation. We can first dispense with positional goods. There is, of course, a kind of good which comes from having a power which no one else has. People generally enjoy distinction. However, the good of participation, or the power of controlling one's life, is not such that it is damaged or eliminated by its possession also by others. We want control. We want to realise our wills. As was seen in the last chapter, this is precisely a reason for general participation. However, there is nothing in the process of participation which means that, if one person has it, another cannot. It is not a positional good.

We might of course want unequal distribution of this good in order to get more of another. But this is just the familiar question of comparing one good with another, which we have already examined, and to which we shall return. There remains the possibility that we might want unequal distribution of the good in order to get more of the good itself, just as unequal distribution of wealth might go with having more wealth. The possibility to consider is whether we might get more of the good involved in participation if participation is unequally distributed. Here we have to careful about exactly which good is involved. We might loosely call it power. But then it is plausible that there might be a greater amount of power if it is unequally distributed. It is a standard problem about democracies that they are not as fast or decisive as systems in which just a few people have the power of decision. Dictators are even more decisive. However, as was discussed in the last chapter, the power in question here is that of autonomy. It is the power of having control over one's own life. This is not maximised by giving control to a few people, or to one. On the contrary, it is the sort of good for which, the more people have it, the more there is. With more autonomous people, there is more autonomy. So there is nothing about the good which is involved in participation in government to suggest that an unequal distribution is appropriate. The default argument then takes over. If participation is a good, which it is, it is also a good that it be equally distributed.

So we have solved the first two problems. Participation is a good; and it is a good which should be distributed equally. There remains the question of how the goodness of participation compares with the goodness of outcomes, and what sort of distribution is best for these outcomes. Remembering the last chapter, there may still look to be a sizeable problem. For although the expression of power involved in participation may be equal in a democracy, it was seen there that its exercise may not be. Some people, the majority, whose wills are put into effect, seem to end up with more control or power than others. It is presumably a good to have one's will put into effect. It is another kind of power. Yet this is a kind of power which seems to be unequally distributed. So the outcome of democratic choice still forms a rival to the procedural good of participation; and this still seems to be a good which is unequally distributed.

In effect, this inequality of distribution was also considered in the last chapter. There it was said that, although liberty was a good, the only way that it can be promoted by democracy (or indeed by any government) is if it is possible to trade off liberty. We gain liberty in a democracy by purchasing one bit at the price of relinquishing another bit. Total freedom means no government at all, anarchy. The price of effective freedom is effective government. And the price of effective government is some relinquishing of freedom.

Now this argument may have worked very well in the context of the last chapter when we were considering autonomy or liberty. However it seems to be more problematic in the context of the present one. For what we are now considering is not whether something is a good but, rather, whether it is a good which should be equally distributed. And it seems that we get more of this good if it is not equally distributed. The arguments of the last chapter should, perhaps, be accepted. But accepting these arguments seems to make autonomy a good like wealth. For both, we are naturally in favour of situations in which we get more of them rather than less. Unfortunately, however, these situations are ones of unequal rather than equal distribution. We get as much autonomy or control as we can. We maximise freedom. More people have it with majority rule than have it in a dictatorship or an oligarchy. So majority rule is a better system. Some people, it is true, do not have control. This, however, is a cost which has to be paid if we are to have any government at all.

This may justify it; but the fact remains that people are being treated unequally by the majoritarian procedure. Some of them have power and some do not.

As seen above, this sort of immediate and essential outcome of the democratic process should be distinguished from such more remote outcomes as the distribution of wealth and power. In certain circumstances a majority of the population will bear down unfairly on a minority, taking away their possessions or power. Then, as discussed in the last chapter, this minority will not be free. But this is the case only when there is a built-in majority which can be independently identified. One race or religion may form a separate, self-conscious, group, which is the largest part of the population. With majority voting this group may well remove other, minority, groups from goods or power. Then we have dictatorship of the majority with a vengeance. The outcomes are unequal, and, even if we might only be weakly in favour of an equal distribution of property, it seems to be unfair. If this happens, then there are reasons for limiting the democratic processes in the name of equality or fairness. Such limitation might be attempted by a theory of rights, and I shall return to this question in the last chapter.

This kind of domination by an independently specifiable group, such as the members of a particular race, is quite different, however, from the control by the majority which is an intrinsic part of the democratic decision procedure itself. Only the latter is an inevitable part of the process and, engaged as we are in a factor analysis, it is the only thing which needs to be considered fully here. This, of course, is also unequal. But it is unequal in a different way, which, by contrast, seems to be fair.

In democracy only the input to decisions is equal. Each vote counts equally. The output, however, is not equal. The will expressed in some votes gets put into effect; the will expressed in other votes does not. However, this should no longer worry us. The inevitability cuts both ways. This output (as opposed to the rule of a race or religion) is the inevitable consequence of a system which has equality enshrined in its input. The input, the democratic procedure, is the core of the system. Here equality applies. Part, but only part, of the point of this input is that there should be output. We would prefer, of course, that there should be equal output. This does not normally happen (although there could, exceptionally, be unanimous agreement). But we cannot get any output at all unless this is so. Equality at the output point is not preserved because this is essential for having any input; and so for having equal input.

We can only use the majoritarian system of decision-making, with all the control of our lives which it entails, if some people get more of what they want than others. Yet the democratic input is at the heart of the system. It is essentially what the system is all about. It is the most important thing to consider in a factor analysis; it is democracy's most essential or intrinsic property. Yet here democracy is egalitarian. Equality is at its heart. Equality at this position gives it a moral foundation. It is one of the reasons in its favour. Equality is in the heart of the democratic system, if not, perhaps, its final cause. But final causes are saved for the final chapter.

CHAPTER XII

Threading some Paradoxes

Up to now it has been assumed that there is no intrinsic problem in taking a set of individual desires, preferences and judgments and deriving from them a single judgment which can stand as the democratic judgment of the group as a whole. The questions or problems have all been about the appropriateness of using this judgment as that of the group; whether, for example, it may not infringe individual autonomy or lead to less good decisions than the use of a group of experts would. Problems about the protection of individuals or the protection of minorities may mean that simple majority judgment (of those voting) is not necessarily the most appropriate method of reaching a group decision. Sometimes unanimity, or at least a much higher proportion than a mere majority, may be thought to be appropriate. However, these are again problems about the appropriateness of various sorts of decision procedure. It is still assumed that there is no intrinsic, or technical, problem about deriving these various social judgments from individual preferences. The only problem considered is whether such derivations are desirable or appropriate.

However, for at least two hundred years, it has been known that there are intrinsic problems and paradoxes about majority voting as a group decision procedure. More recently fairly technical research has thrown up numerous problems with all kinds of public or social decision procedures. Anyone who assumes that they can just take a set of individual preferences and derive from them a single social judgment is walking unsuspectingly through a minefield. Of course they may arrive safely at the other side. If there is just a single issue, with two options, to be decided by straight majority preference, then they will get through. Several of the examples in earlier chapters were of this kind. But all the time the mines have been very near. With the cases altered only slightly, we might have run into unsuspected problems. We cannot therefore rely on luck to get us through. So in this chapter, without getting particularly technical, I shall look at some of the intrinsic problems of deriving a social judgment from individual preferences. We must look at some paradoxes or problems to see whether it is a mere matter of luck whether democratic procedures produce other than arbitrary results. Defending democracy against various moral objections will have had little point if this is so. We need to see whether we have so far been sleepwalking through the dangers. We have to see whether there is at least a partially sighted (partially rational) way in which this minefield can be threaded.

The simplest case which illustrates the problems is one which has been known and considered for a long time. Suppose that we have three possible outcomes and we have to reach a group decision about which to adopt. Call these three outcomes *a*, *b* and *c*. Suppose that the group consists of three persons (or can be divided into three equal parts), called X, Y and Z. Now suppose the persons (or three equal parts) have the following preferences:

X prefers *a* to *b* and *b* to *c*
Y prefers *b* to *c* and *c* to *a*
Z prefers *c* to *a* and *a* to *b*

These people clearly differ from each other, but then people do. It must be the business of democracy, as of any significant social decision procedure, to arrive at a unique result constructed out of people's disagreement. It would be just too easy if the decision procedure only worked when everyone agreed with each other, declaring the unanimously agreed choice to be the decision of the community. So disagreement between people cannot be in itself an insuperable problem for a decision procedure. Furthermore the described pattern of preferences is not grotesque. It is a perfectly possible, indeed plausible, pattern. Each person's preferences are, in themselves, absolutely consistent. So here is a pattern of preferences and disagreement which any reasonable social decision procedure should be able to handle. More specifically, if we believe in democracy, we would want there to be a democratically derivable result in cases like this.

The most common democratic procedure is to take votes between pairs of options and adopt as the group decision that option which receives more votes. That is, the option which receives more votes is held to be preferred by the community to the option which receives fewer votes. This is the way in which it was assumed that democracy worked in the last three chapters. However, if we try to use this method of voting on pairwise comparisons in the present case we are obviously in trouble. Suppose we have a vote on *a* and *b*. The winner is *a* by two votes to one. Then we try *b* and *c*. This time *b* wins by two to one. Finally, for the last pair, *a* and *c*. Here *c* wins over *a*. Suppose we now try to put this together to see what the decision of the group should be, as derived by majority voting. Clearly, it would seem, *a* is to be preferred to *b*, which is to be preferred to *c*, which is to be preferred to *a*, which . . . . We are in trouble. Nor is this trouble which we can get out of by saying that the social choice (the decision of the community) is indifferent between the three outcomes. Although that might seem, on the face of it, the just result, it does not follow from the votes just given. For they showed (using majority decision-making) that the community actually preferred having *a* to *b*, actually preferred *b* to *c*, and so on. In each case one was judged to be better than the other. So it cannot be said that the result is indifference. It seems more obvious that the result is a contradiction: *a* is better than *b*, which is better than *c*, which is better than *a*.

This looks bad for democracy as a method of social decision-making. Perhaps we should try other methods of voting. We could, for example, take any one of the particular outcomes and vote on whether to have it or whether to have either of the others. However, each one would be defeated by two to one. Whatever is chosen, there is a majority against it. This can scarcely make us think that the result is democratically sanctioned. Or, alternatively, if we want results to be democratically sanctioned, we still do not seem to have a result. We could extend this procedure by first running one of the outcomes against both the others, as just described, and then, if the others win, run them against each other. This now does give a result. For example, if we start with *a*, first the others win, then *b* beats *c*. The question is whether the result is appropriate. It would have been different if we had changed the order of voting. If, for example, we had first run *b* against the others, then *c* would have won; if *c*, then *a* would have won. The result depends entirely on the apparently irrelevant or random fact of which order the vote is taken in. This cannot give us much confidence in its fairness or validity. A similar thing happens if we treat the vote like a knock-out competition, giving one outcome a bye into the second round. Whichever outcome is given the bye wins (if c is given the bye, a beats b, and then is beaten by c in the play-off). Again the result depends upon the apparently arbitrary fact of the order in which the votes are taken. Again the result can surely not be invested with any particular democratic significance.

It may be thought that too much has been made here of just one example. After all, any proposed system which is to work in the real world may have difficulties with one or two cases. The preferences in the hypothetical example clearly have a symmetrical, cyclic, structure which is going to make it hard for any decision procedure. Since they seem to be balanced, any answer is likely to seem arbitrary, favouring the views of one person over others for no particularly good reason. This fortunate one person will seem to be in the position of a petty dictator, laying down the general social policy so that it mirrors their own individual preferences and is completely impervious to the views of anyone else. But perhaps we just get occasional dictators. Perhaps these quirks just happen. Perhaps this case should be dismissed with the assumption that at least majoritarian democracy works unproblematically most of the time, but that occasionally it will not produce an intrinsically satisfactory answer.

Whether it is just a quirk or not does depend on how frequent (or likely) this sort of case is. This in turn depends upon the nature of the individual preferences which the democratic machine is meant to turn fairly into a single social judgment. Unsurprisingly, it is their cyclical nature in the above example which does the damage, and it has been shown that if everyone's preferences can be placed on a single scale so that each person ranks their preferences according to the distance from their preferred point, then this kind of problem will not arise. Even if they have different preferred points on the scale, as long as each set of preferences has this structure, then there will be no problems in their aggregation. For example, suppose that the decision is about the amount of money to spend on something. The preferences here can be placed along a single dimension from more money to less money. People may have different most-preferred points, but the important thing is that they rank their preferences according to the distance from their own preferred point. One person may prefer: best, spend a lot of money; next best, spend a middle amount of money; worst, spend little money. Another might reverse these preferences. All that is important is that they rank outcomes according to the distance from their preferred point.

What does the damage is if someone thinks that the ideal order is something like: best, spend a lot of money; next best, spend a little money; worst, spend a middling sum of money. Such a person's preferences are not, in the jargon that applies to this area, single peaked. If such a person exists, then we are in trouble. This is what happened in the original example with Z. If we think of the outcomes *a, b,* and *c* as amounts of money, then both the choices of X and Y are single-peaked. Both X and Y, that is, have a preferred sum of money and rank the others compatibly with the distance away from this preference. X wants to spend a little money, and the more that would be spent the less it is preferred. Y wants to spend a middling some of money, ranks it top, and the others after. If a graph were drawn of either of their preferences, it would have a single peak, with the other outcomes falling away from it (although the peak would be in a different position). But Z is like the person just described who thinks that the worst thing would be to spend a middling amount of money. He or she prefers either of the end points to the middle. Viewed along a single dimension, the preferences peak twice. Once the democratic machine tries to incorporate them, it is in trouble.

My presentation has been informal, but the result can be formally demonstrated. Assuming that this is so, let us now consider what light it throws on whether the original example was just a quirk. This obviously now depends upon the answer to the question of how likely, or how plausible, are people with preferences which are not single peaked. We can continue to consider this in terms of spending sums of money, since there is then an obvious single dimension (more or less money) and since this is a very common type of political decision (that is, it is not arbitrary or artificial). It might seem at first that anyone having other than single-peaked preferences was being irrational or arbitrary. Surely, the first thought might be, if there is a dimension and a preferred point, then the other outcomes should be ranked according to how far away they are from this point. We are relying on spatial metaphors here, and this is normally (although not universally) true if we are literally moving to points in space. If I am trying to get to central London then, generally speaking, I prefer a method of travel which would take me near the centre to one which would land me in outer London, and prefer that to one that would land me in Birmingham. Yet even here it is not difficult to think of cases in which this is not so (communications from Birmingham may be faster than from the outer suburbs; I may have other reasons why I dislike the suburbs; and so on).

Once we turn to money, this is even more obvious. Money may form a single dimension, but the preferences which are turned into preferred sums of money may have many sources, and this may mean that the way the order of preferences comes out pays scant respect to the dimension of money. One common thought, expressed in many aphorisms, is that there is no point doing things by halves; that if you are in for a penny, you are in for a pound; that being in the middle is the worst of both worlds; and so on. In other words, you may find it difficult to decide whether or not something expensive should be done (building a hospital, getting a new defence system, engaging in a local improvement). But you may be certain that, if it is to be done at all, then it should be done properly. That is, whether or not it is decided to do it, what is pointless is both to do it and also to skimp it. In these circumstances, the preference order will be double-peaked along the dimension of money. Whether the small spend or the large spend option is the highest, they are both higher than a middle amount of spending. The preferences are like Z in the first example. Yet what we have here is a frequent and surely not irrational preference order. So the cases in which we have such non-single-peaked preferences can hardly be dismissed as being mere quirks or oddities.

This example used money, where at least there is a natural dimension. If selection of the dimension itself is also somewhat arbitrary, then we are even more likely to get such results. Suppose the choice before X, Y and Z was that between three candidates a, b and c (for an election to some kind of representative council or parliament). There are many factors, toughness, cleverness, honesty, integrity and so on, each of which might allow the candidates to be placed on a dimension (a is cleverer than b, who is cleverer than c). However, X, Y and Z may disagree about the relative importance of the factors expressed in these dimensions even if they agree how the candidates rank on any particular dimension. This could easily lead to their having all kinds of preferences. They might agree, for example, that the right way to rank them for cleverness was best: a; next b; next c. Their preferences might even be single-peaked along each dimension (even though, as before, it would be perfectly possible to prefer someone who was totally honest or totally dishonest to one who was half honest; the thought being that if someone is going to be dishonest, they might as well make a good job of it). Yet X, Y and Z might still disagree about whether toughness was more important than cleverness, integrity than toughness and so on. Each could think that a different factor was supreme. So in spite of all their agreement they might still arrive at the preferences in the original example. We would be in trouble again.

I claimed at the start that the preferences in the original example, austerely oversimplified as it may be, are quite plausible. Nothing since suggests to me that I was wrong. So I do not see that in general this sort of case could be properly ignored as being a mere quirk (although of course any particular example may always be brushed to one side). Therefore, rather than ignoring these kinds of cases, it seems that a theory of democracy should be able to handle them. It might seem that the simplest way to do this would be something quite close to ignoring them. This would be to recognise the existence of problematic cases, but then dismiss their relevance. Democracy, it could be claimed, is a partial decision procedure. It should not be expected to get an answer the whole time. However, I think that this is an unsatisfactory response. By its nature, it refuses to produce answers at times when we might like them. More seriously, it is not possible to tell whether a particular case is one to be dismissed in this way or one for which there is indeed a democratic decision. Think again of the first example. On some suggested ways of handling it there was indeed no answer (or any answer was obviously inconsistent). These, perhaps, could be dismissed. But, on other ways of handling it we did get a (consistent) result. The problem was rather that the result we got seemed to be totally arbitrary. It depended, for example, on the irrelevant fact of the order in which votes were taken. So just dismissing cases when there is no answer is not enough. We need some way of distinguishing the cases where there is an answer into those which are proper operations of the democratic procedure and into those which are not. And for this we need more theory. We cannot just say that democracy is a partial decision procedure which sometimes does not produce answers. We have to discover more about what sort of decision procedure it is, and when it may reliably be applied.

This is not therefore a useful solution. However, even in the original case it seemed that we could do better than this. Rather than not reaching an answer at all, it seemed that there was a perfectly good answer. This is that the right social choice of the group is that it should be indifferent between the three outcomes. The preferences, that is, seem to be perfectly balanced. Each outcome seems to receive exactly the same measure of support, being one person's first choice, another person's second choice, and someone else's last choice. If the three individuals are treated equally, therefore, as good democratic theory requires, and if we have to produce a single social decision out of this, surely the right decision is that all the three outcomes should be ranked equally; society is indifferent between them. Notice this is quite different from saying that there is no decision, or even from saying that they should be counted equally because there is no decision. Here there is the positive judgment, derived from the individual judgments, that they should count equally.

If this instinct about a possible solution is correct, then we should not try and handle this kind of case, in which there are more than two alternatives, by simple pairwise comparison. Instead it would seem to be preferable to use a more sophisticated method, which collects more information, such as the so-called Borda count. (The paradox we started with is sometimes named after Condorcet; both Condorcet and Borda were late eighteenth-century Frenchman interested in the theory of voting.) In the Borda count, everyone assigns points to their preferences, giving most points for their first preference, one less for the second and so on. It can easily be seen that if the three people (or groups) in the original example voted in this way, then the three outcomes would come out equally, each having the same number of points. Something like the Borda count, then, would seem to accord better with the intuitions lying behind democratic decision theory. However, we are not out of the minefield yet. As will be seen, there are problems about the Borda count. Merely adopting it does not mean that we need think no more; we could still run into an explosion. First, however, let us examine why the Borda count might satisfy our intuitions better.

One way it could be considered is as a sort of satisfaction score with a particular outcome: the most favoured outcome would give three units of satisfaction, the next two units, and so on. So what we would be trying to discover by voting is how various outcomes would satisfy people. As such, the Borda count may remind us of the utilitarian defence of democracy in which it was supposed that people's votes revealed what would give them satisfaction (or utility) and that following the majority leads to the greatest happiness of the greatest number. With the Borda count it has been made more sophisticated: we do not just get the result that a particular outcome would satisfy someone but also some measure of how much it would satisfy them. But measurement is grist to the utilitarian mill. Adding up these scores, treating everyone equally as in traditional utilitarian theory, we are even more likely to be approaching the holy grail of the greatest happiness of the greatest number.

Once we realise that the Borda count has similarities to the utilitarian defence of democracy, we are in familiar territory. So familiar objections to utilitarianism can be redeployed against it. It can be objected, as it was in Chapter VI, that votes do not reveal potential satisfaction but evaluative (or moral) judgments. However suppose we waive these kinds of objections for the moment and concentrate on what is surely the central question. This is the viability of the key assumption that it is possible to derive a single judgment about social utility, or welfare, given people's individual utilities. Distinguishing this key assumption means that we are, once again, in well-trodden territory and so can benefit from the considerable amount of precise and careful work which has been done in this area. The central idea here is of a social welfare function, a function which would take sets of functions relating the welfare of individuals to possible outcomes and produce from them a combined single function. The central result is the famous Arrow impossibility theorem which shows that, if very modest assumptions are made, then it is not possible to have such a function. It is Arrow's results which lie behind some of the conclusions presented episodically so far, and this is recognised when the impossibility theorem is called the Condorcet-Arrow theorem. Given Arrow's assumptions, it can be presumed that his result follows. So, for our purposes, the most important thing is to see what these assumptions are, and what they and the conclusion mean. If we understand the assumptions, we then know what we have to avoid if we wish to avoid his conclusions.

One of Arrow's assumptions is what he calls non-dictatorship. This is the assumption that the group choice should not be dictated by the choice of one member. Obviously if we were allowed dictatorship, we could always reach social decisions: we would just nominate one person and say that their preferences were to count as the social choice. We could, for example, reach a social decision in our original example by saying that only X's preferences were to count. However the interesting question is not whether social choice is possible or impossible but, rather, the conditions of its possibility. That is, the plausibility of the assumptions from which impossibility follows. Dictatorship is a nasty name and, in barring it, we want to make sure that we are not barring something which is really more innocent. What non-dictatorship actually means in this special context is that it must not be the case that the social decision mirrors the preferences of one individual, whatever the others' preferences were. In proofs of Arrow's theorem we do not get nasty individuals strutting around and ordering other people about; we only get a demonstration that certain correlations must hold between the preferences of one individual (or group) and the preferences of society as a whole. A mere correlation might not seem to deserve such a harsh name. After all, in a straight vote on a single issue, using the majority decision method, if I am in the majority my preferences are mirrored by society. I prefer *a* to *b,* and this is correlated with society's preferring *a* to *b.* However, in such cases, I am not a dictator in Arrow's sense. For if other people had changed their preferences, I would then have been in a minority. So my preferences are not decisive, whatever anyone else's preferences are. The correlation that the assumption rules out is the correlation between one person's preferences and that of society, whatever anyone else's preferences are; and it may seem more plausible to call this dictatorship.

Once this has been spelled out, then this does seem to be a reasonable assumption, whatever it should be called. Luckily, however, we do not need to try and establish this here since what we are interested in is only the application of Arrow's theorem to the theory of democracy. And, whatever is the case generally, we certainly do not want a democratic decision procedure to be an example of what Arrow calls dictatorship. The whole point of democracy is that it should take the opinions, or votes, of many people (of all the people) and use them as a basis for a decision about what society should do. In this decision they all have, in some way, to count; every individual participating has to have some sort of status. If we just solved the original problem by deciding to do everything which X said, this would always give us a decision; but it could not be a democratic decision because in it the views of Y and Z would be totally ignored. Whatever they thought, on whatever occasion, could necessarily never affect the result. So I think that, for our purposes, we can accept the assumption of non-dictatorship as specifying one aim of democratic procedures. If we are to avoid Arrow's conclusion, this is not the assumption which we should set aside.

We should therefore move on to other assumptions. Arrow assumes rationality. He assumes that preferences are consistent. This narrows the task of the social welfare function, or social decision procedure. The job is to take individual profiles of preferences, which are in themselves consistent, and produce a consistent public profile from them. Rationality and consistency mean that *a* cannot be preferred to *b* and also *b* preferred to *a*. (What I call preference here and throughout is called by the experts strict preference; strict preference just means that something is actually preferred; that is, it rules out indifference.) Rationality also includes the transitivity of preference. That is, if *a* is preferred to *b* and *b* to *c*, then *a* has to be preferred to *c*. In the particular example with which we started, one way of putting the problem was that the preferences which were democratically derived offended against this requirement: *a* was preferred to *b*, which was preferred to *c*, which was preferred to *a*.

Listing these assumptions shows ways of avoiding Arrow's result. Surely, it might be said, individuals are not consistent like this. So why should it be supposed that they are; and why should society be required to be more consistent than individuals sometimes are. In this spirit we might just accept the result of the original example. What society's judgment was, we would say, is that *a* just is preferred to *b*; *b* just is preferred to *c*; and *c* just is preferred to *a*. However, it seems to me that this would be a highly unsatisfactory response. Individuals are indeed sometimes inconsistent, but we cannot allow them very much inconsistency before it becomes very doubtful what their preferences actually are. Notice that in my first formulation here I just took it as obvious that if *a* is preferred to *b*, then *b* cannot also be preferred to *a*. Yet, if we allow transitivity, this is exactly what happens in the original example. Society prefers both *a* to *c* and *c* to *a*. If we block this by denying transitivity then we cannot say what society's preferences are. In the individual case, if someone tells me that they prefer *a* to *b*, *b* to *c*, and *c* to *a*, it seems to me that I have no idea what their real preferences are. Indeed, it is doubtful if they have any. I am certainly not inclined to think that they just happen to have these funny preferences. (Notice, as before, that all this is quite different from saying that they are indifferent between them; here someone claims really to prefer *a* to *b,* and so on.) If we do not assume rationality in the individual case then we cannot really attribute preferences to individuals, since to do this we have to assume that preferences are reflected in behaviour, and this assumes a fair amount of consistency both in the preferences themselves and between preferences and action. If we cannot do it in the individual case, I do not see why it should be any different for society.

So, it seems to me, this is not the way of avoiding Arrow's result. We should move on, and try and find an assumption that is easier to resist. The next assumption made by the proof is that of unrestricted domain; that is, that no profiles of individual preferences are to be barred. If the social welfare function, or the social decision procedure, is to work then it must be able to start with any combination of preferences. In the democratic application of this, the assumption is that we can start with people voting in many different ways, and the problem is to construct a machine which turns these into a social decision without barring some preferences in advance. This was obviously behind the discussion of the particular example at the start. Arrow's result, just like that particular application, can be avoided by barring certain combinations of consistent preferences. For example, it is again enough to insist that the individual preferences are single-peaked. However, as I argued before, it seems arbitrary to exclude perfectly good and consistent sets of preferences, particularly when some rationale can be given as to why it is quite natural to have them.

Of course the assumption for Arrow is that all consistent sets are admissible, whereas the argument given before was only for the admission of a particular kind of set. However, it has been shown that this is the crucial kind, and in any case the onus of proof lies on someone wanting to show that a particular class of preferences is to be inadmissible. Given the widely varied nature of human preferences, when we are considering democracy we should start with the assumption that all consistent sets of preferences are to be allowed. If democracy is to work, if it can be justified as being technically feasible, then we would hope that it could take this manifold variety of individual life and turn it into social decisions. So it is time for another assumption.

The next assumption is that there is some sort of weak correlation between individual and social preference. That is, if an individual finds something better, then, other things being equal, so should society. For example, if everyone is indifferent between two options, then we would expect the decision of society (if it exists) also to be indifference. If someone now changes so that he prefers *a* to *b*, and no one else changes at all, then this should have the effect of making society prefer *a* to *b*. Certainly it would seem wrong to prefer *b* to *a*. Thinking in welfare terms, moving from indifference to choosing *a* is Pareto superior; that is, it makes someone better off without making anyone worse off. So, if we are thinking in terms of welfare, or similar things to welfare, this principle seems hard to resist.

However we need to be careful, for this principle includes other assumptions. For example, it contains the assumption that the social decision between *a* and *b* needs no other input than individual preferences between *a* and *b* (for the assumptions about indifference and preference just made were only about *a* and *b*). This should be remembered in what follows. This principle, often called the weak Pareto principle, delivers the result about unanimity just presumed tentatively. For if everyone prefers (say) *a* to *b* but society was supposed indifferent between them, then an improvement to someone's welfare could be made without any harm to someone else's by making the social preference also that of *a* over *b*. Where there is conflict between individuals then there will be many Pareto superior positions; that is, points at which someone cannot be made better off without making someone worse off. That is why it is normally thought of as such a weak principle; in most cases it cannot identify a unique result. But if there is total agreement, then there is a unique Pareto superior position: whatever everyone agrees about will, if it is adopted, make everyone better without making anyone worse. So adopting the weak Pareto principle means that we get that a proper social decision procedure should declare as the social decision those things about which everyone is in unanimous agreement. This seems harmless, indeed seems to be a transparently correct conclusion. Notice, however, as before, it assumes that the social result about *a* and *b* can be derived entirely from individual preferences about *a* and *b*. Unanimous agreement about *a* and *b* serves to fix the social decision about *a* and *b*. Nothing else needs to be considered.

I stress this point, as the next assumption which Arrow's proof requires is the one which most people who do not like the result resist. This is what Arrow calls the independence of irrelevant alternatives. This is that the social preference between any pair of alternatives should be based only on the individual preferences about those alternatives and nothing else. Preferences on other alternatives are irrelevant. At first sight this seems quite plausible and, more importantly, it has just been pointed out that the normally accepted Pareto principle makes this assumption for special cases. (The assumption of independence from irrelevant alternatives is quite general, and so is needed as an extra assumption in the proof; the weak Pareto principle only assumes something like it in special cases, such as unanimity.) So this assumption is not, perhaps, as easy to get rid of as people think. Let us, however, test it, first by looking at why people have disagreed with it and then by considering an unexpected, probably surprising, democratic application of it.

Amartya Sen, to whom I have been indebted throughout for the most lucid treatment available of these matters, thinks of Arrow's theorem as arising from a poverty of information. It is not possible to have a general decision procedure producing social judgments from individual preferences because the assumptions limit the information available for such a task. The impossibility arises from an informational famine; we are just not allowed to know enough to do the job. But this is a poverty of information, not of facts. The food is there, we are just not allowed to eat it. Alternatively, relaxing Arrow's austere presuppositions about knowledge should give us all public bread. This is my metaphor rather than Sen's; but, as Sen sees it, the informational shortage arises as follows. Arrow operates in a welfarist context (hence, for example, the Pareto principle) which means that non-welfare information is excluded. Then, for welfare information, we are only allowed to know the order of individual people's preferences. More precisely, we are not allowed to know their relative intensity nor how one person's preferences compare with another. The classical utilitarians, working in a welfarist context, had no trouble deriving a best social state. For they supposed that there was something (utility, happiness, pleasure or what have you) which could be counted so that it could be said quite simply that X had more of it than Y, and that Z's increase in it today was greater than it was yesterday. More technically, they assumed that there could be interpersonal comparison of utilities and that utilities could be measured on a cardinal rather than an ordinal scale; that is, a scale which measured not just the order of the preferences but also the relative size of the gaps between them (a measure of intensity). (In fact, as Sen also proves, it is interpersonal comparison rather than cardinality which is important, but here I shall continue to consider them both together.) Being restricted to welfare, but not being allowed to know much about it, the impossibility result follows.

In this restriction, the independence of irrelevant alternatives axiom, innocuous as it may seem, plays a crucial role. For what it prevents is comparison between the preferences under review and some standard method of measurement, which could form a way of comparing people's preferences with each other, and of comparing intensities in more than an ordinal manner. In traditional utilitarian theory, for example, we could imagine an origin so that all positive utilities counted as pleasures and all negative utilities counted as pains. The origin could be assumed as being the same for everyone. In this context it can easily be said that it is better that John has some pleasure $(+1)$ than Jane has some pain (-1); better that his tooth is removed today (-5) and he has to detour to the dentist (-2) in order to avoid dreadful aches for the next two months (-15); even that it is better that Jane gets the last bit of cake than John $(+3$ for Jane, -1 for John if she gets it, total $+2$; $+2$ for John, -2 for Jane if she doesn't, total 0). Of these only the visit to the dentist is resolvable if we can only consider ranking of individual preferences (we examine the preference between the first pair and the painful two months). All the others involve comparison between people's utilities. Yet the comparison between the particular option and the baselines or points of contact allowing such is ruled out by the principle of the independence of irrelevant alternatives.

This might be thought to mean the end of Arrow, and, in one sense, perhaps it does. If we really think that we can gain the extra information (that is, that we really can compare people's utilities) then Arrow's theorem will not block deriving judgments about total public welfare from knowledge of individual welfare. However our present interest is not public welfare, or social welfare functions, but the particular applications of these matters to democratic theory or practice. And here we should be more careful. For whatever is true elsewhere where someone (some official or god) has to derive a public judgment from knowledge of individuals, the characteristic input in democracy is people's votes. In these votes we just get individual judgments about an individual's own preferences. There is no point of comparison between one individual and another. Also, the standard methods of voting just give ordinal information. They just say that an individual, X, prefers *a* to *b*. They don't say how much he or she prefers it, whether they are nearly indifferent or whether they feel strongly that one is better. So there is no interpersonal comparison and no cardinal measure of intensity of preference. Therefore, whatever may be the case elsewhere, the poverty of information on which Arrow's theorem relies applies in the normal democratic cases. And it was just because of this, of course, that the example with which the chapter opened was possible. Given nothing but individual votes over pairs, in some contexts a set of preferences will not reveal a consistent social preference (either unrestricted domain or rationality will be transgressed).

We can also now see in more general terms what would need to be done to alleviate this. If we could impart cardinal information, and allow some kind of comparison then, perhaps, we could get a result. We can get a result if the idea, in utilitarian fashion, is to maximise individual satisfaction. For perhaps individual X in the original example cares much more about all the outcomes than Y (we shouldn't just assume that their top point is the same), or perhaps the distance between *a* and *b* for X is much greater than the distance between *b* and *c* for Y. If we could start importing all this information then we could start getting results (at least if the desired result is finding the decision which gives most satisfaction). However, the original method of voting does not allow it.

In this context it is interesting and instructive to return to the former way in which we broke the deadlock, the use of the Borda count. It will be remembered that the idea was that each person gave a certain number of points to their first preference, one less to their next, and so on, and then the points were totalled. This seemed to produce a fair result. We can now see, if this is so, the assumptions on which it rested. It was assumed that each person's three, say, was equal and that the distance between the preferences was the same for each person. As has just been seen, there is in fact no reason why this should be so.

Questions about the Borda count can also be brought out in the following (related) way which should also help us to think better about the independence of irrelevant alternatives axiom. The Borda count does give a decision. But the decision it gives may differ if other preferences are added or removed from those considered. For example, suppose as before that we have X, Y and Z deciding, only now between four alternatives. Suppose that they still keep the same order of preferences between *a, b* and *c* as in the original example, but the way that *d* fits in is as follows (where the top line is the most preferred):

X	Y	Z
d	*d*	*c*
a	*b*	*a*
b	*c*	*d*
c	*a*	*b*

Here, on a Borda count assigning four points to the first preference, three to the next, and so on, *a* scores seven, *b* gets six, *c* gets seven, and *d* scores ten. So there is a clear winner, *d*. This would also have been the winner on other, simpler, systems. (It obviously would win on a first preference straight vote, and it also beats each of the other three in pairwise comparisons.) So, with a clear winner, it would seem that there should be no problem. But, something funny has happened to *a, b* and *c*. Before, they counted equal, now *b* is a point behind. So what does the Borda count show? If it is supposed to make a social decision, then it is sensitive to whether options are included or excluded. For example, if a committee is using it to select the candidate for a job, then it will be important who is on the short list. Perhaps this is more visible if the additional option is, in general, less preferred. Suppose, for example, the preferences had been:

X	Y	Z
a	*b*	*c*
d	*c*	*a*
b	*a*	*d*
c	*d*	*b*

As before, the *a, b, c* preferences are exactly as in the original example. This time *d* is ranked distinctly lower, indeed might easily have been dropped from the short list. Doing a Borda count on this gives *a* nine points, *b* seven points, *c* eight points, and *d* six points. We have a winner, *a*. Indeed, whereas before all got the same score and so produced (by Borda) social indifference, now each outcome gets a different score and we have a strict preference ranking of all four outcomes, *a* is better than *c*, which is better than *b*, which is better than *d* which comes last. Poor *d*, he never stood a chance. He was lucky not to have been left off the shortlist. But if he had been left off, we would have been back with indifference; *a*'s victory is solely due to the lowly *d*. But this might not be the end of the story. Perhaps there is another candidate, *e*, who was nearly included. If she had been added, the results might have been changed again. For example, keeping the preference order of the last example between *a, b, c,* and *d* the same, *e* might appear as follows:

X	Y	Z
a	*b*	*c*
d	*c*	*e*
b	*e*	*a*
c	*a*	*d*
e	*d*	*b*

Here the scores are *a* ten, *b* nine, *c* eleven, *d* seven, *e* eight. Indeed *e* is lowly; she was a marginal inclusion on the short list. Again, *d* has not done too well. But the interesting thing is who has now got the job. Before it was *a*. Now it is *c,* even though there has been no change at all in the preferences between *a, b, c* and *d*. If lowly *d* put *a* in with victory, lowly *e* gives it to *c*. I have illustrated this enough (although I should mention that there is not the slightest difficulty finding such examples). With the Borda count, if possible outcomes are added or deleted, then the social preference between the other outcomes may be affected.

We can now see, briefed by Arrow, why the Borda count works (that is, why it reaches decisions). It offends against the assumption of the independence of irrelevant alternatives. The social preference between *a* and *b* does not just depend upon individuals' preferences between *a* and *b,* but also on how they rank them against some other (so-called irrelevant) alternative, *d*. But so far, this may not be a problem. This, after all, was the assumption which we were going to dispense with. However, the way that the result swings about, depending on the possibly quite arbitrary or irrelevant fact of how many options there are, may well make us think that there is something in Arrow's assumption after all. Surely, we might think, how a committee decides the order between candidates *a, b* and *c* should depend upon *a, b* and *c* themselves and not upon whether or not they are comparing them with a quite separate candidate *d* (who might not have existed, or applied for the job or whatever). Yet if we adopt this plausible line, we have adopted all of Arrow's assumptions and so are stuck with his result. This would have the consequence that democracy could not be held to be, in principle, a reliable procedure for reaching social decisions once there were three or more people and once there were three or more issues to decide between.

The preferable alternative is to think that the Borda count does not go far enough. After all, cardinality and interpersonal comparison also offend against Arrow. The problem with the Borda count is that it mimics these properties without fully producing them. The order of people's preferences is supposed to reveal, roughly, the intensity of their feeling, and the more preferences they exhibit, perhaps, the more accurate this is (with only two preferences they can reveal little about the amount they prefer a to b; if they rank them among twelve others, though, it may be assumed that the number of options falling between them gives some measure). Obviously, though, this is highly imperfect, which is why new options so easily upset old patterns. Ordinal information is being used to make cardinal judgments.

Perhaps this can be remedied (and obviously we can set up more sophisticated systems). The other, more important, desideratum was interpersonal comparison. Here I think we have a moral argument which fills the gap caused by the shortage of psychological infor-mation. We can draw a conclusion from the last chapter. It is right to treat people equally. So it is right that people's first preference should be given equal weight. But if this is right and we can use equality to plug the gap like this, then perhaps the Borda count is back in business after all. For perhaps we could say the same about the fifth preference. Perhaps it, also, should be treated equally. Equality, then, may hold the key. Equality emerged; was submerged; emerged again in the last chapter. Long and tortuous as it was, it left questions about equal treatment and fairness untouched. From equality we came: it is now to equality that we must return.

CHAPTER XIII

An Impartial Conclusion

It has been seen how complex the relation between other sources of moral value and democracy can be. Democracy has been seen to be good for reasons and also bad for reasons. Indeed the same kind of value, such as equality or liberty, has been found at different times to be ranked on both sides of the evaluation, counting both for and against democracy. Any overall assessment of democracy, therefore, has to be able to take account of such complexity. It has to be shown how we may navigate morally while under the pull of several competing forces. This chapter starts by looking more closely at moral conflicts and at the paradoxes and problems this poses for the valuation of democracy. From amidst such swirling seas, another aspect of equality will eventually emerge: impartiality.

Although uncomfortable, the idea that reasons are complex and conflicting is quite natural. This happens quite apart from morality. Purely prudential or self-interested reasons are often in conflict. This might be thought not to be a theoretical problem, since it might be thought that such conflict is just resolved by the stronger force winning out. But this would be to presuppose that all prudential reasons are of the same kind and therefore can be set neatly one against the other. In fact, prudential reasons apply not only at different times but also in different manners. I might have a choice between an immediate desire (such as to stay lying in bed in the morning) and a long-term desire (such as to make myself healthy by getting up and taking exercise). Here is a conflict which does not seem just to be between opposing forces, as if I were merely being tugged between two desires which can be set neatly one beside the other. Indeed the conflict may well appear to be a conflict between reason on the one side and desire on the other. I may tell myself that

I ought to get up (that is, that there are good reasons for me to get up) in spite of my desire to lie in bed. So although only prudential matters are involved, we already seem to need something more than a simple meter registering the strength of the varying desires to resolve the case. We need to be able to think of reasons as being more than mere brute forces to describe it adequately.

This becomes even more obvious when moral reasons are involved. Typically, there are conflicts between what is perceived to be morally correct (such as being just) and what is thought to be in someone's interest. In most people's views, when there is this sort of conflict between morality and self-interest, the decision about what should be done should not depend merely upon which is the strongest desire; that is, the desire with the greatest immediate tendency to propel the person into movement. In this context people are not well modelled as objects tugged simultaneously by several pieces of string. I may, for example, want to lie in bed; but I feel that I ought to get up and feed the rest of my family. Here I have a conflict between my sense of moral obligation and my felt self-interest. I can, of course, say that I have conflicting desires, the (moral) desire to feed my family and the (self-interested) desire to stay in bed. But, again, it does not seem that these are desires which can be simply placed beside each other, letting the strongest win out. To resolve the conflict I need more than a meter which registers the strength of the two conflicting pressures on me.

Automatic solutions have, of course, been provided to such dilemmas. It has been held that there is no ultimate conflict between self-interest and morality, so that to do the one is (automatically) to do the other. But this is implausible; at least this is not how it appears to most of us, where sometimes such conflicts are only too real. I feel really caught between my desire to stay in bed and my sense of my duty to my family. My desire to stay in bed feels much more immediately strong than my desire to feed my family. But this is not the end of the matter. I try to reason myself out of bed. I tell myself that, whatever I might feel like, this is just something which I have to do. It is not a conflict I resolve merely by giving way to the immediately felt strongest desire.

In the conflict between immediate desire and appreciation of long-term self-interest, it is not as if we were just being tugged by the cigarette on one side and by prudence on the other. In the conflict between morality and immediate desire, it is not as if we were just being tugged by morality on one side and a craving for a cigarette on the other. That is, it is not just that I crave moral approbation and I crave rest in bed and, unluckily, can't have both. It is, rather, that I think that I have a good reason to act in a way which does not match my apparent strongest immediate desire. My desires give me reasons, but there are other reasons, and all these reasons conflict.

Different features of a situation give different, potentially conflicting, reasons for action. Some of these conflicts are moral, where different moral reasons lead in different directions. I have just rejected one way of solving the problem which this provides; that is, to treat all these reasons as being different desires which can be simply compared one with another and summed for their overall strength. There is no simple, resultant desire. There is, however, another way in which to try and solve the problem which conflict of reasons provides. This is to say that the conflict is ultimately only apparent, not real. It is not that the reasons can be simply summed together in the way that different impacting forces can. But it may be that whether different factors are really reasons or not can be discovered by analysing these apparent reasons in the light of a single overall and fundamental reason.

To hold that there is a real conflict in moral reasons is to assume that morality is pluralistic in character. It assumes that there are many different goods, which provide different reasons for action, and which may therefore come into conflict one with another. But, it might be urged, morality is actually fundamentally monistic. Therefore, any conflict between moral reasons can only be apparent and not real. This would be the case if there were only one final good in terms of which all other goods make sense. Indeed there may be one such final good. For, standardly and famously, such a good has been proposed. It is utility.

After its entry in the first analytical chapter, on foundations, utility has not had a striking part to play. Its possible fundamental character was noted; then it subsequently more or less disappeared. At the very least, it might be thought, there should have been a chapter on utility and its relation to democracy. For even if it is not the final fundamental value it seems at least to be an intermediate one. Whatever someone's moral views, to say that something creates happiness or utility is, other things being equal, an argument in its favour. Among the arguments for the goodness of democracy, its tendency to produce utility (or otherwise) should surely feature. Yet we have now reached the end of the book and there has been no such chapter. Or, more accurately, there has not been one in this second, analytical, half of the book. Utilitarian arguments can of course be given for the goodness of democracy. In fact, they have already been given. They were given in the historical half of the book, in Chapter VI. The general shape of a utilitarian argument for democracy is clear enough. In its simplest form it is that the greatest number looks after the greatest number. Of course, it is possible to be much more subtle than this. We can conduct economic analyses of types of decision procedure and examine what happens when supposed self-interested agents are placed in various structures. Some of this, indeed, has also already happened. It formed part of the analysis of different voting systems in the last chapter.

It is important, however, in discussing such voting systems to distinguish between the problem of combining many individual wills into a single public will and the problem of combining many individual utilities into a single public utility. The former is intrinsic to the nature of democracy, whatever one's views about utility. As such, it was discussed throughout the last chapter. The latter is only important if it is thought important that utility be maximised. Then, assuming that voting reveals utilities, voting may be thought to be a method of achieving such maximisation. Hence, perhaps, the move-ment towards systems that might be better able to reveal and combine utility information at the end of the last chapter. However, as was seen there, these systems are still an inferior substitute. The most attractive way of solving the problem of interpersonal com-parison of utilities is to reach for a moral assumption of equality rather than psychological evidence. It is right that people should be assumed to be equal in this respect, whatever their actual utilities might be.

This brings back the question of equality. It also shows, used like this, that the utilitarianism has ceased to be monistic. There is no longer now one value, utility. For there is also another value, equality. As well as the primary value, there is also the question of how it should be distributed. We have already got into more than one good, and so we have already moved into potential conflict of reasons. We may, for example, be in a conflict between greater total utility and more equally distributed utility. The famous formula, 'the greatest happiness of the greatest number', which Bentham plucked out of the surrounding utilitarian air, was in fact dropped by him at the end of his life precisely because it seems to suggest such dual maximisation. As a pure monistic doctrine, all that should be maximised is happiness; which is why Bentham changed the formula to 'the greatest happiness', *simpliciter*. But this formula says nothing about distribution. If we bring in distribution, we are bringing in another value.

This means that the pure utilitarian argument for democracy is not as simple as 'the greatest number will look after the greatest number'. We need rather the claim that the happiness of the greatest number (as achieved in majority voting) is also the greatest happiness. On certain assumptions, such as that people are roughly equally concerned about the issue in question, that they are roughly equally capable of feeling pain or gaining pleasure, and such like, this does follow. However we may easily have situations where things are not equal in this way. The minority might get much more utility or disutility out of a particular decision than the majority. The minority might feel passionately about an issue which is only of slight concern to the majority. In these kinds of cases following the majority's views will produce the wrong answer, from a utilitarian point of view. Hence what I have just described as the most attractive solution. We don't count different people's utilities equally because of some dubious psychological assumptions about equal capacities to acquire utility. Instead, we base this equal treatment straightforwardly on moral foundations. But this, of course, is to bring in another source of value.

In fact, how we operate in actual decisions is (potentially) with many different sources of value. This has been applied in the last few chapters. These showed that it is completely natural to take several different goods, or sources of value, and use them for assessing democracy. It is true that these were dubbed 'intermediate' values, and it might be theorised that they all derived from some one fundamental value. Well, they might. Or they might not. Either way, the important point is that there is the appearance of many different reasons. A world of potential moral conflict is, at the very least, the phenomenal moral world. It is the world in which we move morally and have our being. It has to be understood, and we cannot acquire such understanding by concentrating on the possibly purely hypothetical case of there being only one value.

There is an additional reason for not concentrating only on utility when discussing the value of democracy. This is that the particularly difficult, central problems of utilitarianism in its application to a particular subject area are empirical. To find out whether democracy does, or does not, tend to increase utility is better done by empirical (or semi-empirical) survey, rather than by a priori analysis. We can, for example, survey varying countries by different types of regime and compare this with their performance on indices which may be assumed to be positively correlated with utility. We can, for example, see in which countries and in which situations people starve, and so lack the most basic of all sources of utility. The facts, such as they are, seem to favour democracy. However the point is that any such empirical analysis is far beyond the scope of this book. Therefore a more complete study of utility would only get into this book by further use of a priori models, and there has probably been quite enough of that in the last chapter.

I shall continue, therefore, to assume that there are several sources of value, such as knowledge, equality or autonomy. These give varying reasons, and so possible conflicts. The problems, however, do not stop here. For, as well as these different sources of value, we have different opinions about them. We have different ideas, different positions, different points of view. We have different people. Many of the problems in democracy, and in political theory more generally, come from a comparison between our own position and the position of other people. From where we are, things look a certain way. We make moral assumptions. Yet we can see that there are other people, who are in a way quite like us. They also have a point of view. They also, presumably, make moral assumptions. From a certain point of view, these are no doubt as valid as our own. Yet they are also sharply different. Theirs are theirs and ours are ours. If we are right, they are wrong. If we believe in our opinions, we believe them to be right; so, for anyone who disagrees, we must also think that they are wrong.

So what am I do to if I think that I am right, but I find that other people disagree? How should we decide as a society? I may have one view about what we should do. But I discover that other people have other views. If I consider their views equally with my own, and if there are more of them, then it seems that I should follow their views rather than my own. That is, I should decide democratically, following the majority decision. On the other hand, I do have my own view. If this is different from the majority view, then it must follow that I think that the majority decision is wrong. So it seems that it would be crazy for me to do what the majority thinks. That way, I would be doing what I think is wrong. Surely, it might well be said, that cannot be correct, at least for any autonomous moral agent. Indeed, even if it were correct, I myself cannot think it to be correct. For what the majority say should happen is something which I think to be wrong. If I think that it is wrong, I cannot think that it would be right for me to do it.

In Chapter IX, on knowledge, we considered Plato's problem of why we should follow the democratic view rather than following the people who know. There were several answers to this, some of which depended upon the difficulty of identifying who it was that knew. If, however, we put the problem not in terms of knowledge, but of belief, we get a first-person analogue to this problem. Even if I may not have the truth, or knowledge, I do have my own view about the world. I have my beliefs. This is the truth, as I see it. Included in this view is my view about other people's views. Suppose that most of them disagree with me. Then the truth (as I see it) about them is that they are wrong. So, for me, following the majority rather than me is analogous to, in Plato's case, following the majority rather than the people who know. In both cases, it seems mad or at least inefficient to follow majority decision. But in the present case, I don't have the problem which arose with Plato of identifying the knowers in order to discover whose views should be primarily considered. For the person primarily to be considered by me is readily identifiable. It is myself. I am already there.

This dilemma has been thought to reveal something deeply puzzling, or contradictory, about the nature of democracy. Richard Wollheim calls it the paradox of democracy. As he puts it, it becomes a question of what I think ought to be enacted. Suppose, to avoid the problems of the last chapter, we take a simple situation with a single issue with only two alternatives, to be decided by majority decision. Suppose that I think that *a* ought to be enacted. So I vote for *a*. The majority, however, vote for the alternative, *b*. So they think that *b* ought to be enacted. But suppose that I am also a democrat. Then I also think that what the majority thinks ought to be enacted. This is *b*. So I think that *b* ought to be enacted. But *b* is incompatible with *a*. So I seem to think both that *a* ought to be enacted and also that it is not the case that *a* ought to be enacted. I seem to have contradictory beliefs about what ought to be done.

Wollheim himself traces and dismisses various ways of relieving the dilemma. I could of course regard the vote that I feed into the democratic machine as a sort of guess about what the majority will think, which I happily revise once I discover that I am wrong. However, in many situations, a democrat's commitment to particular issues is not like this. Such a view would not explain why democrats turn out to vote in elections in constituencies when they know in advance that the other side will win by a large majority. I do not (normally) just want to find out what the majority thinks in order to decide what is right. I already have a view about that, and that is the view I express in the vote. In a British General Election I might think, for example, that the Conservative candidate should win. But I might live and vote in a large Welsh mining constituency. I know that the Conservative candidate does not stand a chance. Nevertheless, I turn out and vote for the Conservative candidate. Whatever else I am doing, I am not engaging in a tentative guess about what the majority will say, or offering a revisable opinion which I will withdraw once I have heard the result. I knew what the result would be before I voted. When the predictable result has eventually been declared, I still think that the Conservative candidate should have won.

So the paradox cannot be relieved by making the democrat's commitment on the particular issue merely tentative or prima facie. But neither can it be relieved by making the commitment to democracy non-real. Of course, people have different opinions about the goodness of democracy, just as they have about other matters of value. Some people may not morally approve of it, but merely use it because it is there. For them, there is no problem about their moral views. They believe in the particular issue and, even though they voted in the hope that their view might come about, they have no separate reason to think that what the majority voted for should be enacted. However, not everyone is like this. There are also people who believe in democracy. The question is not whether everyone faces a paradox but whether these people face a paradox. *Ex hypothesi*, they value democracy. But, as seen, they (often) also value other things. So it seems that, for them, the paradox must arise.

Wollheim's own solution to his paradox depends upon distinguishing between what he calls direct and oblique moral principles. The subject matter of direct moral principles is picked out by general descriptive expressions. Examples would be 'murder' or 'telling lies'. The subject matter of oblique moral principles is picked out by what Wollheim calls 'an artificial property bestowed upon them either as the result of an act of will of some individual or in consequence of the corporate act of some institution' (p. 85). An example would be 'what is commanded by the sovereign'. Wollheim then suggests that two principles are not incompatible if one of them is asserted as a direct principle and the other as an oblique principle. So there is no incompatibility in the case of democracy. My commitment, as a democrat, to the particular issue is direct. My commitment to the principle that 'what the majority votes for should be enacted' is oblique. End of paradox.

I do not think that this solution works. If *a* and *b* are incompatible, then they are incompatible. This cannot be talked away by saying that they are different kinds of principle. If *a* and *b* cannot both be realised, then they are incompatible. The incompatibility comes from their contents, not from the origins of these contents. Yet Wollheim's 'direct' and 'oblique' are different ways of marking the origins. They cannot, therefore, touch or alleviate the incompatibility.

It is true, of course, that there is no necessary conflict between an oblique and a direct principle. This is one thing which is gained by Wollheim's device of pointing out the different ways in which they identify the subject matter. 'What the majority want' and *a* are not necessarily incompatible in the way that *a* and *not-a* are. Sometimes the majority will vote for *a*. Sometimes what they want and what I want is the same. Nevertheless, when I, on moral grounds, have voted for *a* and the majority have voted for *b*, then I, as a democrat, seem to be saddled with incompatible moral beliefs. I think both that *b* ought to be enacted and that it ought not to be enacted. And I don't get out of this incompatibility by giving each of these beliefs a different kind of theoretical description, or other fancy name.

So the paradox still needs to be dissolved, or resolved. Or, rather, it does if such incompatibilities are fundamentally debilitating, or important. However, I think that once we have moved as far into moral pluralism as the start of this chapter promoted, such resolution is not so important. At least it means that there is nothing especially difficult or defective about democracy. The fact that different evaluative beliefs that I hold may result in conflict because of the particular nature of the world is something that naturally comes from having several values. As the world is, I cannot realise all these values simultaneously. Faced with conflicting reasons, I have to decide. I have to balance liberty with autonomy, equality with welfare. Indeed, even when considering only one value, as we have seen, choices still have to be made. The unfortunate mother of the chapter on equality was faced with such difficulties and conflicting reasons, even though she only wanted to promote equality between her children. Equality was both a reason for giving her children equal pocket money and also a reason against. Considering only equality, she was caught between conflicting reasons; multiplying the values could only have made worse her plight.

So I do not think that the conflict that Wollheim has diagnosed in democracy poses any particular problems; or indeed tells us anything particularly special about democracy. We have different values, and, in particular cases, these may provide conflicting reasons. But this is part of the everyday phenomenology of moral life, whatever we might think about the theoretical possibility of reducing such pluralism to a single ultimate value. For example, I make someone a promise that I will go to see them at a particular time. Here is something which I ought to do. However, on the way to the meeting I see someone who needs help. Here is also something which I ought to do. I ought to do both. But I cannot do both. I am caught between conflicting reasons. They conflict, but they are both genuine reasons for action; they are both things which I ought to do.

Similarly when I as a democrat vote in the minority. I think that my view ought to be enacted. That is something which ought to happen. I also, as a democrat, think that the majority view ought to be enacted. That is also something which ought to happen. Both ought to happen. But, given that I am in the minority, both cannot happen. The particular way that the world happens to be has prevented it on this occasion. Another time I will be more lucky. Just as, another time, to keep my promise would not produce a moral conflict. But, in the present case, I am caught between conflicting reasons. However, just as with the example of the promise, this particular conflict does not mean that they are not both genuine reasons. They are both things that ought to happen.

This avoids the way of trying to resolve the paradox by saying that I am not really genuinely attached to one of the two principles which have come into conflict on this particular occasion. For, as seen, I may be really (morally) committed to the particular issue on which I vote. It is not just a prima facie commitment. It is a genuine moral belief expressing what I think ought to happen. This makes sense of, and justifies, how I might still campaign for my view and attempt to persuade people of its correctness even after I have been beaten. On the other hand, as a democrat, I also genuinely think that the majority's view ought to be put into effect. This explains, for example, why I might go along with it, respect it and obey it. I am in a moral conflict, and have to resolve it as seems appropriate to the particular occasion, just as with the duties to keep my promise and to help.

This may well be thought to be fine as a formal solution; but it may also be felt to lack an explanation of what makes democracy special. For it may be felt that Wollheim is right to suggest that there is a special reason why democracy should lead to such conflicts in values. To see whether this is so, we have to look again at whatever special value there may be in the democratic answer to set against the value of my own answer. After all, the paradox of democracy, or the conflict of reasons in this case, is only real when both the reasons in conflict are real. Both of these reasons have to be such that there is something to be said for them. They must both be proper sources of value. For my own view, given that I am holding it as a moral view, this is automatic. It is my view about what is right. It is, so far as I can judge, what rightness is for me. So I must think that it declares value. The problem, rather, is why I should give any separate acknowledgement to other people's views about value (as are expressed, for example, in the majority view when I happen to disagree with it). There will be an answer to this only if there is a reason for taking other points of view as being of importance as well as my own.

Even when our concern is only with assessing moral truth, there might still be such a reason. As we saw in Chapter IX, given roughly equal abilities, consulting other people is more likely to make each of us right than would be the case working on our own. We saw how this happened with roughly equal competence in simple mathematics, where the most efficient procedure was for us all to do the sums and then to vote on the right answer. Here it is appropriate for me to consult the majority as my best means of discovering the right answer. However, in the present context, this is at best only a partial answer. This corresponds to the case discussed above in which people put preliminary or tentative views into the voting machine and are ready to correct them when they find out what is the majority view. I might do this with simple sums. I might even do it with matters of moral concern when I am uncertain about the answer. But, as seen, I may still decide to operate democratically even when I am convinced that I already know the answer. The paradox only arises when there is no question of my consulting the democratic machine in order to find out the right answer. As long as we are considering only moral truth, and as long as I am myself already convinced about what this truth is, then it seems that there could be no reason at all for valuing or putting into effect the contrasting views of others. So if there is nevertheless a reason for putting these contrasting views into effect, this reason cannot be that they are, or are likely to be, true.

At first sight, it might seem that there could be no such other reason. But there is. The people who may differ from me in this particular disagreement are like me in being moral agents. As moral thinkers and deciders, they have an equal claim to be considered. We ought to be impartial between them; and we ought to be impartial between them and ourselves. Hence equality re-emerges as important; this time in the guise of impartiality.

Central to our idea of morality is that it involves what Kant called legislation for all law-making members. This is a metaphor; but with literal legislation the same points apply. We think, in formulating the law, that it should apply to everyone. We think, in discovering or deciding the moral law, that, similarly, it applies to everyone. We are all what Kant called law-making members. For Kant this means that we are all to be treated as ends in ourselves, not as means towards the satisfaction of other people. If we are moral, then we should show an equality of moral respect to all other moral agents.

From this equality of respect the argument for democracy directly follows. If all moral agents are to be equally respected, then I must give weight (or moral consideration) to everyone expressing their moral views. If they are doing so by voting, then I should give these votes equal respect. If I give these votes equal respect, then the view I should respect as superior is the view supported by the majority. Every vote counts equally and that is the view with more votes. So, independently of my particular view of the matter, and therefore independently of whether I happen to be in the majority or the minority on this occasion, I have a reason for respecting the view of the majority. Here, then, is a reason why the majority's view should be enacted, quite independently of any view I myself may have about the truth of the matter. Here is a separate reason which may come into conflict with my own particular estimation of the matter. Hence we have a well grounded separate reason. Hence we have a potential conflict of reasons. Hence we have the kind of problem which was dubbed the paradox of democracy.

That reasons could be found for democracy itself, to set against reasons for action on the particular issue, is not in itself surprising. After all, the last few chapters have examined, in turn, several separate sources of value and their connections with democracy. Any of these can provide reasons, and so lead to such conflict. However, there is something special about the kind of equality of respect just mentioned. It is not like some of the kinds of equality discussed in Chapter XI which may be disputed or disregarded, such as the equalisation of property. This use of equality is very central to the idea of morality itself. So, if we are aiming to be moral, or if we are looking for what to do when there are conflicting moral reasons, this one is hard to ignore. It is a kind of second order equality. It doesn't say that goods should be distributed equally. It doesn't even directly recommend egalitarian practical procedures. But it does say that, when considering anything at all, equal respect should be given to all moral agents. Therefore, as well as our own natural first personal perspective and position, it urges consideration of an independent or impartial position.

Unless we can also see things from the outside, in which our own view is just one view among others, then we are not thinking fully morally. On the other hand, unless we can also see things from our own position, we cannot be coherent people or agents. We have to act. We have to deal with the world as it is for us. So, as moral agents, we have to be aware of both perspectives. The external, impartial perspective leads naturally to the equality of respect which gives reasons why the majority view should be enacted. Our own, individual, perspective gives our own direct appreciation of the situation, giving reasons why our own view should be enacted. Unsurprisingly, these may conflict. When they do, in certain respects I may treat this just like any other moral conflict, deciding it on the particular facts of the situation. However it is also important to realise that in the case of democratic conflict both of the conflicting reasons are strongly supported. The conflict is so deeply rooted that it is difficult to avoid. In this sense, democracy is not just one conflict among others.

The considerations based on equality of respect give reasons for following the majority view. But they also place limits on it. Exactly the same basis can lead to the view that there are fundamental rights which should be secured to each person (or to each member or citizen) whatever the majority may determine. If we just start with democracy as a value, and then think that it comes into conflict with other values, such rights may seem simply undemocratic, and hence, at least to this extent, wrong. If, however, we think that the value of democracy can be derived from other sources, then these other sources, as well as supporting democracy, also place limits on it. If the reason for the goodness of democracy is the equality of respect that is due to all moral agents, then this democracy should not be allowed to do anything which conflicts with such respect. We may therefore shield individuals with rights to prevent such depredations by the majority. This may be undemocratic; but it is as morally justified as democracy itself is.

We can make this more precise. If democracy is a good, then its proper exercise is a good. Hence those things necessary for its proper exercise can be secured against itself. So we may properly have democratic rights which may not properly be removed by the vote of the majority. Each member should be allowed the vote, and should be allowed access to those things necessary for the proper working of democracy, such as free discussion and communication about matters being decided. Such things should be entrenched as rights not subject to control by the majority. Again, it might be thought that this was wrong, because it would be undemocratic. For, it might be thought, democracy means majority rule; and majority rule means that the winner takes all. If the majority decide, therefore, that a particular group should not be allowed to vote or publicly present their views, then that is what, democratically, should happen. Everyone would still be equally respected, because there is equal respect when the majority's views are followed. However, if we look further at the equality of respect argument on which this suggestion is based, it can be seen to be fallacious. Equality of respect has supported the goodness of the democratic machine. If the machine is good, then it has to be allowed to work. So equality of respect forms an argument for protecting the machine against self-destruction. It leads to entrenched democratic rights which the majority may not alienate without losing their own moral legitimacy.

This removes other paradoxes surrounding democracy, such as the majority's right to abolish democracy itself (which, as was noted in Chapter II, happened in classical Athens). Again, if the goodness of democracy just means that the majority is always right, then if the majority decides to have a dictatorship, it would seem that there should be a dictatorship. But, again, the goodness of democracy does not in fact mean that the majority is always right. It is important to keep the levels separate. If we ask why democracy is a good, then one powerful argument, such as has been proposed in this chapter, says that equality of respect means that in cases of difference of opinion, the majority view should be followed. However, this is its basis. It is because this is a good thing that democracy is a good thing. It is this basis which allows the majority view to be followed. However, if the majority wish to abolish democracy, this goodness would also be abolished. The majority would no longer have a say, and there would be no longer equality of respect. Hence equality of respect argues against this. The majority view should indeed be followed, except where it does things which undermine equality of respect. Given the argument from equality of respect to democracy, this means: except when it undermines democracy. So democracy is not allowed, democratically, by majority decision, to vote itself away. The arguments for democracy are also arguments for rights, or other entrenched provisions, controlling its operation and preventing it eliminating itself.

This argument can be taken further. So far the rights being considered are particularly democratic rights, or entrenched provisions which directly affect the operations of democracy itself. But if the source of the goodness of democracy is equality of respect, then this source supports other rights which are not so directly connected with the preservation or operation of democracy. If everyone is equally to be respected as a moral agent, then it is wrong for anyone to be killed or reduced to such an impoverished or miserable form of life that they are incapable of acting as a moral agent. Hence everyone (every member of the community being considered) may justifiably be held to have whatever rights are necessary to protect them individually against such a miserable position. Again, just as with the more obviously democratic rights, these rights come directly from the idea of equality of respect. Since this is the source for them as well as for democracy itself, democracy cannot legitimately overturn them. So, again, whatever the majority wish, they cannot act against such rights without losing their own legitimacy. Hence, in certain particular areas, the minority is properly protected against the majority, by the same reasons which give the majority their normal legitimacy.

When discussing foundations in Chapter VIII, it was suggested that various ideas of equality stood behind both of the rival supposed fundamental sources of value, rights and utilities. As was seen, these two sources tend to pull in opposing directions, with utility going to the control of the majority and rights to the support of the minority. In Chapter XI, it was seen that this can lead to confusion about the question of whether equality is a support or a criticism of democracy. However, we have now located a particular idea of equality, which is especially central for the idea of morality itself, namely equality of respect for all moral agents. Using this particular idea, we can now locate more precisely both how democracy can be supported and how it can be controlled or limited. Equality of respect means adoption of an external perspective which gives independent reasons for following the majority. So much in support of an argument from equality to majority rule. However, equality of respect also means that there are certain things which a majority must not do. So much in support of an argument from equality to fundamental rights and protection of minorities.

So the search for a fundamental basis in equality, which started in the 'Foundations' chapter, returns here at the end with impartiality. This is now, as the persevering reader can easily see, the end. We end with impartiality. Impartiality is the last offering of the author. The impartial author should, no doubt, reflect at this point on all the important things which have not been covered, but ought to have been. The present, embarrassed, author thinks that that might be unnecessarily impartial. There are so many areas that I have not covered in this second, analytical, part of the book that it would be indelicate to draw any of them at this late stage to the reader's attention. I have restricted myself, until the penultimate chapter, to a very simple model of democracy. I have considered cases in which small groups use direct democracy. I have taken cases in which there is a single issue with only two options to be decided by straight majority voting. This is highly over-simplified compared with the real world problems of representation and a multiplicity of inter-connecting issues. However, even these simple examples have provided problems enough for the overall question of whether democracy can be given a foundation; that is, whether it secures such intermediate goods as knowledge, autonomy or equality.

As has been seen, the relation between these intermediate goods and democracy has been complex. The defence of democracy has been both teasing and tortuous. These other values have interacted both negatively and positively with democracy. Democracy at times has been morally battered. However, I hope that it does ultimately emerge with several different possible foundations. If not, perhaps, sufficient to give it uplift, these should be sufficient to keep it intact. Difficulty and dispute is only to be expected with a system which has not only been repeatedly criticised but also regarded with deep suspicion throughout most of human history.

Indeed this long history of distrust, with which the book began, might be thought to provide a final shot against democracy. Impartiality, with which we have ended, might be thought to be on the other side. For the ambitiously atemporal impartial observer might think that this variability of esteem should dispose of democracy. For, otherwise, it might be thought, we are overvaluing the present time and the accuracy of its access to truth. We happen to live at a time when democracy is in fashion; but history tells us that this is not the normal state.

Or so, perhaps, it could be argued. But, on the other hand, the present is where we actually are. However impartial we may be, we must also have our own particular perspective, and this is it. Whether it be fashion or otherwise, democracy is something that we have got (at least to a limited extent and in a few areas). And having got it, it can be defended. Indeed, even if we try with full impartiality to go beyond our own parochial starting point, impartiality turns out to be one of democracy's best defences. Impartially considered, democracy is a good. What we happen to have, we have good reason to hold.

Notes

1   Self-rule

There is a long-standing discussion about whether, and with what effect, there are two concepts of liberty. Leading points in this include: Isiah Berlin 'Two concepts of liberty', in his *Four Essays on Liberty* (Oxford: Oxford University Press 1969); Gerald MacCallum, 'Negative and positive freedom', in P. Laslett and W.G. Runciman (eds), *Philosophy, Politics, and Society, Fourth Series* (Oxford: Blackwell 1972); Charles Taylor, 'What's wrong with negative liberty', in A. Ryan (ed.) *The Idea of Freedom* (Oxford: Oxford University Press, 1979); Thomas Baldwin, 'MacCallum and the two concepts of freedom', *Ratio* 26 (1984); Quentin Skinner, 'The idea of negative liberty: philosophical and historical perspectives', in Richard Rorty, J.B. Schneewind and Quentin Skinner (eds), *Philosophy in History* (Cambridge: Cambridge University Press, 1984); and Quentin Skinner, 'The paradoxes of political liberty', in S. McMurrin, (ed.) *The Tanner Lectures on Human Values* VII (Cambridge: Cambridge University Press and Salt Lake City: University of Utah Press, 1986). A recent detailed attempt to see how the distinction might apply to two emblematic nineteenth-century thinkers is Richard Bellamy, 'T.H. Green, J.S. Mill and Isiah Berlin on the nature of liberty and liberalism', in Hyman Gross and Ross Harrison (eds), *Jurisprudence: Cambridge Essays* (Oxford: Oxford University Press, 1992). For the problem of the criterion for membership of a state, see Michael Walzer, *Spheres of Justice* (Oxford, Martin Robertson, 1983), Chapter 2.

II   The Greeks

The most detailed recent accounts of the workings of the *ecclesia* are by Morgens Hansen. He wrote a series of articles in the 1970s usefully collected in *The Athenian 'ecclesia'* (Copenhagen, 1983). Before then was *The Sovereignty of the People's Courts in Athens in the Fourth Century BC and The Public Action against Unconstitutional Proposals* (Odense University Press, 1974), describing the relative power of the *ecclesia* and the courts. Hansen has now written *The Athenian Democracy in the Age of*

Notes

Demosthenes (Oxford: Blackwell 1991). Other recent books include R.K. Sinclair, *Democracy and Participation in Athens* (Cambridge: Cambridge University Press, 1988); J. Ober, *Mass and Elite in Democratic Athens* (Princeton NJ: Princeton University Press, 1989); and David Stockton, *The Classical Athenian Democracy* (Oxford: Oxford University Press, 1990).

Hansen's detailed treatments supplement and revise older accounts such as A.H.M. Jones, *Athenian Democracy* (Oxford: Blackwell 1957). Commentators from this period to the present seem to think that their predecessors were over-influenced by Greek contemporary commentary, and hence were over-severe on democracy; by reaction they themselves have been fairly sympathetic. This applies to Jones, W.G. Forrest, *The Emergence of Greek Democracy* (London: World University Library, 1966), Finley (see below), and the two monumental books by G. de Ste Croix, *The Origins of the Peloponnesian War* (London: Duckworth, 1972), and *The Class Struggle in the Ancient World* (London: Duckworth, 1981). M.I. Finley's *Democracy Ancient and Modern* (London: Chatto & Windus, 1973) paints a vivid picture and is concerned in Chapter 1 to distinguish between Greek and modern democracy by emphasising the closeness between leaders and followers in the ancient democracy. His later *Politics in the Ancient World* (Cambridge: Cambridge University Press, 1983), however, rather reverses the emphasis by bringing out the full-time, or professional, activity of the leading politicians, and the above text relies on this (although this point is also made by de Ste Croix (1981: 125). Both of de Ste Croix's books have interesting pages on democracy (1972: 348–9; 1981: 284–5, 414–15). On the dependence of democracy on empire there is a dispute between Jones and de Ste Croix on the one side (which is the position followed in the text) and Finley (1973) on the other; see de Ste Croix (1981: 602). De Ste Croix also thinks that Athenian democracy did not have long term stability, and its departure was merely because 'the basic economic situation asserted itself in the long run, as it always does' (1981: 97). On the other hand, this is merely an expression of de Ste Croix's a priori economic model, and de Ste Croix himself says that the class struggle (which was meant always to assert itself in the long run in this way) was 'very muted' in Athens during the democratic period (1981: 290).

For primary texts the translations used here are, for Plato's *Republic*, that of F.M. Cornford (Oxford: Oxford University Press, 1941) and for Aristotle's *Politics* that of Ernest Barker (Oxford: Oxford University Press, 1948). Aristotle's *Constitution of Athens* is from the translation of J.M. Moore in his *Aristotle and Xenophon on Democracy and Oligarchy* (London: Chatto & Windus, 1975); this also includes the translation used of Pseudo Xenophon's *Constitution of the Athenians*. There is a useful general collection, M.H. Crawford and David Whitehead, *Archaic and Classical Greece: A selection of Ancient Sources in Translation* (Cambridge: Cambridge University Press, 1983); the second translation used of Herodotus' *History* in the text comes from here and the standard nineteenth-century translation referred to in this context is that of Rawlinson (reprinted in Everyman's Library, London: Dent, 1910). Xenophon's *Memorabilia* is in the Loeb Library (Cambridge, Mass.: Harvard University Press, 1923).

Notes

For Demosthenes, Aeschines and Pericles I used the translation by A.N.W. Saunders (1975), and for Plutarch that of Ian Scott-Kilvert (1960) (both Harmondsworth: Penguin).

Secondary works on the great Athenian thinkers are too numerous to mention. However Cynthia Farrer's *The Origins of Democratic Thinking* (Cambridge: Cambridge University Press, 1988) not only treats Thucydides, but also makes him out to be much more supportive of democracy than the main text implies.

III Hobbes and Locke

Hobbes' *Leviathan* was written in English. The *De Cive* was in Latin, and quotation is from the contemporary translation usually, but inaccurately, attributed to Hobbes himself. The best recent edition of *Leviathan* is that by Richard Tuck (Cambridge: Cambridge University Press, 1991) and the quotations are taken from it; reference is given to the chapter numbers, followed by the page number in Tuck. Editions of the English *De Cive* are edited by B. Gert (Doubleday, 1971; reprinted Brighton: Harvester, 1978) and by Howard Warrender (Oxford: Oxford University Press, 1983). The standard edition of Locke is *Locke's Two Treatises of Government*, edited by Peter Laslett (Cambridge: Cambridge University Press, 2nd edn, 1967; new edn, 1988). Quotations are taken from it, and it is referred to by chapter and section number.

The brief raid on Hobbes and Locke in the text for the purposes of democracy neither used nor needed secondary material. However, for those interested, Hobbes has been a much fought-over figure. There was a famous Marxist interpretation of Hobbes (and Locke) by C.B. Macpherson, *The Political Theory of Possessive Individualism* (Oxford: Oxford University Press, 1962), which has produced more critics than converts. Other older controversial and discussed interpretations are those by Leo Strauss, *The Political Philosophy of Hobbes*, translated by E.M. Sinclair (Oxford: Oxford University Press, 1936; reprinted Chicago: Chicago University Press, 1952); and by Michael Oakeshott, *Hobbes on Civil Philosophy* (Oxford: Oxford University Press, 1975). Hobbes has been made out to be much more of an upholder of natural law than allowed in the main text (see Howard Warrander, *The Political Philosophy of Hobbes* (Oxford: Oxford University Press, 1957)); but this is another much-criticised interpretation. Jean Hampton situates him in the social contract tradition from the point of view of modern games theory in *Hobbes and the Social Contract Tradition* (Cambridge: Cambridge University Press, 1986). Three good brief treatments from different periods are Richard Peters, *Hobbes* (Harmondsworth: Penguin, 1956); D.D. Raphael, *Hobbes* (London: George Allen & Unwin 1977); and Richard Tuck, *Hobbes* (Oxford: Oxford University Press, 1989). Two stimulating works on Locke are John Dunn, *The Political Thought of John Locke* (Cambridge: Cambridge University Press, 1969) and James Tully, *A Discourse on Property* (Cambridge: Cambridge University Press, 1980). John Dunn has also written a short general treatment, *Locke* (Oxford: Oxford University Press, 1984).

Notes

IV Rousseau

The quotations in the text from the *Social Contract* are from the G.D.H. Cole translation (Everyman's Library, London: Dent, 1963). References are to book and chapter number, allowing reference to any edition.

On the secondary material, J.C. Hall, *Rousseau; an Introduction to his Political Philosophy* (London: Macmillan, 1973) is a careful, analytical short account; R. Grimsley, *Jean-Jacques Rousseau* (Brighton: Harvester, 1983) contains considerable quotation from less accessible sources; other recent books are James Miller, *Rousseau, Dreamer of Democracy* (New Haven: Yale University Press, 1984), which gives biographical and cultural context as well as analysing the thought, and John B. Noone, *Rousseau's Social Contract: a Conceptual Analysis* (Athens GA: University of Georgia Press, 1980) which concentrates on the text discussed in the chapter. On this there is also Hilail Gilden, *Rousseau's Social Contract: The Argument* (Chicago: Chicago University Press, 1983). In a different style, and as a leading representative of French work, there is R. Derathé, *Le rationalisme de J-J. Rousseau* (Paris, 1948). J. Shklar, *Rousseau, Man and Citizen* (Cambridge: Cambridge University Press, 1969; 2nd edn, 1985) gives competing images of Rousseau, and also brings out the totalitiarian implications, as did the earlier work of J.L. Talmon, *The Origins of Totalitarian Democracy* (London: Secker & Warburg, 1952).

The similarity between Rousseau and Kant has been queried by Stephen Ellenburg in his contribution to R.A. Leigh (ed.), *Rousseau after Two Hundred Years* (Cambridge: Cambridge University Press, 1982); however, the comparison can be found not only in E. Cassirer, e.g. *Rousseau, Kant and Goethe* (Princeton NJ: Princeton University Press, 1963) but also in such more recent work as Andrew Levine, *The Politics of Autonomy: A Kantian Reading of Rousseau's Social Contract* (Amherst: University of Massachusetts Press, 1976). There is also Edna Kryger, *La notion de liberté et ses repercussions sur Kant* (Paris: A.G. Nizet, 1978). For Rousseau's influence on the French Revolution, see N. Hampson, *Will and Circumstance: Montesquieu, Rousseau, and the French Revolution* (London: Duckworth, 1983), or the shorter account in Chapter 6 of Miller.

There is a good analysis of the idea of public interest, which refers to Rousseau, in Brian Barry, 'The public interest', in Anthony Quinton (ed.), *Political Philosophy* (Oxford: Oxford University Press, 1967). Marxist readings of Rousseau can be found in G. della Volpe, *Rousseau and Marx*, 1964, translated and introduced by John Frazer (London: Lawrence and Wishart, 1978) or L. Colletti, *From Rousseau to Lenin* (London: Lawrence & Wishart, 1972). There is a recent general treatment of Rousseau's philosophy by N.J.H. Dent, *Rousseau* (Oxford: Blackwell 1988).

V Revolutions, Liberty and Law

Quotations from Polybius are from the Loeb translation (Cambridge, Mass.: Harvard University Press, 1927); those from Charles I and Algernon Sidney are from the collection of texts in David Wootton (ed.), *Divine Right and*

Democracy (Harmondsworth: Penguin, 1986). Page numbers given of Hume's *Essays* are to the edition of E.F. Miller (Indianapolis: Liberty Press, 1987). Translation of Montesquieu's *The Spirit of the Laws* is by Melvin Richter, as included in his selection *The Political Theory of Montesquieu* (Cambridge: Cambridge University Press, 1977). I had started using the edition by Anne Cohler, Basia Miller and Harold Stone (Cambridge: Cambridge University Press, 1989), which does have a complete text; but I found that the English in it flowed less well and was less clear. Translation of Constant is from Benjamin Constant, *Political Writings*, edited and translated by Biancamaria Fontana (Cambridge: Cambridge University Press, 1988). Quotations from Madison's *Papers* are from *The Papers of James Madison* (Chicago: University of Chicago Press, vol. IX, 1975; vol. X, 1977). The edition of the *Federalist Papers* which I have used is that edited by Isaac Kramnick (Harmondsworth: Penguin 1987). Page numbers refer to this edition; however I have also always given the numbers of the papers, which should enable reference to any edition. Reference to and quotation from the ratification debates (such as from Mason) is taken from *The Documentary History of the Ratification of the Constitution*, vols VIII and IX (Madison, Wis.: University of Madison Press, 1988 and 1990). The page numbers of Paine refer to the Penguin editions (*Common Sense*, 1976; *Rights of Man*, 1969). Rousseau is from the G.D.H. Cole translation as listed for the previous chapter. Burke is from the Everyman edition of *Reflections on the Revolution in France* (London: Dent, 1910).

VI Bentham and the Mills

The best editions of Bentham's *Constitutional Code* and *First Principles Prefatory to Constitutional Code* are in the new *Collected Works* (1983, ed. F. Rosen and J.H. Burns and 1989, ed. P. Schofield, respectively; both Oxford: Oxford University Press). Page numbers given here are to this edition. Earlier, inferior, versions are in vol. IX of the nineteenth-century edition of the *Works*, edited by John Bowring (Edinburgh: Tait, 1843). The *Plan of Parliamentary Reform*, as yet, only exists in the old edition (vol. III), and page numbers here are given to that. Of other work of Bentham more briefly referred to, the *Introduction to the Principles of Morals and Legislation* and *The Fragment on Government* both exist in modern editions, edited by J.H. Burns and H.L.A. Hart (London: Athlone Press, 1970; Cambridge: Cambridge University Press, 1988, respectively). Quotation from Bentham's correspondence is from *Correspondence*, vol. IV in the new edition, J.R. Dinwiddy (ed.) (London: Athlone, 1980). The English translation of Helvetius referred to was published in London in 1759 with the title *De l'Espirit, or Essays on the Mind*. There is a useful collection of 1973 edited by B. Parekh and called *Bentham's Political Thought* (London: Croom Helm). The chief secondary study of this material is F. Rosen, *Jeremy Bentham and Representative Democracy* (Oxford: Oxford University Press, 1983); but there is also L.J. Hume, *Bentham and Bureaucracy* (Cambridge: Cambridge University Press, 1981); R. Harrison, *Bentham* (London: Routledge, 1983); and P.J. Kelly, *Utilitarianism and Distributive*

Notes

Justice (Oxford: Oxford University Press, 1990). David Lyons' classic work, *In the Interest of the Governed* has recently been reissued (Oxford: Oxford University Press, 1973; revised edn, 1991).

As regards James Mill, there is a separate edition of the *Essay*, edited by E. Barker (Cambridge: Cambridge University Press, 1937) and a useful collection which contains both it and Macaulay's reply (and then subsequent replies to replies) by J. Lively and J. Rees (eds), called *Utilitarian Logic and Politics* (Oxford: Oxford University Press, 1978). Page references are to both editions; in each case they are given in the order Barker, Lively and Rees.

There are many editions of J.S. Mill's *Considerations on Representative Government*. Page references here are to the edition in the new *Collected Works* (Toronto: Toronto University Press and London: Routledge). Mill's 1838 essay 'Bentham' is also quoted from this edition. There are also many editions of *On Liberty*. The 'tyranny of the majority' can be found on p. 68 of the Everyman edition (London: Dent, 1910) or p. 8 of that by Stefan Collini (ed.), (Cambridge: Cambridge University Press, 1989).

VII Hegel and Marx

Quotations from the *Elements of the Philosophy of Right* are from the translation by H.B. Nisbet (Cambridge: Cambridge University Press, 1991, edited by Allen W. Wood) and those from the *Lectures on the Philosophy of World History* are by the same translator, with an introduction by Duncan Forbes (Cambridge: Cambridge University Press, 1975). The latter is an edition of the *Introduction* to the *Lectures*, a part which is also known as *Reason in History*. The complete *Lectures* are only available in nineteenth-century translations. References in the text to the *Philosophy of Right* give section numbers as well as page numbers, which should allow reference to any edition. Another standard, authoritative, translation is that by Malcolm Knox (Oxford: Oxford University Press, 1941). The minor political writings are given here in Knox's translation, from *Hegel's Political Writings* (Oxford: Oxford University Press, 1964). Also interesting are the theological writings, although they are not quoted above; in particular the discussion of Greek political life around p. 154 of the edition and translation of Knox, *Early Theological Writings* (Chicago: University of Chicago 1948). Other interesting material not discussed is in the *Phenomenology of Spirit*, in particular Hegel's meditations on freedom and terror. The most recent translation of this is by A.V. Miller (Oxford: Oxford University Press, 1977).

Secondary material on Hegel's politics includes Allen Wood, *Hegel's Ethical Thought* (Cambridge: Cambridge University Press, 1991); and two collections edited by Z.A. Pelczynski, *Hegel's Political Philosophy: Problems and Perspectives* (Cambridge: Cambridge University Press, 1971) and *The State and Civil Society* (Cambridge: Cambridge University Press, 1984). Pelczynski has also written a long introduction to the edition listed above of *Hegel's Political Writings*. Two accessible general treatments are S. Avineri, *Hegel's Theory of the Modern State* (Cambridge: Cambridge University Press, 1972) and R. Plant, *Hegel* (Oxford: Oxford University Press, 2nd edn, 1983).

239

Notes

The translations of Marx used for the *Critique of Hegel's Doctrine of the State, On the Jewish Question,* and the *Economic and Philosophical Manuscripts* of 1844 are by Rodney Livingstone in Karl Marx, *Early Writings* (Harmondsworth: Penguin 1975), with an introduction by L. Colletti. The edition used of *The German Ideology* is that of C.J. Arthur (London: Lawrence & Wishart, 1970). The short *Critique of the Gotha Programme* has been published separately by Progress Publishers of Moscow (1937), or is substantially reprinted in D. McLellan (ed.), *Karl Marx: Selected Writings* (Oxford: Oxford University Press, 1977).

The secondary material on Marx is enormous and conflicting. Two recent treatments of Marxist thought on democracy are Chapter 9 of Keith Graham, *The Battle of Democracy* (Brighton: Wheatsheaf, 1986) and Chapter 4 of David Held, *Models of Democracy* (Cambridge: Polity, 1987). There is also Michael Levin, *Marx, Engels and Liberal Democracy* (London: Macmillan, 1989). Consistently interesting on Marx's general politics is John M. Maguire, *Marx's Theory of Politics* (Cambridge: Cambridge University Press, 1978).

The quotation form Nietzsche's *Untimely Meditations* is from the translation by R.J. Hollingdale (Cambridge: Cambridge University Press, 1983).

VIII Foundations

The formal structure of rights in the text depends mainly on Robert Nozick's *Anarchy, State, and Utopia* (Oxford: Blackwell 1974); and the reference to 'side constraints' is on p. 29. Nozick also refers to the 'utilitarianism of rights' (p. 28). Following his general theory (and also the point of the main text above), he is against it. However, such a view is defended as being superior to either pure rights or pure utilities in Amartya Sen, 'Rights and agency', *Philosophy and Public Affairs* 11 (1982). The general idea of Ronald Dworkin's analogy between rights and trumps is in his *Taking Rights Seriously* (London: Duckworth 1977). It is also the title of a paper of Dworkin's printed in Jeremy Waldon (ed.), *Theories of Rights* (Oxford: Oxford University Press, 1984). This can also be taken as a useful general collection on the subject of rights. Also recommended as an introduction is Michael Freeden, *Rights* (Buckingham: Open University Press, 1991).

X Autonomy

The quotation in the text from J.S. Mill is from Chapter 5 in his *On Liberty*, p. 158 of the Everyman edition, (London: Dent, 1910); or p. 103 of that of Stefan Collini (ed.), Cambridge: Cambridge University Press, 1989).

XI Equality

The quotation about each counting for one and no one for more than one is from Chapter 5 of Mill's *Utilitarianism*, p. 58 in the Everyman (London: Dent, 1910); or p. 257 in the *Collected Works* vol. X (London: Routledge,

1969). Although attributed to Bentham, it seems that Bentham never said it in so many words.

XII   Threading some paradoxes

There is an enormous recent literature on social choice, as well as much detailed work on Arrow's and other imposibility theorems. Arrow's work originally appeared in K. Arrow, *Social Choice and Individual Values* (New Haven: Yale University Press, 1951; 2nd edn, 1963). Recent work on social decision and elections was also stimulated in the 1950s by Duncan Black, *The Theory of Committees and Elections* (Cambridge: Cambridge University Press, 1958), which rediscovered the work of Lewis Carroll about nineteenth-century elections to Oxford fellowships. Amartya Sen's *Collective Choice and Social Welfare* (San Francisco: Holden-Day, 1970) became a standard treatment, and among the best recent commentaries, or introductory guides, are Dennis C. Mueller, *Public Choice* (Cambridge: Cambridge University Press, 1978; now *Public Choice II*, Cambridge: Cambridge University Press, 1989); A. Sen, 'Social choice theory: a re-examination' in Sen, *Choice, Welfare and Measurement* (Oxford: Blackwell, 1982); and Peter C. Ordeshook, *Games Theory and Political Theory* (Cambridge: Cambridge University Press, 1986). There is also Michael Dummett, *Voting Procedures* (Oxford: Oxford University Press, 1984), another work which deals, in passing, with elections to Oxford fellowships.

I have found all these useful; although Dummett is too attached to the efficacy of the Borda Count for my taste. Ordeshook gives the most complete account of various paradoxes and results (such as the order in which agenda are taken), seemingly rendering rational public choice frighteningly difficult or impossible. Mueller gives the fullest treatment of the basic results in their application to actual political choices, analysing when in practice problems might appear. Sen is continually interesting about their possible significances. I append a sketch of the Arrow proof, which may, at least, show its strategy. This version assumes strict preference; a more complicated one would also allow for indifference. This sketch is a combination of the four authors just mentioned, but is closest to Ordeshook.

The proof proceeds in two stages. In the first it is shown that if a group (or individual) is decisive over *any* x/y pair, then it is also decisive over *every* pair; the preference rankings which lead to the former can be extended so that they lead to the latter. In the second stage it is shown that, if any group is decisive, then an individual is decisive (and one group, the whole, must be decisive by definition).

In the first stage we take a decisive group, U, and suppose it to be decisive over x/y. Call everyone else NU. So we can suppose, for example, that U prefers x to y and that NU prefers y to x. Since U are decisive, we have that the social preference is x to y (call this xPy). Now we can, consistently with this, have a ranking on another possibility, z, so that U prefers x to y to z and NU prefers y to z to x. Since everyone prefers y to z, yPz. Hence, by transitivity, xPz. (I haven't noted the axioms used here; but that we can consider all the rankings comes from unrestricted domain; that if all agree, this is also the social decision that comes from unanimity – or weak Pareto; and transitivity comes from rationality.) However, if we look at these preferences we find that U, and only U, prefers x to z; everyone else prefers z to x. The axiom of independence of irrelevant alternatives says that the social preference order for x and z must depend only on individuals' preferences between x and z. No other preferences can count. Hence U is decisive over x and z. That is, its choice determines the social choice over x and z whatever anyone else's choices are, or however they might change. (Any change in preference about other than x and z is irrelevant; any change members of NU have about x and z itself cannot alter the position of x with respect to z, since x is already preferred to z even in the worst case when the whole of NU prefers z to x.)

The proof that if a group is decisive over any pair, it is decisive over every pair follows easily from this. For we can, similarly, show that, if they are decisive over x/y, then they are decisive over w/y. Given that they are decisive over w/y and over x/z for any w and z, it is easy to show that they are decisive over w/z; i.e. if decisive over one particular pair, x/y, then they are decisive over any pair, w/z.

For the second stage of the proof we take the smallest set which is decisive over all pairs and show that it contains one member; that is, that we have a dictator. If a set is the smallest decisive set over one pair, then it is the smallest decisive set over all pairs. (This bit of the proof is often left out; but, from above, if it is decisive over x/y, it is decisive over w/z. So no *larger* set than it can be the smallest decisive set for w/z. But if a *smaller* set were decisive over w/z it would also be decisive over x/y, contradicting the assumption that we had started with the smallest decisive set.) Now, take the smallest decisive set, U (and we know that there is one because the whole is decisive). Either this set has a single member or it does not. If it has, then we have a dictator immediately. If it does not, we divide it into the set containing only the person i (UI) and the rest (UJ). Suppose the rest of the population, if any, are in UK. Now the unrestricted domain assumption says that we can assign any preferences. Suppose that these were that UI prefers x to y to z and UJ prefers z to x to y. Suppose UK prefers y to z to x. Now both parts of U, UI and UJ, prefer x to y. Hence U prefers x to y and, since U is decisive, we have xPy. Now consider z/y. If zPy, then UJ would be decisive (everyone else, UI+UK, prefers y to z). This would contradict the assumption that U was the smallest decisive set. Hence yPz; but, since we have xPy, by transitivity, xPz. Now we have UI prefers x to z but everyone else, UJ+UK, prefers z to x. Hence UI is decisive. Hence we have a dictator.

Notice that the second stage depends upon dividing the population into three parts (two parts which form the supposed smallest decisive set, and the rest). These are then assigned preferences in the cyclical manner first discovered by Condorcet, and as illustrated in the main text. Transitivity does the rest; and we get a dictator over a pair. But Arrow has already shown that, if an individual or group is decisive over any pair, then it is decisive over every pair.

XIII   An impartial conclusion

Richard Wollheim's paradox of democracy was presented in his paper 'A. paradox in the theory of democracy', in P. Laslett and G. Runciman (eds), *Essays in Philosophy, Politics and Society,* second series (Oxford: Blackwell, 1962). It spawned a considerable literature shortly afterwards, including a treatment by Brian Barry in his *Political Argument* (London: Routledge, 1965); Marvin Schiller, 'On the logic of being a democrat', *Philosophy* 44 (1969); D. Goldstick, 'An alleged paradox in the theory of democracy', *Philosophy and Public Affairs* 2 (1973); Ted Honderich, 'A difficulty with democracy', *Philosophy and Public Affairs* 3 (1974).

Index

Index

fraternity 115, 126
freedom 9–10, 17–8, 28, 35, 37–8, 49–50, 52–4, 58–60, 63–73, 114, 117–18, 125–7, 144–5, 147, 161–77, 178–9, 181, 193–5

general will 54–7, 59, 110
Geneva 51
good, the 26
guardians 28–9, 33, 99, 174

Hamilton, Alexander 62, 65–6, 71, 82–5
happiness, greatest 29, 90–1, 99–100, 108, 221; *see also* utilitarianism
Hegel, G. W. F. 9, 113–30, 147
Helvetius, C. A. 89, 92–3
Herodotus 17
hidden hand 130
Hobbes, Thomas 9, 36–47, 49, 52–3, 55, 63, 115, 143, 171
Hume, David 35, 70–3, 77, 81, 83, 85

impartiality 139–40, 217–33
independence of irrelevant alternatives 210–15
individuals 26–7, 36–41, 44, 49, 85, 115, 119–21, 129, 135
interest, common 54–6, 59, 77, 85, 108, 110–11; real 8–10, 54, 57, 59–60, 174; self 92, 94–5, 102–3, 117
intermediate values 144–7, 221, 232–3
interpersonal comparison 211–12, 216, 222
isegoria 17–18
isonomia 17

Jay, John 82
Jefferson, Thomas 75, 77
judicial review 84
justice 31–3

Kant, Immanuel 51, 57, 164, 167–8, 228

knowledge 27–9, 33, 59–60, 99, 102–4, 145, 148–61, 223

law 21, 71–2
leisure 24
liberty *see* freedom
Livy 36
Locke, John 9, 36–7, 43–9, 53, 115–16, 135, 147
lot 19–20, 61, 86
Luther, Martin 116
Lycurgus 68

Macaulay, T. B. 94–5, 98, 100–3
Machiavelli, Niccolò 36
Mackintosh, James 100
Madison, James 63, 65–6, 69–71, 73–88, 90, 132, 146
majority 5–6, 29, 33, 43–4, 47, 75–9, 109, 139, 178, 195–7, 230–
Marshall, John 84
Marx, Karl 9, 31, 35, 113, 116, 123–32, 188–9
Mason, George 65
metics 16–17
Mill, J. S. 101, 105–12, 135, 152, 167, 177–8, 189
Mill, James 66, 94–103, 105–6, 108–9, 135
Montesquieu, Baron de 51, 64–5, 67–8, 70–4, 80, 83, 86
motor of history 123–31

nature, law of 38, 44; state of 26, 37, 44, 49, 53–4, 116, 170
Necker, Jacques 94
Nietzsche, Friedrich 123–4
non-voters 5–6, 166
Nozick, Robert 9, 138

Paine, Thomas 49, 64, 71
paradox of democracy 223–7
Pareto principle 210–11
Pericles 17–20
Pitt the Elder 68–9
Plato 15, 18, 20, 22–3, 25, 27–9, 36–7, 99–100, 103, 145, 147–61, 223

Lightning Source UK Ltd.
Milton Keynes UK
UKOW050620020112

184578UK00001B/48/A